India Rising

Oliver Balch is a UK freelance journalist specialising in business
and world affairs. He work has appeared in a wide range of
international publications, including the *Guardian*, the *Financial
Times*, *Condé Nast Traveller* and *The Traveller*.

His first book, *Viva South America!* was shortlisted as Book of
the Year at the UK Travel Press Awards.

www.oliverbalch.com

India Rising

Tales from a Changing Nation

OLIVER BALCH

faber and faber

First published in this edition in 2012
by Faber and Faber Limited
Bloomsbury House,
74–77 Great Russell Street,
London WC1B 3DA

Typeset by Faber and Faber Ltd

Printed in the UK by CPI Group (UK) Ltd, Croydon, CR0 4YY

A CIP record for this book
is available from the British Library

ISBN 978–0–571–25925–0

FSC
www.fsc.org
MIX
Paper from
responsible sources
FSC® C101712

10 9 8 7 6 5 4 3 2 1

For Mum and Dad

Contents

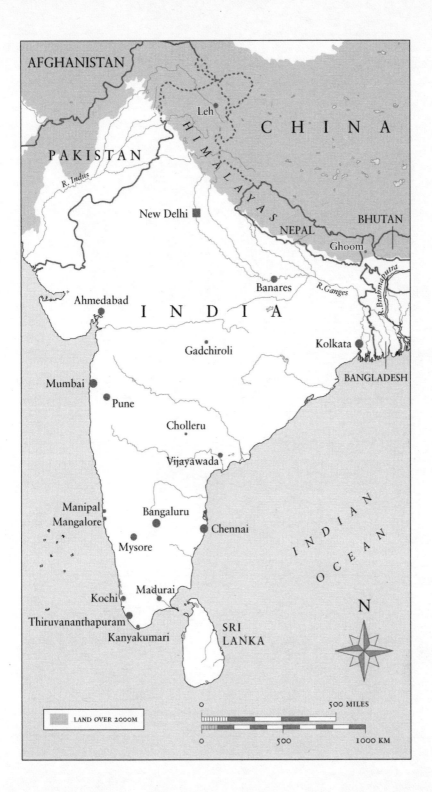

Introduction: Lifespaces

'We used to live right there, man. Now, it's all business. India is
at the centre of the world now, bhai. And I . . . I am at the centre
. . . of the centre.'
  Salim, *Slumdog Millionaire*

'Please, make yourself at home. I'll be with you in just a minute.'

With a hospitable wave of the hand, the president of Mahindra
Lifespaces directs me to a sofa on the far side of his penthouse
office.

A dapper gent of India's old school, Mr Nanda is close to retirement. He is wearing an immaculately tailored suit and exudes
a refined yet roguish charm.

On the desk in front of him sits an orderly pile of paperwork.
He leafs through the pages, signing some with a flourish and pushing others to one side.

A long bank of windows runs along the side of the room. I gaze
out at the muddling cityscape of Mumbai, a conglomeration of
vertical skyscrapers and horizontal slums. I am surprised to see a
flower garden on the rooftop below.

The company president puts down his pen and strides across
the room. His steps are long and his leather-soled shoes leave a
visible trail in the thick carpet, like the tracks of a small mammal
on virgin snow.

He takes a seat in the high-backed armchair opposite me. It is
late morning. He has a lunch appointment. What would I like to
know?

I explain about a visit I'd made to Mahindra World City a few
weeks beforehand. Touted by Mahindra as India's first 'integrated

business city', the multi-million-dollar real-estate project is Mr Nanda's brainchild.

The futuristic township lies on a sprawling patch of wasteland outside Chennai (formerly known as Madras), one of a cluster of mega-cities that Indians affectionately refer to as their 'metros'. It took an hour to get there from the airport. A clogged line of commuter traffic crawled slowly into town in the opposite direction. Heading against the flow, we'd sped along.

I had gone at the behest of a business magazine, which had got wind of the project's eco-credentials and asked me to check them out. Through a perfect white smile, a PR girl had used the drive to laud the company's environmental achievements. An earnest delegation of local management then spent the remainder of the day reinforcing the message. Our tour took in the tertiary water-treatment plant and biodegradable waste unit, the rainwater catchment systems and smart-drip irrigation processes. The development's large natural lake and protected forest stood untouched, they'd insisted.

The magazine's editor was impressed. So was I. Not just because of the City's green innovations. Everything about the place, the whole package, struck me as extraordinary. A scale model in the City's visitor centre mapped it all out in miniature. On one side, hundreds of modern duplexes pointed towards a puddle of blue paint depicting the lake. Some are already complete, others still under construction. A circuit-board of private roads connects driveway to driveway. Within the community gates no convenience is overlooked, from the international school and shopping arcade to the restaurant court and leisure centre. All are for residents only. A fence runs around the site's perimeter to ensure outsiders remain just that.

The City is registered as an Export Processing Zone and sets its clock by business hours. Whole neighbourhoods hum to the sound of machinery. Automotive suppliers occupy one entire district. Apparel manufacturers, another. Their factories churn out brake parts and branded underwear for the global market. The brightest and the best of the City's corporate residents live in

'Cybervale', Mahindra's stab at an Indian Silicon Valley. The high-tech enclave houses some of the country's largest information technology firms. Their gargantuan offices of glass and steel rise incongruously from the surrounding scrub.

Mahindra World City is almost as exceptional for what it lacks as for what it contains. The privately owned metropolis boasts no temple or cremation ground, no market stalls or rickshaws. Public commons are absent, replaced by landscaped verges and impossibly green lawns watered by timer-controlled sprinklers. The grass is trimmed by motorised lawnmowers, not grazing cows or goats. Sixth Avenue, the main boulevard, is free of India's usual bustle and flurry. Tropical palms are set at perfect equidistance along its route. It has no footpath. In Mahindra World City, everyone drives, cycles or travels by company bus.

I have visited India on several occasions, the first time as an adventure-hungry school-leaver fifteen years ago. Mahindra World City is different from anything I saw on those previous trips. The scale of its ambition, the breadth of its vision, the size of its budget – all would have been inconceivable a decade ago.

Yet there it is, taking shape in the Tamil countryside. Not a mirage, but a functioning fragment of tomorrow. How could that be? That's what I want to know.

The company president tugs stiffly at the cuffs of his shirt and clears his throat. If I don't mind, he'll start with the big picture. India has over five thousand towns and nearly four hundred cities, he begins. Between them, they accommodate more than three hundred million people, just over a quarter of India's population. The country's urban residents are set to nearly double over the next twenty years.

'Imagine, two hundred and forty million more people. Our cities are already bursting at the seams as it is.'

He pauses to allow me to digest the figures. Roughly four times the population of the UK. The numbers, indeed, are baffling. But then numbers in the world's second most populous country often are.

Next come the demographics. In debonair tones, the real-estate boss tells me of India's 'demographic dividend'. More than half of all Indians are currently under the age of twenty-five. With the youngest working population on the planet, India has the potential to become the world's factory. Get it right and it could become its chief service provider too.

Neither outcome will materialise, he stresses, unless the country sorts out its cities. India's metropolises, not the countryside, will provide the jobs of tomorrow. For that to happen, the existing urban infrastructure must be completely overhauled.

The president checks his watch. He has a couple more minutes. His focus narrows.

Mahindra Lifespaces cannot remodel India's cities alone. What it can do is create 'islands of excellence'. The World City, he hopes, will prove to be exactly that. The Indian-owned property-development firm is already pouring billions of rupees into a second such project outside Jaipur, the capital of Rajasthan. Mr Nanda's urban archipelago of next-generation cities is taking shape.

There is one more motivation he'd like to share. Just quickly. It is of a more personal nature. He was sitting at his desk one evening, pointing across his spacious office, when an up-and-coming manager knocked on the door. 'We had some business to wrap up. It was late.' In the paternalistic way of old-style managers, the president had asked after the junior's family. The question brought unexpected tears to the younger man's eyes. He had a newborn daughter, he'd explained. He barely got to see her.

The president believes India's talented youth merit more. A two-hour commute, a tiny flat on the edge of town, a complete lack of family time. Is that the sum of all their efforts, what the citizens of New India have to look forward to? 'This poor kid graduated from a good engineering college. He's got a good MBA. He deserves better.' Which is where Mr Nanda's vision for the World City comes in. Everything under one roof. A place to Work, Live, Learn, Play, as the company's motto puts it.

'Now you will excuse me, I trust. My lunch appointment is calling.'

Returning to India was never going to be easy. Much had changed, me included. No longer was I a carefree singleton with a backpack. This time, I came with a wife and two small children. The country had moved on too. I had read about the enormous transformations of recent years – about the country's software boom, its expanding megalopolises, its nuclear weapons, its soaring stock markets, its millionaire entrepreneurs, its expanding middle class, its global stature. India's economy is booming, the headlines trumpet. Asia's elephant is finally awaking. After years in the economic doldrums, it is slowly but surely making good its potential.

Yet could so much have changed? Changes sufficient to create something as grand, confident and frankly un-Indian as the World City? No, that I hadn't expected. Perhaps in a Gulf state or Southern California, but India? This was the land of choked thoroughfares and magnificent old palaces, of bearded sadhus and bedi-smoking beggars, of rattling trains and clapped-out buses, was it not?

Of course, as images go, mine may be off the mark. After all, my earliest impressions of India started out-of-date: some yellowing photographs of a grandfather who served in the dying days of the Raj; stories of my mother's premature birth in the blood-soaked weeks after Partition. Then little else for years bar bedtime stories of Mowgli and the childhood friendship of a few very anglicised, second-generation émigrés.

Not until late adolescence would my perspective on India be updated. For almost a year, I taught English and travelled. The first activity took me to a monastery outside the Himalayan tea-station of Darjeeling. The second led me all over. With hindsight, both offered only a partial view of the country. My teaching experience, because it was spent primarily with a monastic order of Tibetan Buddhists. My time on the road, because I was too wrapped up in my own agenda. I longed for something Other, something enchanting, something utterly different from anywhere else I knew. I was determined that India should be that place and subconsciously resolved to see it so. Any evidence to the contrary, I edited out.

I returned home smitten and lovingly pasted photos of mahoots and mystics into an album. There my image of India languished: a land of wonder and exoticism, happily and securely detached from the world around it. Anything I read or experienced thereafter, I saw through this basic prism. Specific events forced some amendments, naturally. A more recent trip introduced me to the ubiquity of mobile phones and the expansion of cheap air travel, for instance. These I treated as rare exceptions: contemporary phenomena that didn't alter India's age-old essence.

Mahindra World City and the company's smooth-talking president have now left me in a quandary. What kind of country could create such a place? Its modernist pretensions and international flavour share nothing whatsoever with the India of my imagination. Either the City is an anomaly, a freakish invention that runs against the grain, or my perceptions are misplaced – it had to be one or the other.

A hunch pointed me towards the latter. The instinct grows as I look about me. As though for the first time, I see the quantity of people wearing Western clothes and driving foreign cars. The more I probe, the more I sense a shift in people's attitudes, and a new-found confidence too. Is this the 'New India' of which writers and commentators are beginning to speak?

Until now, I had not given the term much credence. Only a few years ago, all the talk was of 'Shining India'. This idea of a glowing nirvana always struck me as premature at best and downright mendacious at worst. India's economic growth rate may be riding high, but many millions of its citizens continue to live unresplendent lives dulled by poverty. Likewise 'New India' has a presumptuous ring to it, as if the Old had upped and gone.

Yet, if the country is indeed changing, then perhaps New India is as good a name as any. A transitory place, not necessarily divorced from the Old, yet not wedded to it either. Nor must the term be entirely material. Could it not point to a change in spirit, a shift in perception? That notion of a country on the move would certainly fit with the evolving dream of Mahindra Lifespaces' president.

The idea excites me. For many years, India has exerted a compelling pull on my imagination. That is as true now as when I first visited as an impressionable teenager. Privately, I'm keen to update my understanding of the country. The integrity of my memories, if nothing else, demands that I take a fresh look.

Broader issues attract me too. The world, not just India, has changed much since my first visit in the mid-1990s. The East is on the rise. Alongside China, India is predicted to become an increasingly important player on the global stage. If and how that happens depends on many factors. Some will originate outside the country – issues of global finance, world trade, geopolitics and the like. The most important, however, will unfold within India's own borders. The connotations of how New India sees itself and what makes it tick could therefore be profound, both for the sub-continent itself and for the world looking in.

Drawing any definitive conclusions from a collective of more than one billion individuals is a treacherous task. In India, even the exceptions run into millions, as the late Bengali writer Nirad Chaudhuri once said. This book provides no comprehensive macro-narrative nor any catch-all explanations. My intent and direction lie elsewhere. My overarching goal is to gain a flavour of this place, New India, through its people, through their hopes and their passions, their opinions and their perceptions. Given that New India's future will be written by its youth, it is their voices that I seek out primarily.

Such an approach is unapologetically subjective. Anecdote is not analysis. Nor should it be. Yet as a way of taking a nation's temperature, of prodding and seeing what gives, I can think of no better.

New India is taking flight and I resolve to scramble on board. As a point of embarkation, I head to Bengaluru. I have an appointment with Captain Gopinath, the man who gave the nation wings.

Part I

Enterprise

1

Self-Made Sahibs

[entrepreneurialism]

'Apparently, sir, you Chinese are far ahead of us [Indians] in every respect, except that you don't have entrepreneurs. And our nation, though it has no drinking water, electricity, sewage system, public transportation, sense of hygiene, discipline, courtesy, or punctuality, does have entrepreneurs.'
Aravind Adiga, *The White Tiger*

Bengaluru

Captain Gopinath offers me a cold beer. As he prises off the bottle-top, the whoosh of gas disturbs Leo, his one-year-old Labrador, who looks up alarmed from the pillow of his big black paws. Seeing all is calm, he returns to his slumbers, nodding off at his master's feet to the rhythmic buzz of insects around the poolside light.

It's close to ten o'clock. We're sitting on the paved garden terrace of Captain Gopinath's heritage-status bungalow. The night has crept in on us, stealthily, the glow of a million street-lamps cheating the evening of a graceful farewell. My host apologises for the time. It's been back-to-back meetings all week. Tomorrow morning, he's leaving for a business trip to the US. Another round of funding. 'But now, now's good,' he says. 'So let's talk.'

I expected him to have a commanding presence, but his demeanour is modest and his tone warm. Legs crossed, he is dressed in an ankle-length dhoti. The cotton garment is entirely white but for a narrow navy line running along the trim. His back is impeccably straight, a throwback to his army days as a younger man. He slowly strokes his greying moustache. His other hand reaches into a bowl of masala chips.

The house is located down an exclusive cul-de-sac just off Vittal Mallya Road in central Bengaluru. The ambient noise is remarkably hushed, as if the tree-lined garden were somehow soundproofed. The grand, two-storey building looks squat beside the towering apartment blocks that now surround it. Captain Gopinath is a recent arrival to the neighbourhood and has just given the house a tasteful refit. Inside, thriving ferns stand tall in empty corners and loom behind sofas like the feathers on a peacock. The presence of so much greenery gives back to the listed building something of its original colonial feel.

Captain Gopinath – 'Please, call me Gopi' – is in ebullient mood. A recital of his favourite Carnatic folk music earlier that evening has warmed his senses. He directs our discussion to the content of his bookshelves. 'My father was a published poet, did you know?' Since his student days, he's cherished a fondness for Tolstoy and the Russian greats. Emerson's essays. Mandela's *Long Walk to Freedom*. Tagore, of course. No management books, though. Only a few biographies of business people that he particularly admires. Vernacular authors occupy a section to themselves. At school, he was taught in the regional Kannada language. His daughter, on the other hand, is studying English literature at Liverpool University. Both facts are points of pride for the one-time village boy.

'But you haven't come to natter about books. What is it you would like to know?' he says, reaching for his own glass of beer.

Gopi's colourful curriculum vitae is already well known to me from his autobiography. A recent best-seller, *Simply Fly* sticks faithfully to the rags-to-riches storyline: started out with nothing (born into a remote village in Karnataka, Brahmin parents educated but penniless, walked to school), escaped his fate (winning a place at the distinguished National Defence Academy, joining the army, rising up the ranks, fighting in the Indo-Pakistani War of 1971), had an early-life crisis (injured in a climbing accident, bedridden, much spiritual soul-searching, resigning his papers, buying a motorbike, travelling the US and India), found his purpose (becoming a farmer, getting into debt, getting out of debt, finding a wife, winning acclaim as a silkworm cultivator), changed direction (setting up a motorbike dealership, buying a small hotel, establishing a stockbrokerage firm, launching an agricultural consultancy, running for public office), took a risk (moving to Bengaluru, purchasing a helicopter, purchasing another, starting to ferry rich clients around), struck on a good idea (pioneering low-cost flying, opening new routes to small towns, taking on the big boys, becoming India's largest domestic airline), and made his millions (selling up, pocketing a fortune). And, come the closing chapter, India's aspiring classes have themselves a modern-day hero: the self-made man, the archetypal Indian entrepreneur.

A smartly attired houseboy appears from the shadows with two hot chicken kati rolls. My host waves towards the cutlery. 'You must try the dhal too,' he insists, pushing a small bowl of lentil paste across the glass-topped table towards me.

I had arrived at the electric gate of Gopi's home with two parallel images of the successful Indian entrepreneur. The first finds its origin in real life. From India's rich list, in fact. Men – they are predominantly men – like steel tycoon Lakshmi Mital, planetary industrialist Mukesh Ambani and his sibling Anil, and beverage giant Vijay Mallya. Cut-throat deals and takeover bids occupy their days. Rich food and private clubs, their nights. They are the rough-handed, handsomely attired heirs of Old India, cast into the New with weapons of wealth and patronage, confidence and contacts. Every bit as imperious as the most powerful of the maharajas who preceded them, they are the Entrepreneur Monarchs.

The second image owes even less claim to reality. Its voice is that of the bustling marketplace, its stride that of modern India. It finds its essence in Balram Halwai, the fictional owner of a Bengaluru-based taxi firm. My introduction to him came via Aravand Adiga, in his fast-paced novel *The White Tiger*. The son of a rickshaw-puller and a one-time chauffeur, Adiga's creation is frank and ambitious, street-smart and irreverent. He is also a murderer. He slits the throat of his employer Ashok, and pockets a suitcase of his money to get his foot on the business ladder. It's not the crime that dominates my mental picture of Balram, but his hunger: a hunger to escape his social confines, to move up in the world, to break out of the prison of poverty in which his birth has trapped him. He is the entrepreneur who longs to be rich so that he may no longer be poor. He is the one I see staring back at me from the traffic lights, eyes filled with hurt and hate and vengeance. He is the Famished Entrepreneur.

Gopi's ease has disarmed me. His hospitable welcome, the singular way in which he looks me in the eye as he talks, the absence of flash cars in his driveway, the works of local artists on his walls, the fact his wife runs a bakery – all speak of a different character from those occupying my imagination.

Then my memory triggers a phrase from his autobiography. I read it back to him from my notebook. 'My story is the story of New India.' The words had sounded trite when I first read them, an all-too-obvious trope scripted by his marketing people. I ask if he might flesh out the phrase in his own words. What does it mean to him?

India's Mr Ryanair sits forward, suddenly animated. His homeland, maybe for historical reasons, whatever, has always been a 'diffident country', he explains. When he set up Air Deccan in 2003, India was emerging as a new nation. 'You could feel it, you could touch it.' He grabs at the air, clenching his fist and turning his wrist as he does so. 'It was vibrant, resurgent. There was a spring in its step. These were all things that were not there earlier.'

He talks quickly, in soft, precise English. After a brief pause, he recollects an experience to illustrate his point.

'I remember once driving through one of the villages close to my farm. I found a board in the centre of the village saying "Computer School". So I parked up. I found a young guy there from the village, who had done his diploma in computer science. He hadn't found a job when he graduated so he'd started a school. Running a business doesn't seem odd because of examples like this. The vision of business as a preserve of the rich, of privilege – it's changing.'

I enjoy the anecdote. It turns out that he has a cupboard-load of them. He reaches into the drawer and pulls out another. This one also features a journey, on this occasion by helicopter. He was flying over a village in a nearby rural district when he saw something glinting in the sun below, dozens of silver pools refracting the light. His curiosity piqued, he dropped down to get a closer look. Could I guess what it was? I couldn't, eh? They were TV-dish antennas, dozens of them. Star TV, Tata Sky, Airtel Digital, Sun Direct, all now inextricably built into India's rural landscape. Could I believe it? 'Oh my God,' I thought at that moment. 'This is a different country.'

The fact that things are changing is not lost on me. Anyone who arrives in Bengaluru International Airport cannot escape the fact. Fifteen years ago, I had rocked up in the same city on an overnight train from Chennai. Back then, travel was, almost by definition, a hot and time-consuming experience. But it was one you shared with millions of others, which, in a sense, made it endurable, even enjoyable. Today, for many new arrivals to Bengaluru, the grit and grime have gone. They drop in from the sky on cheap chartered planes and taxi up to a shimmering terminus. 'Welcome to Karnataka: the knowledge hub of Asia,' a huge advertising hoarding in Arrivals tells them. '700+ MNCs [multinational corporations] have reaped Karnataka's abundance,' another proclaims.

'But, tell me, how does your story in particular reflect this new India?' I ask, trying to move the conversation on to more personal ground.

By 'your', however, he hears 'Air Deccan'. In that sense the two stories are symbiotic. India is a country of a billion or more hungry people, he continues. At the same time, it can be seen as a billion or more hungry customers. That's what the TV dishes taught him. In the future, India will have just one class: the consumer.

Cue his big idea: modern people like to fly; what they need is a low-cost model to help them do so.

Within four months of his inaugural flight, he was presiding over India's largest airline. His fleet of aircraft expanded by a plane per month throughout the first four years. It quickly became, to use the former army captain's own words, 'a massive business'. More than that, it proved the precursor of a gigantic industry. India's no-frills airlines now transport over fifty million passengers per year, more than the entire population of Spain. Many of them have never flown before.

There's a metaphor here, surely? A symbol of the nation taking off? I put the suggestion to the aviation pioneer.

He responds with another anecdote. Again, it is travel-related, this time about a passenger on a flight from Delhi to Bengaluru. 'She was an uneducated lady. As we were disembarking, she recognised me from my picture in the in-flight magazine. She looked towards the cockpit and pointed to the pilot in the seat. Then she quoted a passage from the Ramayana. The bit when the Hanuman carries a mountain in his hand . . .'

I look quizzical.

' . . . Hanuman, you know?'

I nod. The Hindu deity, a loyal defendant of Sri Lord Rama and avatar of Shiva.

'Well, because he was so powerful, he was sent to a mountain in the Himalayas to get a life-restoring herb. Lakshmana, the companion of Ram, was unconscious and had to be revived. But Hanuman didn't know which herb to take, so he took the whole mountain instead . . .' Quick thinking.

I nod again.

' . . . The woman made a sign like this . . .'

He cups his hand, as if weighing up a juicy melon at the market.

' . . . All the old calendars and pictures show Hanuman like this, flying with the mountain in his hand. She imagined that scene. And she kept telling me the pilot who was flying the plane was like Hanuman . . .'

I find myself smiling. There is something of the raconteur about this inveterate entrepreneur. He speaks with his facial muscles as much as his larynx. Storytelling comes naturally to him.

The memory of the old lady prompts him to recall other notable passengers. The Dalai Lama tops his list. Tibet's spiritual leader used to fly regularly from the base of his exiled government in Dharamsala to the Indian capital, Delhi. In fact, a photograph of the beaming monk sitting by the emergency exit appears in Air Deccan's early publicity materials.

The village-boy-turned-entrepreneur has a vignette or phrase for all the famous people with whom he's crossed paths: the Indian guru Sai Baba ('He has his little kingdom'), British entrepreneur Richard Branson ('He had a notebook and he kept writing and writing'), and *Men are From Mars* author John Gray ('He was crazy for temples and swamis').

I ask about the celebrity businessman Vijay Mallya. The question brings the line of conversation to a sudden stop. The brewing magnate happens to live next door to Gopi's bungalow. It's his father's name that's attached to the main road at the end of the street. Gopi and Mallya's back gardens meet. Their minds, however, do not.

By late 2007, the dreams of the cheap-flights pioneer were taking a nosedive. Competition had grown fierce. Air Deccan pilots and engineers were deserting to rival companies. Passengers were migrating. The airline needed more planes. Gopi needed more money to buy them. For months, Mallya had been making overtures towards him. The Air Deccan founder recounts the 'awe' he felt on entering his palatial home to discuss a possible deal. But for Gopi, a merger was a non-starter. Mallya wanted too much control. Old Money India, the ex-army officer foresaw, would quickly swallow the New. The Kingfisher boss promised otherwise. With losses of one crore (ten million) rupees a day, Gopi's room for manoeuvre was shrinking. Then the Indian stock market crashed. Reluctantly, the aviation entrepreneur sold his stake.

The businessman in him rationalises events as best he can. 'The market was white-hot,' he says. 'I didn't have the right to gamble on other people's money.' Captain Gopinath, the self-made man, is still smarting though. In person, Mallya is 'charming, very generous', he admits. In business, forget it. 'He becomes a very different man. He is very clear about what he wants to do.' And it didn't involve poor Gopi. Air Deccan was subsumed and the airline's founder sidelined. Just as predicted.

It does not require a military strategist to have seen the ugly end of the Kingfisher–Deccan 'alliance'. Culturally, the men are miles apart. Mallya, the Entrepreneur Monarch, is not for sharing. Overweight and over-the-top, the millionaire's son revels in his self-concocted image as 'King of the Good Times'. For the price of a small regal state, he has pegged his whisky brand to a Premier League cricket team ('Royal Challengers') and his philosophy to a Formula One team ('Force India').

Gopi, in contrast, doesn't really do sponsorship. Creating jobs in a country that lacks them: that, in his mind, summarises his main social contribution as an entrepreneur. Nor does he go in for brash branding. Plastered on the fuselage of Deccan planes rode an image of The Common Man. Forever dressed in a dhoti and checked coat, the well-loved, homespun creation of *Times of India* cartoonist R. K. Laxman represents the very antithesis of excess and frivolity. The Common Man champions the poor and lampoons the powerful. He abhors corruption and espouses good sense. For Gopinath, Laxman's comic creation points to the 'true wealth' of India, to 'those who till the land, make the bread, turn the lathe'. No, the two neighbours were never destined to get along. They inhabit different orbits.

The serial entrepreneur breaks off for a second or two. He looks up at the night sky. The moonlight blinks between the clouds, rebounding off the black-blue surface of the swimming pool. It's close to midnight and his thoughts, at last, turn upon himself.

If he had to define his career, he says reflectively, then it would be that of a 'first-generation entrepreneur'. The term is fundamental to his self-perception. In a country of business dynasties, his rookie status sets him apart. He started with nothing, only his wits and a willingness to work hard. There was no one to bank-roll his early ventures or pick up the bill after his mistakes. Not that this was a total disadvantage. In the long run, he credits his lack of resources for making him 'hungrier and faster and more innovative'.

The connection between necessity and invention is irrefutable, he insists. Personal experience has taught him that. The belief explains one of his stranger-sounding business maxims: 'Your business will succeed only when you can't pay your rent, you can't pay salaries, you can't buy your wife a sari.' Of course, the wealth and contacts that come with inherited affluence have their advantages. Yet equally they can act as a drag, turning the lean fat and the agile lazy. As he sees things, it's a 'rise and fall of the Roman Empire kind of scenario'. Sat indoors on Gopi's study shelf, Gibbon would be pleased.

Hunger, as well. Starting with zero, constantly playing catch-up, standing alone, just you and the world. First-generation entrepreneurs know this well. And it gives them an appetite and energy for success. 'There was no exhaustion in me,' he says about his sale of his low-cost airline. 'I didn't say, "Oh my God, I've finished Air Deccan and now I'll do nothing, just sit back and have lunch."'

He credits his fellow countrymen with the same hunger. 'If you go to any road junction in India, people come and sell you things – flowers, mobile-phone cases, books, goggles.' I smile in assent, recognising the scene only too well. He is right. India has no need for out-of-town shopping centres. Most items are laid out, ready for purchase, on the country's roadsides. 'No one is begging for alms.'

The point is exaggerated, but the underlying message clear: Indians are industrious. He rams home the point. 'I get a million letters a day asking me to give their father a job or their sister a job or their son a job. Whatever, it could be a job as an office boy, or as a clerk, or as a pilot. It doesn't matter. What matters is that everybody wants to work.' Again, the observation proves hard to dispute. Rarely do you see idle hands in India. There are too many mouths to feed, for one thing. And too little help to call upon, for another.

Optimism, as well. Of all the aspects of his story and facets of his character, for Gopi, this is the characteristic of his New India that overrides all others. The former farmer talks of 'plunging headlong into new ventures'. He is forever 'throwing himself unthinking into things'. He likes to boast of never having commissioned a business plan. Self-belief and gut instinct convince him of success. 'You don't need a McKinsey report to tell you.' His optimism has a naive, almost foolhardy edge to it. A driving force of his thinking, he admits, is 'an innate reluctance to analyse the negatives'. That's how it was when he left the army to set up a farm on land he'd never seen and with soil he'd never tested. So, too, when he applied for a commercial license to fly a helicopter that he had no money to buy, or when he started an airline service for people unaccustomed to flying, travelling to places without airports. 'It's sometimes like jumping off a cliff and then trying to figure out a way of landing.'

Not that he is repentant. Far from it. He even confesses how his 'blind, inextinguishable optimism' has landed him in trouble. The hurt from overstretching himself at Air Deccan and being forced to sell stings to this day. He refuses to dwell on it, though. 'In fact, it's also what's got me where I am,' he counteracts.

The circle is repeating itself once more. Express logistics, the undaunted enthusiast believes, is where the future lies. He throws out the numbers. In the US, it is a fifty-five-billion-dollar industry. In Europe, thirty-five billion. In China, seven billion. 'And in India?' He waits for a response. 'A mere six hundred million.'

The Captain, at the helm, embarking on a new voyage, is intoxicated with hope. 'I see things so clearly. This thing just can't fail.'

A few weeks later I am heading across town. It is rush-hour in Bengaluru, a phrase of which India's rapidly expanding cities make an absolute mockery. The traffic does not rush. Ever. It crawls. And it does so interminably, hour after hour, day after day.

Out of the window, angry horns scream. Sweat gathers on the line of my collar. The taxi's fan, a minute, stick-on contraption robbed from an office desk, whirrs noisily. It provides a steady flow of tepid, unwanted air. I look around at the cars and buses and trucks and bikes, all wedged in beside me on the road, jolting together in a slowed-down staccato. The Great Indian River Dance of Traffic edges forward.

Since my poolside chat a fortnight before, I've been pondering on Captain Gopinath the Metaphor. He fits neither of my earlier preconceptions. That is no bad thing. For one, timing is on his side. Entrepreneur Monarchs may still abound, but their star is waning. New India casts itself as an open-opportunity enterprise. Its citizens are not subjects. They are masters of their own fate. Nor is Gopinath Famished as such. Hungry, yes. But India's aviation pioneer is no Balram Halwai. He takes risks, not retribution. He concentrates on being upbeat, not downtrodden. Hope, not hurt, directs his entrepreneurial energies. New India is the same. He is, I'd settled, the epitome of the Optimistic Entrepreneur. But how characteristic is he of his times?

The previous week, I'd fought the same downtown traffic to make the acquaintance of some of Bengaluru's other stellar entrepreneurs. My first stop saw me deposited in an industrial zone along the Hosur Road highway at the forecourt of a large hospital. The no-frills healthcare complex does not look like the venue for one of India's most innovative businessmen, but then Narayana Hrudayalaya is no ordinary hospital. A pioneer in the Walmart-isation of medical treatment – high volumes, low costs, quick turnarounds – its world-class clinicians perform about ten times the number of cardiac surgeries as the average US hospital. And they do so at about half the cost. To ensure equitable access, the hospital's administrators take the fees of the rich to subsidise the operations of the poor. Couple that with a micro-insurance scheme, which counts over three million low-income members, and this Robin Hood of healthcare is on the way to bringing heart surgery to all – regardless of a person's ability to pay.

The mastermind behind Narayana Hrudayalaya is Dr Devi Shetty. The former physician to Mother Teresa, he is one of Asia's top cardiologists. We'd talked in his consulting room. All the while, the heart of his previous patient had been beating methodically on a wide-screen electrocardiogram behind him. Handsome, intelligent and charming, Dr Shetty is the kind of man every mother dreams of for their daughter. He'd talked passionately about his ambition of 'disassociating healthcare from affluence', of bringing heart surgery to the ninety-two per cent of Indians who currently can't afford it, and of ushering in a generation of medical professionals who could differentiate between 'need and greed'.

The plan is taking off. The charismatic medical entrepreneur has similar units in Kolkata (formerly Calcutta) and Hyderabad, and new ones going up in Jaipur, Jamshedpur and Ahmedabad. He's exporting his low-cost model too. The blueprints have already been drawn up for a cardiology facility in the Cayman Islands aimed at low-income Americans.

Another stop in my tour brought me to the gates of 24/7 Customer. The round-the-clock 'business processing outsourcing' firm, or BPO, was one of the earliest Indian companies to jump on board the call-centre boom. In the glass-walled atrium of the company's headquarters, the security staff had divested me of my laptop, phone and voice recorder. For the sake of data protection, they even compounded my memory stick. 'Your Customer. Our Passion', read a banner above the reception counter, as large as a sail.

Nagarajan ('Nags'), the founder and 'Chief People Officer', is a fit, smooth-talking man with an American twang and expensive spectacles. By his own confession, he lives and breathes customer service. And he expects his eight and a half thousand employees around the world to do the same.

He'd made his millions by thirty-five after selling his California-based software start-up in the late 1990s. Deciding that he was 'too young to retire', he'd moved back to India and started 24/7. The company kicked off with twenty staff answering customer enquiries for Altavista. Now, it carries out over eight million 'transactions' a month and counts the UK's three largest banks and insurance companies among its lengthy client list. To keep ahead of the pack, Nags is ploughing money into an 'innovation labs division' to design apps for iPhones, Twitter and the like. 'The idea', he'd explained, 'was to predict when the customer would call and why.' It's a frightening, ground-breaking thought.

Both Nags and Dr Shetty had struck me as inspiring and ambitious. Visionaries in their fields, they had – like Gopi – succeeded in creating something from nothing. Together, the entrepreneurial trio shared the same drive, the same audacity to go against the tide and, most importantly, the same unassailable conviction that India's time was *now*. The combination had seen them achieve much in their respective careers. It had also helped them land a ton of cash.

As individuals, they abounded with optimism. And why not? As a triumvirate, they could claim impressive track records. Although none showed signs of slowing, they had each, in their own way, arrived. Students pore over their business models. Management commentators treat their opinions as 'insights'. Everywhere they go they are 'somebody'.

What about the nobodies? What about the fledgling entrepreneurs who are starting out at the bottom? Do they show the same qualities, the same ambition, the same optimism?

It is with this question in mind that I am making my way out to the Golf Links Business Park to meet Naveen Tewari.

Founder of InMobi, a technology start-up selling ads for Internet-enabled phones, Tewari belongs to a new, upcoming breed of Indian entrepreneur. In a sense, Gopi, Dr Shetty and Nags tee up the story of New India. They laid its foundations. They wrote the introduction. Now, it falls to the next generation to continue the tale and make it their own.

I arrive forty-five minutes late. Mr Tewari is waiting, his secretary informs me. Accustomed to latecomers perhaps, her voice carries no reproach. I go through to the company boardroom. A sparse, square room, it is decorated with a bachelor's eye for functional furniture and foreign-made electronics. Pride of place is given to a Polycom teleconference machine. The space-age contraption has a protruding plastic arm, fixed to the end of which is a spherical socket containing a roving eyeball. A wilting fern occupies the corner.

My test case is tapping his fingers.

The gridlock traffic and my subsequent delay have ruffled me. So too has the business park. Arriving via the architectural bedlam of unplanned Indian suburbia – improvised housing, crumbling storefronts, pavement-less streets, chaotic wiring, endless concrete, overworked sewerage, real life – the business park comes as a shock.

Sectioned away from the cluttered arterial road and shielded from outsiders by uniformed security, the world of Golf Links is neatly boxed. Here, corporations reign. Microsoft, Yahoo!, Dell. Blunt yet powerful acronyms dominate the skyline, writ large in designer script. KPMG, ANZ, LG, IBM. Glass and chrome abound. The buildings are big. The lines straight. The grass cut. The bushes sculpted. The roads empty. The people near-absent. Order, of a very Germanic kind, has been restored. Or, more accurately, imposed. The world shrank and righted itself when we drove in. It could have been the miniature demonstration model back at Mahindra World City that we were driving through.

Thrown off kilter, I kick off by asking the thirty-three-year-old entrepreneur about the photograph by the door. It's the boardroom's lone wall-hanging. The scene is a happy one: fifty or so employees in matching polo shirts, standing with their spouses on a golf fairway. A handful of children run amok. Stick-on smiles spread across every face. Palm trees provide the backdrop to an idyllic day out. These are his 'superstars', Tewari tells me.

I look out of the window. All the superstars are now busy at their laptops, plugging away at keyboards in narrow cubicles. Each booth is equipped with a small whiteboard splattered with rushed arithmetic, sales targets and holiday dates. Bathed in the pale luminosity of artificial lighting, that happy summer day must feel like a lifetime ago. Mr Tewari insists this isn't the case. His workforce is charged. They have something to prove. They are young. They have drive, passion, energy. They believe in his industry, in the potential of Internet-enabled mobile-phone advertising. 'You can do a lot if you get the right energy in place.' I take a second look out of the window. Perhaps he's right? Maybe the drab decor and uniform workbenches are camouflaging a hidden ambush of tigers, gnashing at the bit and thrusting at their prey? My senses, I have to concede, are still awry.

The discussion about his employees gives me an opportunity to get a brief measure of the man sitting across from me. In appearance, Tewari is unexceptional. He is tall, but fleshy, with jowly cheeks framing a face that looks younger than the rest of him. His comfy, kick-about jeans and brown-striped office shirt point to a relaxed but work-focused ethos. It occurs to me that the uniform also suits teleconferencing – the old newscaster's trick of smartening only what's visible to the camera.

I enquire about his background. The start-up owner plays with his phone as he talks, turning it on its end then spinning it around between his fingers, repeatedly. I picture him as one of the kids who would doodle through class, yet still come out top in all the tests.

As techies go, Tewari was born with a silver spool valve in his mouth. He has pedigree. His grandmother was the first-ever female professor at Kanpur's prestigious Indian Institute of Technology. His father became dean of the same elite institution. Under his watchful eye, the young Tewari passed out with honours in mechanical engineering. After graduation, he joined management-consultancy firm McKinsey, part of its first intake of Indian trainees. For four years, he dedicated himself to writing the type of report that Gopi refuses to read. Then, after an MBA at Harvard, he struck out on his own.

Today, sitting in his own boardroom, treating his employees to off-site awaydays on the golf course, it looks like a logical decision. The hard numbers give substance to the impression. InMobi is now the world's second largest ad operator for mobile Internet. Tewari's fledgling company already has international offices in London, Singapore, San Francisco, Tokyo and Johannesburg. The Kanpur graduate is riding high. His seventeen billion ads reach one hundred and eighty million consumers in one hundred and nine countries every month. The figures are growing by the week. He can count Ram Shriram, the original investor in Google, among his early-round financiers. It all reads very scripted, very *Forbes* magazine, for the Poster Boy Entrepreneur.

So it surprises me to hear that the Tewari tale is not without its abrupt commas or paragraph breaks. As the conversation unfolds, several factors emerge that could easily have derailed him from what looks like a predestined path. Not least was his family. Tewari's parents saw his success in the entrance exams for the Indian Institute of Technology – a feat that hundreds of thousands fail annually – as confirmation of the glittering academic career that awaited him. They were, he says with marked understatement, 'disappointed' at his decision to go into commerce, a world still considered a trifle grubby by India's traditional educator class.

Then his father died. Tewari had just left Harvard. Being the eldest son, social convention prescribed that now was not the time to set off on a hare-brained new venture. Yet he did it anyway. For middle-class Indian families like his, he explains, job security is 'placed on a pedestal'. The mindset comes with other ingrained truths: earn a little and make do; follow, don't lead; welcome change, don't provoke it. He chose to ignore these too.

To complicate matters further, he had recently married. In Old India, it is the man of the house who earns the keep. Not vice versa. The idea of the wife leaving every morning for a desk job and making sure the monthly bills get paid is anathema to traditional thinking. Yet for the first years of their marriage, that's exactly what happened. Mrs Tewari kept him afloat.

The weight of expectations did not stop at the family hearth. The fresh-faced entrepreneur had his own inner demons to confront. Money talks. Finishing his MBA aged twenty-six, the Harvard graduate had every prospect of making stacks of it. He spent a week in California attending job interviews, which resulted in employment offers from a variety of select private-equity firms. All his peers told him to put off going it alone. '"Wait a couple of years," they told me. "Get some more work experience."' The idea, he admits, sorely tempted him. It would mean more cash in the bank, a more comfortable lifestyle, a fancier car, a juicier bonus. But the prospect unnerved him too. The longer he waited, he realised, the harder it would be to jump ship. So he picked up the phone to his would-be employers, thanked each of them in turn for their generous offers, and said, regretfully, that he had to decline.

That takes guts. Throwing everything after a dream. Putting heart before head. If *Simply Fly* has any guiding themes, it's qualities like these. My thoughts turn back to the aviation entrepreneur by the pool. The two men come from different stock and different generations. Gopi, at least to begin with, had less to lose than the McKinsey man. As Tewari talks, however, I hear unmistakable echoes of the older man's voice. It's there in both men's inner compulsion, in their embrace of the seemingly irrational. 'I'd always kick myself if I didn't give it a go,' the InMobi founder says at one point. It's the Graduate stealing the Captain's lines.

I probe further into the InMobi story in search of other similarities. Two practical factors hampered the company's creation. First, Tewari had no working capital. Second, he had no InMobi. As with Gopi, the colt entrepreneur began with the second problem. The money, he figured, would come later. What he needed was his 'big idea'. To find it, he headed for San Francisco. His plan was to work with 'very, very small companies', help build them up and then flog them on. A year later, nothing. The ventures had either bombed or stalled.

Feeling low, he headed back to India for a month-long break. Sitting on the couch at his mother's house, bored, he sketched out a business plan. His idea centred on 'mobile search'. The intention was to design a service enabling phone users to send an SMS requesting information – say, for the location of a restaurant or the number of a plumber – and receive an SMS back with the answer. That was the breakthrough idea. It looked good on paper, he says in retrospect. It 'got trashed' in practice. Yet it opened the door to what he is doing now. By early 2008, a prototype version of his InMobi product offering hit the market. And the rest, as they say, is history.

Tewari was right about the money too. It came. First in dribs and drabs, then in ever-increasing volumes. He remembers his meeting with Ram Shriram, of Shertalo Ventures and Google fame. The Technology Midas was joined by a representative of Kleiner Perkins Caufield & Byers. Together, they represented two of the biggest venture-capital firms in the world. Twenty minutes into Mr Tewari's presentation, Shriram raised his hand for him to stop. 'Right, we're investing,' he said. The InMobi owner stood there stunned. He looked down at the remains of his slide presentation. 'What about the revenue model, the pre-money valuation?' The details can wait, the investment guru responded. 'For now, let's roll up our sleeves and discuss what you're going to do after this.'

An hour later, the boy from Kanpur found himself sitting in a cheap rental car in a Silicon Valley parking lot. When he had woken up that morning, InMobi had officially run out of money. For three months, he and his five colleagues had been pooling their private credit cards. No one was collecting a salary. Then, from one moment to the next, he was over seven million dollars richer.

'How did you feel in that moment, sitting there in your car?' I ask, imagining the exhilaration he must have felt.

'I was very happy,' the modest entrepreneur replies, allowing himself the slightest of smiles. 'I thought, "I'll drink to this." So I cracked open a Coke.'

Mysore

Manjunathea presses 'Play' on the video software that sits expectantly on his computer screen. I'm back in another bare, business-like meeting room. Only this one is located on the edge of Mysore and measures about four times the size of InMobi's. It also has a name: The Taj Mahal Conference Room.

As the introduction of the corporate video plays out, my toes begin to curl. The script is packed with business-speak and fulsome phrases, all of which are read out in cloying tones by an over-dramatic narrator. 'Behind the brand is a story of excellence,' the commentary starts. I have a foreboding of what's to follow. The predictable ad agency behind the film does not disappoint. The company 'explored new domains', became a 'mission-critical transformation partner' and, at the end of it, still emerged with 'the courage to dream'. It's wince-making stuff.

Sitting across the conference table, forty-four-year-old Manjunathea is looking elated. In a sense, he has every reason to be. For the last fifteen years, the subject of the video – IT giant Infosys – has been his employer. Narrative style aside, the story is indeed extraordinarily impressive. Starting with two hundred and fifty dollars in cash and seven founding members, Infosys has grown to become one of India's most successful firms. A genuinely global player in the IT industry, it now employs over one hundred and thirty thousand people in ninety countries.

The whole operation stands as a testament to entrepreneurial vigour and enterprise. Back in 1984, Infosys anticipated the market by switching from mini- to mainframe. It introduced the 'Global Delivery Model', arguably the genesis of India's multi-billion-dollar outsourcing industry. It was the first Indian company to list on the NASDAQ exchange and the first to offer stock options to its employees. Today the best known of its founding fathers, Narayana Murthy and Nandan Nilekani, command worldwide respect for their creative genius. They deserve it. As their employee explains, the pet project that they had kicked off in Murthy's front room now boasts annual revenues of over six billion dollars, more than that of the entire state of Goa.

'Now it is my pleasure to spend the next forty-five minutes to an hour talking you through the learning programme for our freshers,' Manjunathea says, before quickly correcting himself. 'Sorry, our "fresh entrants", I should say.'

He scrolls his keyboard mouse across to the PowerPoint icon and brings up a set of slides on the projection screen. Like Tewari, Manjunathea is a graduate of Kanpur's Indian Institute of Technology. The two have little else in common, however. The grey-moustached Infosys manager is undoubtedly smart and articulate. Dressed in his 'crocodile' chinos and prescription black shoes, however, he isn't what the corporate video would call a 'game-changer'.

Before his current post, he spent fifteen years as a software developer. Everything about him, from the leather mobile case on his belt to the pens in his breast pocket, speaks of a steady, dependable, meticulous employee. Manjunathea is the kind of man on whom successful corporations depend: loyal in his affections, unstinting in his work ethic and essentially content with his place on the career ladder. He is, I realise, the perfect candidate to be training Infosys's new employees.

The first slide shows a graph with the total number of graduates in India. Once more, I steel myself for what's to come. 'So there were eighty thousand graduates in 2000, around two hundred and fifty thousand in 2006 and, if I had to estimate the current rate, I'd say it would be around three hundred thousand.' The figures have a purpose. He wants me to understand the dilemma facing contemporary India: 'quantity versus quality'. If you were to handpick ten tomatoes, he explains, you can choose carefully. If you pick ten thousand, you cannot. It's meant as a generic truth, which he then applies to his employer. Infosys finds itself in the second bucket. The IT giant recruits between fifteen and eighteen thousand graduates every year. 'Ensuring the best level of quality is what we try and achieve on this campus.'

He flicks to the next slide, which outlines the core components of the three-month training course: technical competency, soft skills, process orientation, English-language fluency. 'The ultimate goal', he says with a flurry of his hands, 'is to make a person production-ready.'

He makes the new stock of trainees sound like computer microchips, readying themselves to be commoditised, marshalled into line and then shunted out of the factory gates. As he continues through his slides, the impression grows. Twenty-four days of basic IT training. Twenty-two days' tech-specific instruction on JAVA, .Net and a variety of Open Software Frameworks. Ten days' POST: Project Organisational Standards Training. All the while, the new recruits are expected to be busying themselves with technical assignments, case studies and group projects. Libraries and computer labs open twenty-four hours a day. There are no discos, alcohol is forbidden and curfew falls at eleven o'clock. It's Tech Boot Camp in all but name.

Slide Six deals with 'Building a Conducive Learning Environment'. Again, Infosys's desire to manufacture the country's smartest programmers covers every angle. All the classrooms have 'smart' whiteboards linked to the trainer's computer and on-desk terminals for each student. The company's combined intelligence – essays, think pieces, programming advice, reviews, et cetera – is all accessible through KSHOP, Infosys's online knowledge portal. Furthermore, the teachers are 'A1 professionals', as good as any university faculty.

'Conducive Learning', Manjunathea clarifies, includes close attention to the new recruits' private lives as well. Students are housed in plush chalet rooms with maid service and the latest mod cons. For meals, they have the choice of seven food courts. As for leisure, Manjunathea reels off a selection of the facilities: a fully equipped gym, a swimming pool, four squash courts, a bowling alley, a full-size cricket stadium, a soccer pitch, tennis courts, an athletics track, a huge sports hall, a snooker hall, a health club, even salsa classes.

Occupying more than three hundred acres of once barren land on the edge of Mysore city, the campus has the feel of an upmarket seaside resort. The list of other amenities makes life more or less self-contained: a launderette, a hairdresser, a Domino Pizza restaurant, a supermarket called Loyal World, a health centre, Vodafone and Airtel stores, an outlet of fashion retailer Indigo Nation, several banks and a one-thousand-four-hundred-seat cinema. Partially submerged, the latter looks akin to a gigantic metal golf ball plugged in a bunker. As with Mahindra World City, there is no temple or mosque, no whiff of religion whatsoever. At Infosys, the gods are quiet and every miracle made by human hand.

At the end of the extensive briefing, Manjunathea offers to take me for a quick tour. To facilitate transportation around the sprawling campus, Infosys puts five thousand bicycles at the disposal of its fresh-faced trainees. We take a golf cart. He shows me the library first. The shelves hold sixty thousand books. Prominent on the 'Advised Reading' display is Narayana Murthy's collection of speeches, the optimistically entitled *A Better India: A*

Better World. I wander over to the magazine rack. For downtime, students can pick between *Dataquest, Developer IQ, PC Quest* and a host of other technology titles. I thumb through a copy of *Visual Studio.* 'Code # Contracts in .NET 4', the headline article reads. I scan the first few paragraphs and put the magazine back. The contents might as well have been in Klingon.

From the library, we make our way to the Global Education Centre, known on campus as GEC 1. Groups of young graduates are making their way to class. Boys and girls walk separately, segregated by cultural instinct rather than corporate edict. We briefly sit in on the last of the morning sessions. There are roughly a hundred 'fresh entrants' in the theatre-style classroom, all sitting behind an Acer Computer watching the lecturer on the stage. She speaks quickly. '. . . structure members are accessing the dot operator . . . a structure can be embedded in another structure; a pointer can point to a structure . . .' She loses me immediately.

We head to an open-air cafe, where Manjunathea introduces me to two students on a free period. He asks if they have five minutes to talk with me, a request to which they politely assent.

Pushing aside their open textbooks, they wait for me to start. I'm slightly reticent. From Manjunathea's presentation, I half expect them to be brainwashed programmers capable of responding only in code. Neither does, of course. Indeed, both turn out to be extremely personable and highly fluent. Twenty-one-year-old Amrutha describes herself as an electronics undergraduate from Bengaluru. It's her first time living away from home. I ask her about her experience on campus and she says she felt a 'little bewildered at first, you know', but is more settled now. Her parents, she points out, are 'more than happy' to see her here.

Prianka is one year older and the more outgoing of the two. Originally from Bhopal, she talks of the 'wow factor' that she and all the students feel on arriving at the campus. She's the first in her family to get a job 'in corporate', as she puts it. As with Amrutha, she too feels it necessary to stress the contentedness of her family with her choice of employer. 'They are happy for us to be independent,' she says of her expectant parents, 'but they want us to settle and save our salary too.' Both girls expect to marry in 'four or five years'. I ask if they'll carry on working afterwards. 'It depends,' Prianka says. Depends on what? She doesn't respond, just smiles and hunches her shoulders. 'Just depends.' Both would certainly like to build careers at Infosys, they add. 'The last thing we want to do after studying so hard is to sit at home.' Prianka giggles and Amrutha joins in. They agree that the money is good too. The girls are cagey about telling me exactly what their starting salary is, but Prianka provides an illuminating comparison. 'Put it this way, it took years and years for my father to start earning what I earned in my first week.' I ask what he does. He works for Western Coal Fields Limited, she tells me, 'a quasi-government group'.

Gopi had talked about India's gradual economic liberalisation, about how the state was loosening its grip, freeing the private sector up to grow. Prianka and Amrutha were born at the outset of that process. Not all Indians have seen their prospects improve, but these young women certainly have. Their career hopes and earning power both speak of a remarkable generational transition, a shift that now offers them opportunities inconceivable to their parents.

Sat on a nearby bench, Manjunathea taps his watch face. I thank the graduate pair and leave them to their break time. Looking back from across the quad, I turn to wave. Both are already looking down, however, their noses buried back in their textbooks.

We walk along one of GEC 1's many corridors. Manjunathea has arranged for me to ask a few questions at the end of an IT basics class. We pass by room after room, each overflowing with future Infosys programmers diligently studying their craft. The sheer scale of the operation begins to hit me. Later, my tour would take me to the newly built Global Education Centre 2, a colossal, crescent-shaped structure with Greek colonnades, Indo-Islamic flourishes and, at its centre, a more than passing resemblance to Washington DC's Capitol Hill. Covering one million square feet, the floor plan of the four-storey building reveals one hundred and thirteen rooms on Level 1 alone.

Even here, though, in the modest enormity of GEC 1, I'm struck by the hundreds of people that pass through these corridors every day, all of them bright, industrious young adults like Amrutha and Prianka. Where are they heading? What lies in store for them? What kind of India are they set to inherit? What kind of India do they hope to create?

My eye is drawn to plaques on the classroom doors. As with the conference room, all carry illustrious names. Most derive from the world of business and scientific enterprise: automotive pioneer Henry Ford, General Electric's charismatic former leader Jack Welch, early computer scientist Alan Turing, inspired inventor and polymath Benjamin Franklin. I don't see any rooms dedicated to Narayana Murthy or Nandan Nilekani. Should they exist, their names would not be out of place. After all, it is on their entrepreneurial acumen that the gargantuan Global Education Centres have been built.

Striding some ten yards ahead, Manjunathea ushers me into the last classroom along the corridor. How many of the young graduates inside aspire to be the next Ford, the next Franklin, the next Nadkani? The thought follows me through the door and towards the lectern at the direction of the class coordinator.

'What does Infosys mean to you? What thoughts does it conjure up?' I ask by way of a warm-up question.

Answers are proffered from among the full rows of terraced seating. 'A good career in the IT field,' comes one. 'Excellent training,' comes another. 'Career growth and international exposure,' a third. My follow-up questions receive a similar response. Why Infosys, not Whipro, Tata Consultancy Services or another of India's leading IT companies? 'It's an honour to be here.' 'It has the world's best training.'

Only one deviates from the script, a thin, mop-haired young man on the back row. 'Personal growth,' he says. Then, to the laughter of the class: 'In financial terms, and all.' Reminded of Prianka, I ask for a show of hands. How many of you are earning

more relative to your parents when they started work? Not a hand
stays down. The hope to be working for Infosys in five years' time
is almost universal too.

I had come to the campus of one of India's most famous examples of entrepreneurship in the expectation of meeting a new
breed of business visionaries. It was, I realise now, a naive as-
sumption. India's entrepreneurs have created companies in which
the brightest crop of young graduates can prosper and thrive. Not
all want to go it alone. Very few do, in fact. A mere three hands go
up when I ask who in the class envisions themself setting up their
own businesses in the future. In the US, it would be the majority.
Outside, on the steps of GEC 1, a batch is having a graduation
photo taken. They are 'production-ready' and throw their hats in
their air to prove it.

I leave the Mysore campus with a graphic appreciation of what
Optimistic Entrepreneurs can create. As the taxi pulls away, I
glance back over my shoulder. Through the rear window, the
miniature world of Infosys lies out in the sun, all pristine and
packaged for consumption. Can the country's best brains be
blamed for buying in?

Entrepreneurs are the dashing lead characters in the surging
New India story. They remain the exception, though, not the rule.
Not all Indians can be, or even want to be, the next Captain Gopi
or Naveen Tewari.

Industriousness, in contrast, is more generous in its bounty. It
welcomes all bar the idle. Few in India can afford to sit on their
hands. They have mouths to feed and bills to pay. And, now, at
long last, they have money to make too.

2

Bad Status, Actually

[industriousness]

'Their money is big in America. But in India, people want to get money. They eat, do shit, and then get up and work again. They don't think why.'

Mohammed 'Babu' Sheikh, Mumbai driver

Mumbai

Babu parks his boss's white Maruti Swift on a kerb of loose gravel. With considerable effort, he begins manoeuvring his long legs from the pedals to the pavement. His knees bang against the steering wheel as he twists and turns. Once his feet touch the sun-sizzled tarmac, he makes much of stretching his back and exercising his neck muscles.

'This is not a flashy car,' he says as he bleeps the electronic lock. 'In fact, it has bad status actually.'

The practicality of the two-door hatchback – a small car in a traffic-choked mega-city – is of little consequence to the lanky product of a Mumbai slum. Babu doesn't care that it parks easily or squeezes between lanes. A Toyota Innova. That's what his boss should buy. Seven-seater, SLX. That is the 'best good status car' in his opinion.

As a retained chauffeur, Babu's professional standing is directly linked to his employer's choice of vehicle. As he sees it, the Swift is doing his image no favours. Babu feels that depreciation keenly.

A Muslim (his formal name is Mohammed) in a Hindu-dominated city, the gangly driver already senses himself on the defensive. His niece, for example, who keeps the faith and wears a burkha, recently lost her job as a teacher in the slum. 'After seven years there, they required her to change her religion.' She chose to resign instead.

'In Maharashtra, the party says only Marathi people should work,' Babu remarks, his shoulders hunching in resignation. 'Every government office wants to employ their own man.'

By the 'party', I presume he means Maharashtra Navanirman Sena, a radicalised offshoot of the already ultra-right Hindutva group Shiv Sena. The Mumbai-based party (which enjoys a somewhat turbulent alliance with the nationalist Bharatiya Janata Party) is hell-bent on closing the city's doors to outsiders. The list of unwanted includes Muslims, whether Maharashtra-born or not. If he could, Raj Thackeray, the nephew of Shiv Sena supremo Bal Thackeray, would oblige all Mumbai's taxi drivers to speak fluent Marathi. The sectarian proposal preoccupies the Hindi-speaking chauffeur.

Babu's sensitivity about his status has a more personal edge too. By Indian standards, he is extremely tall – six foot two inches, 'without shoes'. Everything about him, from his nose to his toes, looks one size too big. It's as though his mother had anticipated him shrinking in the wash. He never did. What he is most conscious about is his receding hairline. A protractor-shaped patch of naked skin runs from his forehead to his crown. A bald pate is the source of great anxiety for Indian men. A fulsome crop of hair symbolises virility and general manliness. And not just on the head. There are coffee-table books dedicated solely to the wonder that is the Indian moustache. Babu keeps his hair close-cropped, brushing it forward for an extra few millimetres of coverage. Regardless of his efforts, the taunts of children still hound him through the slum's congested alleyways. 'Ganjaa, Ganjaa,' they shout. 'Baldy, Baldy.' Their parents chide him too. This time for his bike, a rusty Yamaha RX 100. Babu tells them to go to hell, but the jokes bite. He admits that his two-wheeler is old ('1987 model') and rusty and so small that he has to crouch over the handlebars like an overgrown child on a toddler's tricycle.

He has his eye on a 150cc Honda Unicorn. His wife, Jyoti, is needling him to buy one. 'She tells me, "I said nothing about a car. Just a good bike. That's enough for me. To take the kids and go for chapatti."' Babu doesn't know where he'll get the money. The thought keeps him awake at night. 'I tell her, "Don't break my heart and my mind."'

We cross the road towards Ganesh Murty Nagar colony, the crowded slum where Babu lives with Jyoti, his two children – Nabi, aged six, and Sameer, aged four (also known as Ashu, meaning 'fast') – and around ten thousand other people. The community clings to the rocks at the very southern tip of Mumbai, a populous barnacle lapped by the Indian Ocean and encrusted in sea salt and poverty.

Babu suddenly grabs my elbow. I halt mid-stride. As I do so, full laundry bags of dirty linen swoosh by, inches from my face. The bulging bundles are riding pillion on a speeding moped. A blast of hot air fragranced with sodium bicarbonate knocks me back on my heels.

'They used to deliver on bicycles,' Babu says, half-heartedly cursing the laundry man as his rattling dragonfly of a bike drones off down the road. 'Now all is change. Now they have good money.'

The near-miss brings the motorbike dilemma back to Babu's mind. He turns to me once we've safely navigated the road. 'What exactly is a Unicorn, actually?'

I tell him what I know: that it's a mythical creature, like a horse but with a horn protruding from its forehead. I imagine them to be white, but – presumably like the Honda – they could come in other colours too. 'If I'm not mistaken, the ancient Greeks used to believe they originated in the plains of India.'

'Really? In India?' replies Babu, his scepticism alerted by this last point.

He is an avid fan of *Animal Planet*. ('It's true, I heard it on *Animal Planet*' is, I would later learn, one of his stock phrases.) He takes a special enjoyment from watching big cats hunt, 'but they're mostly in Africa only'. India has tigers, but 'we Indians kill them in large numbers and export them. So now no tigers are left.' The revelation is delivered with no sense of regret or remorse.

Babu's evaluation of Mumbai's animal life is equally matter-of-fact. Dogs, cats and cows basically comprise his list, a four-legged fraternity of three. And maybe some pigs (something his secular Muslim nose still turns at). Oh, and an elephant or two as well. 'They come to beg.' But as for unicorns? He thinks he would have heard about unicorns if they really came from India.

Meantime, he has another question: 'What do you mean by "mythical"?'

'Like stories,' I suggest hesitantly.

The explanation seems to please Babu, who nods vigorously. 'Oh, so like cartoons then.'

I had grown used to Babu's questions over the weeks. We first met at Mumbai International Airport. His boss, a friend of a friend, had sent him to pick me up. For the young Englishman on a princely salary, Babu forms part of the expat package, along with a live-in maid and a small militia of sentries at the gate.

New India shows one notable similarity to Old India: it is swarming with foreign officialdom, most of them white and privileged and overburdened with staff. Their allegiances have ostensibly changed. Today, they answer to suits in the City rather than in Whitehall. British India was always a commercial project first, and a political concern second.

Still, I often wonder what it must be like for these modern-day vassals of Empire when their assignments finish. There will be no Babus waiting for them at home, just the jam-packed District Line chugging slowly in from Putney every morning. Will they miss their 'ridiculously over-wrought baroque' lives, to use the words of India's chief foreign writer-in-residence, William Dalrymple?

Babu's life, at least, contains no such dualities. His reality is stark and his life no more wrought than the simplest of iron railings. In the morning, he picks up his boss and drives him ten minutes to his office. Nine hours later, he has to be back at the same spot to retrieve him. In the interim, he twiddles his thumbs or takes a nap in the driver's seat.

His only other fixed task comes at four o'clock in the afternoon, when he has to drop off the maid at Mahalaxmi Racecourse. He waits in the car as she walks the dog. Occasionally, his employer might just have meetings outside the office or require a lift to the airport. Babu's napping may also have to work around the odd errand, such as dropping off a suit at the cleaners or stocking up on dog food.

The nights are different. If his boss is heading out, then Babu will often stay late to ferry him home. He'll eat at a pavement cafe as his boss wines and dines. His knowledge of the city's top eateries ('Did you try the smoked salmon at Olive?') and hottest clubs ('Prive, Fridays. China House, Saturdays') outstrips that of most guidebook writers.

All this for a base wage of just over eleven thousand rupees a month. With his Diwali bonus and overtime, he might add an extra three or four thousand on top. That makes him better off than most in the slum. The average income of his neighbours is around eight thousand rupees, Babu reckons. Still, in a city with some of the highest property rents in the world, his salary doesn't stretch very far.

Indians – poor Indians especially – are unnervingly direct about their incomes. On that initial drive back from the airport, Babu had interrogated me about my income. I answered evasively. Journalism, he resolved, was a poor career choice. I struggled to disagree.

Unperturbed, he offered me in return a full breakdown of his personal finances. His largest single expenditure is his rent, which sets him back two thousand rupees per month. Babu gives his elderly parents a similar figure 'for rations and all'. An extra one thousand goes on their medicine. At home, he has the children's schooling and extra tuition to cover, plus the food and electricity bills. Jyoti, meanwhile, is anaemic and has bleeding gums that require expensive treatment. She's also just started on a weight-loss programme. The course requires a half-kilo jar of diet supplement, at one thousand three hundred and fifty rupees each. 'She's lost one kilogram in a week,' says Babu, evidently pleased with the result. Other than that, he spends fifty rupees every day on petrol going to and from work. Occasionally he buys beer, although he claims to 'hate the alcohol'. He usually skips lunch.

'By the tenth of the month, you are finishing the money. On the fifteenth or twentieth, you ask for advance from your boss. Because money doesn't wait. It has to spend,' he'd concluded philosophically.

During our morning ride to the slum, Babu had been in typically expansive mood. Weaving down the thinning peninsula, the born-and-bred Mumbaiker pointed out the tourist spots. Victoria Terminus ('built by the Britishers, actually'), Churchgate station ('one million commuting people every day'), the University of Mumbai ('India's oldest university'), the Session Court ('today the crime is too much'), Old Maiden ('for the playing of the cricket'), the Lawn Tennis Association ('for the playing of the tennis').

Parallel to his official tour ran a more personalised commentary. He'd shown me the office block at Nariman Point where he'd had his first job, pulping fruit at his cousin's juice kiosk. He'd pointed out the evening college by Metro Cinema where he'd studied English. I'd been taken past the bodybuilder's gym in Colaba where he'd exercised as a younger man ('You know *Shantaram*, the book? The author used to train there actually. Madonna went once. Her picture and all is on the wall'). We'd briefly parked up at the apartment block in Kuffe Parade where he'd met Jyoti. She was working as a maid at the time. Finally, I'd been introduced to the fishing colony where the Mumbai terrorists had landed in 2008 before unleashing their infamous bloodbath on the city.

Now, standing on the doorstep of the slum, his focus is more immediate. Back up the road stands a public park, a precious smudge of green on a bulwark of seaweed grey. A well-worn path runs around the fenced edge. It measures half a kilometre. Babu knows the distance well. He runs the full circuit twenty times every morning, usually before six o'clock. He wears the same sole-worn RB running sneakers to work. The fabric is fraying along the seams. His knees must be shot. Or soon will be.

Across the way is the Spastics Society of India School. Nabi

used to study there, although – as Babu is quick to inform me –
'he is not a spastic actually'. Further down sits the Gothic church
of St John the Evangelist. In years gone by, its pyramidal spire is
said to have beckoned ships into port. Today, its view to the coast
is blocked by the drab apartment blocks of a Navy compound.

We walk past the Backbay Bus Depot, a subdued rectangle of
diesel puddles and idling motors. The access road to Babu's slum
falls under the jurisdiction of the Navy. For decades, the men in
uniform refused to widen it, effectively depriving thousands of
residents of public transport. Three years ago, they got their bus.
No longer do they need lose hours every day trudging on foot to
work or the market.

The bus station is hedged in by an expansive empty lot on one
side and a half-built skyscraper on the other. Both are incongru-
ous in an area where people live bunched, horizontal lives. I ask
Babu about the discrepancies. There used to be houses on the
abandoned lot, he explains, but government bulldozers recently
came and levelled them.

Demolition is a constant threat for Mumbai's slum dwellers.
(That and diarrhoea, which kills nearly one thousand children
every day in India.) Many have lived for years on the same plot,
although often without legal title. This severely weakens their im-
munity against the onslaught of parasitic real-estate developers.
Babu heard that Reliance Industries, India's largest conglomerate,
has acquired the site as a helipad.

If the slum rumour mill is true, developers have their eye on the
rest of Ganesh Murty Nagar too. In exchange for selling up, Babu
and his neighbours are promised homes in soon-to-be-built tower
blocks on the edge of the city. He's not sure whether to believe
the pledge or not. The slum's official neighbourhood committee,
which negotiates such matters, is backing the resettlement plan to
the hilt. They would, Babu observes wryly. 'They receive bribes
from the builders, so we never believe anything they say.' For the
moment, he and everyone else is staying put.

As for the whir of rotor blades, they have yet to add their
particular rhythm to the hubbub of the slum. In the interim, the

empty space is fast turning into a public rubbish dump. A top-soil of plastic and garbage covers large portions, creating a living patchwork of decaying mulch. Young boys still play cricket on the less sullied squares, but their wickets are gradually shrinking. Soon their pitch will be smaller than a long-jump pit, and only pigs, rats and half-famished dogs will occupy the space.

As for the skyscraper, Babu's understanding is that it will act as a retirement home for the Navy's top brass. It is built on top of what used to be the slum's only play park. Babu has no idea how they plan to provide water for such a large construction.

Access to water represents another constant preoccupation for the residents of Ganesh Murty Nagar slum. Babu is keen to brief me on the subject. But first he must 'go do piss'. With his giraffe legs, he lopes off to the public latrines by the slum's entrance. 'Two rupees to go for loo,' he says on his return. 'But piss is free.' He appears content with the economy afforded by his bowels.

The slum is divided into three sections, unimaginatively entitled Zone One, Two and Three. The first has water every day, but old leaking pipes. The other two have newer pipes, but supply alternates between them. Babu lives in Zone Three. 'The water can come any time, but generally it is between mid-afternoon only and midnight,' he explains. The flow dries up after twenty or thirty minutes, so speed is of the essence. If Babu is at home, he will help Jyoti fill the jerry cans at the communal tap. The plastic containers come in two sizes: twenty litres (coloured white) and forty (blue or black). If he's out, she has to fetch their day's supply by herself.

'Sweet water', as Babu refers to the intermittent supply from the mains, is good for drinking. Well water, by contrast, is not. On sale at various water tanks dotted around the slum, a twenty-litre container of the latter costs two rupees and fifty paisa. It used to be two rupees, Babu says, but the price is currently hiked due to summer water shortages. 'This is policy.'

Babu's interest in water is semi-professional. His father used to sell it. 'Not the bottled stuff,' he adds for clarity's sake. His father would buy his sweet water 'wholesale' at Colaba market. He'd cycle over there, fill four forty-litre containers, and walk the two kilometres back with his sloshing cargo dangling from the handlebars of his bike. His margin was three rupees per container. On an average day, he'd make four or five trips. I totted up the maths. He was clearing sixty rupees a day. Babu's driving job is lucrative by comparison.

'Sometimes he'd collect the water from a nearby building that had a leaking overflow pipe,' Babu says, a crook-toothed smile crossing his clean-shaven face. 'It is a military soldier building actually.'

As his father's only son, Babu was occasionally drafted in to help. His inauguration as a water rustler came at age eleven. 'Many times the police were catching us,' Babu admits. First, they'd be dealt a beating. Then the uniformed officers would make them cut the grass or wash their bicycles.

Babu's smile gravitates into a light-hearted chuckle at the memory. What kind of childhood must he have had, I wonder, to recall father-and-son moments like these with such affection?

The thought occupies me as we step into the slum. The entrance comes via a few downward steps and a shack-padded passageway. The path is wide enough for a bicycle but too narrow for an ambulant cow. Neither are considerations to be overlooked in India.

A corner store the size of a small garden shed serves as a sentry post. It is manned by a heavy-set girl called Rochi (meaning 'light'). I stop to buy some Peppy Cheese Balls for Babu's children. Clad in the white smock of a school pupil, the twelfth-grader has proficient English and a keen desire to practise. She plans to do a graphic-design course after graduating, she tells me. She won't marry until she's 'well set' in her career. Her father was a chauffeur for the US Embassy. He lived in New York for a year, but he had to have emergency heart surgery. The operation took place at the city's Bellview Hospital. The last point is shared with a touch of wonderment, as if her father had dined at the Waldorf rather than narrowly escaping death after a massive coronary.

As we press on, Ganesh Murty Nagar opens up – or rather closes in – like a multi-highway rabbit warren. Everywhere there are sharp corners and cavernous tunnels. Babu turns left and right and left again. It is not long before I am totally disorientated.

I concentrate my eyes on Babu's over-exercised sneakers, watching their threadbare tread closely for both direction and dog shit. Head down, life unfolds in my peripheral vision. Curiously, the world at close quarters lodges more as sound than sight: housewives gab, televisions sing, couples yell, children shout, vendors vend, dogs howl. To my surprise, the cacophonous symphony calms my step. It's as if the discordant score were choreographed to match the jumpiness I feel during my stroll through the slum.

Despite the baldy jokes, Babu appears well liked. People recognise him and he, in turn, waves, laughs and jokes with all and sundry as he walks. His stride is confident. His manner, warm. His bike might be rusty and his boss's car a two-door, but at least he has wheels and a job. That counts for something. Plus, he's fit and healthy. In the slum, that's worth even more.

'This is my sister-in-law's house,' he says, stopping by a piece of lurid red fabric hanging over an open doorway. He inches it open, a curtain twitcher in reverse. Cleaning the tiled floor with a mop bends a shadow in a sari. She straightens, smiles the briefest of smiles at the sudden burst of sunlight and returns to her chores. There appears to be little love lost between them.

Babu presses on until we reach a junction of sorts. It's an absurdity to have a clearing in a forest that lacks trees, but that's exactly how it feels: the sudden sense of space, the uninterrupted patch of sky, the ability to breathe. We are, as it were, poking our heads through the warren's principal rabbit hole after days underground.

In reality, the open glade is little more than a widened lane. A myriad of tightly squeezed pathways squirt out of it, identical to the one we've just exited. There is room to move and, as a consequence, it serves as both a market and a meeting place.

Turning into the lane, Babu slows his pace to exchange pleasantries with the bow-legged postman, Mr Jadhav. White-haired and good-natured, the elderly mailman waddles to a stop. He lowers his voluminous satchel to the floor, sending a runaway utility bill into the dust. Diligently, he brushes off the dirt and returns it to his stockpile. Mr Jadhav is an old hand. No one knows quite how long he's been delivering letters around the slum. About as long as the independent Post Office of India has been issuing stamps, most figure.

A thin-faced man in a pressed white shirt hurries past us. Babu shouts at him to stop. 'Can't,' the scurrying figure shouts back over his shoulder. 'Late for work.' Raju, Babu informs me, earns his keep as a chauffeur for global accountancy firm KPMG.

Mr Jadhav returns to his rounds and Babu wanders off. It is not long before he spots another familiar face. Robert is sitting on his haunches, shooting the breeze with a friend. Long of mane and languid of speech, Babu's athletic-looking acquaintance boasts a baseball cap and a single-figure golf handicap. He works as a caddie at the Indian-only United Services Club (popularly, yet confusingly, known as the US Club).

The multiplicity of jobs and evidence of enterprise fascinate me. I turn to Babu and make a remark to that effect.

As he ponders the fact, a knock-kneed man in tatty shorts and flip-flops lollops by. He has a basket on his head full of nail polish, hairclips, brushes and cutlery. He dips into one of the feeder alleys. Just as he does so, a diminutive man emerges with a bulging sack of nylon underwear on his head. The two almost collide, narrowly avoiding what had the potential to become the slum's first female department store.

Shifting his gaze to the flurry around us, Babu seeks to enlighten me to the occupations of his neighbours. 'Most people here are drivers or maids. Or they work as security guards.' He pauses. 'Some do official work.' By which he means that they are on the government's payroll: a tea boy at the municipal water-works department, a ticket-office assistant for the railways, a runner for the court, an underling in the tax office, that sort of thing. Any higher and they'd have the salaries to pay for more desirable accommodation, or the clout to bribe their way to the same. 'The lazy and the sick, they are not so much working actually,' Babu adds, not hiding his disapproval. The water seller's son has been earning for as long as he can remember. He has a loathing for the unemployed, regardless of their personal circumstances. People should work. Final.

'Oh, and others are doing the selling,' he mentions as an afterthought, casually pointing his head up the lane.

Commercial activity – buying, selling, bartering, haggling, hassling, hawking – is so pervasive and public in India that it is understandable that Babu should initially omit to mention it. Hucksters crowd the buses and trains; stallholders stifle the streets; pedlars pack the pavements. India has a wallah for every ware under the nation's white-hot sun. Children, adults, the elderly – none is exempt from the art of exchange, the primordial urge to trade. India's mercantile horde made the country's cities into a virtual marketplace long before the Internet propagated the idea. Who needs eBay when every street corner provides a living, crowded auction site?

The three-man shopping parade next to Robert proves the point. First in line is an elderly fishmonger. Silent yet stoic, the Zenned-out salesman wears an age-lined face as shrivelled and grey as his rapidly spoiling catch.

The second, a jolly fruit seller with apple-red cheeks, appears more animated about his trade. Babu sidles up to him. As the two talk, Babu's two lanky fingers graze on the vendor's grapes. Piled high on a wheeled cart, the driver pops them into his mouth with the casual insouciance of a gambling addict plugging coins into a fruit machine. At the bottom of the cart, a pile of ripening green oranges emits a wispy curl of incense smoke. 'For the flies,' says Babu, through a mouthful of grape juice.

A diminutive Bihari called Mukesh occupies the end of the row. He trades as a barber. His overheads are small: a stool, a comb, an oxidised pair of kitchen shears and a cracked mirror resting on a breezeblock. He charges twenty rupees for a trim. A shave costs ten. The head massage afterwards comes free.

'I take Saturdays off,' he says, when I ask if he works the whole week. 'Hindus don't cut their hair on Saturdays.'

Offending religious sentiment is bad for business. Perhaps that's why Mahindra World City had no provision for public worship? Ganesh Murty Nagar could not be more different. Painted divinities preside over cubbyhole shrines at every turn. The busy lane alone houses a multi-coloured Sai Baba temple, an unsteady mosque of bamboo walls and tarpaulin roof, and a concrete Catholic mission hut built over an old creek.

Babu, for his part, cares little for any of them. 'I am not into the religion actually,' is how he phrases it. Later, when I knew him better, he'd expand on his world-view. His personal ethics reflect a succinct secularity. 'My thing is to have good work, good food, good money and good sleep. Oh, and help the disabled people.' A remnant of gratitude to the Spastic Society, perhaps.

Babu's antipathy towards religion contains the odd exception. He has some sympathy for Christianity, for instance. His affections are in fact more specific. They concentrate primarily on St Anthony, patron of (among other things) pregnant women, sterility, starvation and swineherds. Babu credits the slum chapel's official benefactor for answering his candle-lit prayers and providing him with two sons. He also has the Hindus to thank for allowing him one of their own as his wife (although she's since jumped ship to New Life Fellowship, an evangelical group active in the slum). It is his fellow Muslims for whom he can find nothing good to say. 'I am hating my religion', is as far as he'll venture. Now, I sense, is not the moment to ask why.

'Are there many Muslims in the slum?' I enquire instead.

According to Babu's reckoning, roughly a third of his fellow residents would describe themselves as 'Maharashtran Muslim'. Most of the rest are Hindus. South Indian Catholics and a small yet growing quota of born-again Christians make up the remainder.

However, it is caste – not religion – that Babu sees as the defining characteristic of his community. As we leave the lane and set off down a single-file corridor of a street towards his house, he waves an arm at the maelstrom of humanity around us. 'There are only scheduled castes here. We're all *non-weg* [a common colloquial abbreviation for 'non-vegetarian']. Everyone drinks whiskey. No one eats on banana leaf. So even the Brahmins are only Brahmin in name.'

With that, he strides off. I clatter behind, tripping on duck-boards and bumping into passers-by to prevent his running shoes from speeding off without me.

A few minutes and a dozen hairpins later, Babu draws to a halt. He turns to his left and looks down a stunted cul-de-sac. Sat on a doorstep, a young woman is scouring the scalp of her droopy-eyed five-year-old for lice. Babu wishes both ladies a good day.

'This is my old house,' he says, leaning a hand on the wall of a dingy storeroom.

The one-room house occupies the corner. It is full of empty wa-ter containers. The property measures eight feet by nine and is just tall enough to fit Babu's tall frame without bending.

'And this here', he continues, swapping hands and proudly pat-ting the exterior wall of the opposite shack, 'is my new house.'

Less than three feet separates the two properties.

Babu unties his shoelaces at the door of his new home. 'See? It's much bigger. Ten feet by twelve.' Unlacing my own shoes, I peer inside. Jyoti is sitting on the floor sieving rice for weevils. There is no chair. She is wearing a thin cotton dress over her squat, ample frame. She climbs to her feet. A patch of sweat causes the material to stick to her back, causing it to ride up ever so slightly. Embar-rassed, she pulls at the hem.

I press my hands together to wish her 'namaste', mimicking the universal Indian salutation with which she greets me. I sense her momentarily sizing me up over the tips of her fingers. I wonder what she saw, because she never looks at me straight again.

Babu steps across the torn T-shirt that doubles as a doormat and places a protective hand on his wife's head. His hips are al-most in line with her shoulders.

'This is Jyoti,' he announces with atypical formality. 'You must be excusing her. She is illiterate. But she is learning English speak-ing because she would like to study Bible studies.'

The recent convert to New Life Fellowship grins obligingly.

Only her eyes betray the confusion brought on by her husband's unintelligible little speech. She directs me to sit on the bed as she busies herself preparing lunch.

The bed is the only substantive piece of furniture in the room. Slightly wider than a standard single, it is shoved up against the wall closest to the alleyway. If Babu were to stretch, he could lever the door handle with his foot. The home-made bed has bricks for legs, four of them stacked one on top of the other in each corner. The majority of the family's personal possessions are packed into cardboard boxes and shoved under the hardboard base. Some sheets and a few everyday clothes squash flat underneath two meagre pillows at the head of the bed. Nabi and Ashu sleep on rush mats on the concrete floor. The mats too are packed away.

The house has the feel and shape of a domesticated prison cell. An electric fan and lone light bulb dangle from the ceiling. A tiny alcove opposite the doorway houses the kitchen. It comprises a concrete chopping surface, a gas hob and a metal drying-up rack. The latter sags under the weight of a dozen aluminium plates and cups. Below the sink runs a single shelf. It divides the cooking pans above from the plastic water containers below. In front, a pair of gas cylinders stands squashed together. They look like two bronze bullets squeezed into a firing chamber. In winter the gas hob serves the additional function of heating the house as well as the family's food.

Along from the kitchen, in the other corner, stands a squat lavatory. It is curtained in behind bricks and a wooden door. The size of a phone box, it doubles as a shower room. (Doubling up, I learn, is essential when you live in half the minimum space necessary.) Jyoti refuses to use the in-house loo for reasons of habit and privacy. Instead, she prefers to toilet with her girlfriends in the public lavatory block. She makes her way there every morning in the pre-dawn light, armed with toilet paper, toothbrush and an eagerness to be updated on the latest goings-on in the slum. Still, just having their own lavatory differentiates the house from its immediate neighbours. It's a status thing, much like having a bidet in Billericay.

The most obvious symbol of success balances on a metal support attached to the far wall near the bed. The Samsung colour television presides over the room from just above head height. 'Twenty-one inches,' says Babu. 'Any smaller and my eyes would spoil.' He subscribes to fourteen paid-for channels at a total cost of seventy rupees per month. Most show re-runs of popular Hindi and Western movies. For a year, he has been hassling the local dealer to add the Pix channel to his package, 'but he is not listening only'. When Babu is not watching animal documentaries, he likes action flicks. Sylvester Stallone, Arnold Schwarzenegger and Sharon Stone count among his favourites.

The TV rack holds a Phillips DVD player as well. Babu frequently sits up late into the night to watch pirated films that he buys at one of the many pavement Blockbusters around the city. He has a few blue movies squirrelled away too. These he reserves for the very early hours when Jyoti is asleep. If she wakes, which she sometimes does, she scolds him fiercely for his devilry.

A knot of black wires extends from the back of the Japanese television to four small speakers spread around the room. Babu bought the surround-sound system with his last Diwali bonus. His boss was hoping he'd buy a fridge or water purifier, but to no avail.

Babu comes and sits beside me on the bed. He pulls out a collection of family photos from a plastic bag beneath the bed. The low-resolution scenes, blurred by thumbprints, are typical of such collections: birthdays, first days at school, family outings. Curiously, there are none of Babu's wedding. I ask why. 'No camera,' he explains. He pauses a fraction, as if contemplating what to say next. 'We had a private party only. Nothing fancy.' The wedding breakfast, it turns out, consisted of a six-pack of beers back in the slum.

Mixed-faith marriages, even at the bottom of the social hierarchy, are best celebrated quietly. As it is, Jyoti's family situation doesn't lend itself to happy get-togethers. Her mother died when Jyoti was young, immolating herself with paraffin and a match. The family cried murder, however, and pointed the finger at Jyoti's father. Under pressure from her aunt, Jyoti testified against him in court. Her father was duly imprisoned. She later recanted. It was too late. He'd already died behind bars. Jyoti and her five siblings bounced around family members for a little while, but eventually ended up on the street. 'That's why none of them have a good education and why everybody is doing violence with each other,' Babu notes. Jyoti eventually landed herself the job as a maid in Kuffe Parade. 'Then I got into a love affair with her,' Babu says. His tone is unromantic and everyday. 'And one day I went to get married.'

A soft, metallic thud sounds from the corrugated iron roof, disturbing what has become a rather sorrowful stroll down memory lane. 'Just a pigeon,' Babu says, his ear attuned to every noise and movement in and around his one-room house.

The interruption allows for a welcome change in subject. Babu lays the photos aside. Sometimes kids from his alleyway clamber on to the roof to lie out clothes to dry, he explains, looking up at the roof. 'I shoo them off actually.'

Trespassing children are just one of the daily annoyances that slum life brings. Other people's rubbish dumped on his doorstep vexes Babu too. (Garbage collection is 'privatised' in as much as residents who don't want to dispose of it themselves must pay someone else to take it away.) His biggest grouch is the thieving. Some mornings he tries starting his motorbike, only to find that the petrol has been siphoned out of the tank. 'They do it with a Biseleri bottle,' he explains, in reference to a popular brand of mineral water.

'Is there much crime?' I ask, interested to know how much weight Babu gives to such incidents.

Mumbai's shanties, like shanties in all of India's large cities, have the reputation of being dens of vice and violence. For the tabloid press, the slums always provide the backdrop for grisly murders and massive drug busts. Middle-class friends would often look at me in horror on hearing I'd been traipsing around a slum. 'Tell me you didn't take your watch?' one girl even remonstrated. 'People get stabbed in those places for far less.' It was the term 'those places', spoken with such contempt, that kept me going back.

In my personal experience (albeit limited), social solidarity in the slums often far exceeds that in the atomised worlds of expensive apartment blocks and walled-in communities. 'Close-knit', for Babu, represents far more than just a geographical description of where he lives. The willingness of his fellow residents to band together makes burglary a high-risk business. 'We beat them very badly if we catch them,' Babu remarks. 'There's no mercy for them.' The consensus is simple: if people must rob or deal drugs, then they should do so elsewhere. Not, ever, on their own doorstep.

'How about gangs? Do they operate in the slums?' I enquire.

The question isn't asked entirely blind. Sitting on my bedside table back at my lodgings is an open copy of Suketu Mehta's *Maximum City: Bombay Lost and Found*. A graphic description of the city's teeming underbelly, a large portion of the book is dedicated to the Dawood Idrahim gang. Allegedly based in Karachi, with operations throughout Mumbai, the Indian mafia don oversees a genuine multinational corporation of crime.

'They are no gangs exactly. Actually, they are more like teams,' my host responds, uncharacteristically judicious in his selection of words.

The description makes them sound harmless, as if it were all one big game, a case of supporting one football club over another. If so, then the rules are certainly unforgiving. 'One of my friends was stabbed twice during the last Holi celebrations,' says Babu, his tone almost blasé. The man was a gang member, he adds. It's meant as an explanation, not a description.

The slum is definitely no play park. The spectre of violence is forever lurking in the shadows. Shanties, by definition, host the poor. That impoverishment might give rise to petty theft. It could exacerbate domestic violence too. In some cases, it might even foster organised crime. Yet poverty rarely results in murder. India has religion and politics for that.

Every now and then, India's hard-won reputation for inter-faith harmony and secular plurality takes a blood-soaked battering. The weeks after Independence, when trainloads of slaughtered corpses trundled into Delhi and Islamabad, set a lamentable precedent for what – admittedly, very occasionally – was to come. One of the latest such outbursts occurred in 2002, when intersectarian violence in Gujarat left more than one thousand dead. Unofficial figures put it at double that. The majority were Muslims. Most were poor.

Mumbai's recent history bears the scars of similar inter-communal madness. In December 1992, the destruction of the Babri mosque in Ayodhya (the result of the same religious dispute that sparked the Gujarat riots a decade later) provoked a rampage by Mumbai's Muslims. Hindu reprisals soon followed. Babu was sixteen at the time. For his safety, his mother pulled him out of school. He never went back. 'Riots. Bloodshed. Each and everything happened,' he says, dredging up the events that thrust him into an early adulthood. 'It is in front of my eyes. It is still kept in mind.' He shakes his head, mostly in sadness but, I like to think, partly in an attempt to dislodge the memories. He blames fighting between Hindus and Muslims for depriving him of his education. They spoilt his future, he insists.

Babu clears his throat with an eruption of violent, guttural hacking. Calmly he steps towards the door, leans over the threshold and spits a globule of yellowish-green phlegm into the alley. He turns back. 'For that reason, I am becoming a driver only.'

There is no time to consider the implications of the statement, for in run Nabi and Ashu. Wild and impish, they scream gleefully at the unexpected sight of their father and run open-armed towards him. Each grabs a leg. With much giggling, they attempt to wrestle him to the ground. Babu retaliates with tickles and enveloping bear hugs.

'Boys, stop messing,' barks Jyoti with a well-honed, on-stage anger. The tussling ceases immediately, all three recognising an order when they hear one. The boys dutifully carry out the instructions that follow. Satchels are put away under the bed, hands

are washed and bottoms are parked on the concrete floor in front
of Cartoon Network.

'Now, boys, homework straight after lunch, okay,' Babu chips
in. 'You must grow to become good in the reading and writing.'

The second injunction, spoken in Babu's evening-school English, is said for my sake more than for the boys. He wants me to
know that he takes their education seriously. He would like to see
Ashu become a doctor one day. 'For that, he has to go for good
studies in science.' He shrugs his shoulders. Neither has shown
much enthusiasm for their schooling so far. 'They like many jokes
and having fun.'

As he's talking, Nabi pinches Ashu and a small scuffle breaks
out. Jyoti gives both a sharp clip around the ear and silence
returns. For a brief moment, the only sound to be heard is
floppy-haired Ben 10 gearing up his all-powerful Omnitrix wrist-
watch to do battle with Swampfire and his alien accomplices.
'See what I mean?' Babu says, raising his hands in a what's-a-
man-to-do gesture.

'I want to see my children become good and honest and intelligent men in the future.' His face grows serious. 'This is one of my
dreams, my main dream actually.'

He gazes down at his two children, who are sitting rapt as the
supersonic boy wonder drubs yet another ghoulish baddy. Then
his lips part in a paternal smile.

'But actually for now they are still kids only.'

Jyoti requests her husband to turn off the television. 'Lunch-
time,' she tells the boys, who moan at not being allowed to see
how Ben 10's intergalactic alien-blasting ends. Obediently they
swivel round and, together with Jyoti, begin to eat. In front of
their crossed legs sit two small mess dishes, each with a measured
dollop of dhal and rice. For flavour, the parsimonious meal depends heavily on a splattering of stir-fried okra. The slices of green
vegetable represent the only concession to colour too. The boys
mechanically move the contents of the bland lunch from hand to
mouth, munching unenthusiastically as they go. The same meal is
repeated in the evening, only with chapattis instead of rice ('rice

has gone up to forty rupees a kilogramme,' Babu would mutter in disgust at a later date). For variation, Jyoti sometimes buys radishes because she knows Babu likes them. Meat, however, remains a rarity on the family dinner table.

'I'm not so much interested in non-*weg*,' Babu confirms. 'Egg food, fish food, sometimes the chicken food I like. But chicken, I liked roasted only. Not with curries and all that. That I hate it.'

The truth, I suspect, is slightly different. When Jyoti buys meat, it's at the start of the month; that's to say, in the flush wake of payday. It is cash, not culinary preference (and certainly not caste or religion), that makes the family pious eaters.

Babu indicates that we should be on our way. I'd offered to buy him lunch after the visit. Now I feel guilty for not suggesting he bring his family along too.

As I rise to leave, I remember the cheese balls. There are in my shoulder bag. I reach in and pass the two packets to Jyoti. It's a mistake. The sight of the manufactured pap, glistening with E numbers, causes the boys to lose immediate interest in their meal. 'Now, now, now,' shouts Ashu, hassling his mother for the snack food. He crawls over onto his back in a tantrum when the request is denied. 'Finish your food first,' Jyoti scolds. Babu shouts something strict at him in Hindi, which evokes yet more convulsions. The English word 'stubborn' is used several times. Ashu takes himself and his fit off to an empty patch under the bed. His brother, meanwhile, silent until now, begins to bleat plaintively. Further wailing erupts in response from below my seat on the mattress.

Fortunately, a distraction in the shape of a twelve-year-old boy rescues the visit from the brink of mayhem. Dressed in the pukka uniform of the nearby Navy school, Anand is the bright kid on the block. Momentarily forgetting the cheese balls, Ashu and Nabi jump to their feet to greet their friend.

Anand's bright eyes twinkle intelligence. He is courteous, the product of a mother who has him set for better things. He lives two doors down. As he has no hesitation in informing me, he would like to become an engineer when he grows up. 'Why?' I enquire, expecting something along the lines of a good salary. His answer surprises me. 'I want to build the cheapest money car that poor people can buy so they can go on a long drive.' His expression reveals a steely determination.

I ask if he's heard of the 'Nano'. He says he hasn't. I explain that it is a car designed by Indian automobile maker Tata Motors which costs only one lakh. I had visited the company's headquarters in Pune a few months previously for a test drive. I tell him as much. He doesn't seem impressed. 'One lakh, eh?' he says. I nod. He smiles and with the same resolute look assures me that his car will be cheaper still.

Leaving Jyoti and the boys, we make our way back through the slum's labyrinthine tunnels. We walk in silence. Babu is brooding on something. As we near the corner store where I'd bought the fateful cheese balls, he reveals what's on his mind.

'It won't work on the road, you know.'

'What won't?' I ask.

'The Nano and all. Whoever is buying actually is buying the cheapest car. They are not thinking about safety.'

Something about my conversation with Anand had obviously been eating away at him. I repeat what the Tata engineers had told me about successful crash simulations and side-impact reinforcements.

'One crash and it will break into lots of pieces,' he responds, his mind made up. 'It's unsafe actually. The door will go one way and the body will go another.'

We reach the store. An old man with a grisly beard is occupying the stool where Rochi had previously been sat. I wonder if it's her father, the heart patient.

Babu draws my attention away. He hasn't finished with the Nano. 'They say it will cost one lakh. But they are fooling actually.' He had seen an interview on television with Ratan Tata, the visionary behind India's first low-cost car. 'He himself says that such a cheap vehicle makes profit very difficult.' Babu snorts, appalled that anyone could be gullible enough to be taken in by the Poor Man's Car. He can't honestly see anyone buying a Nano when they can pick up a Santro from Hyundai for three lakhs.

'Anyway,' he says, almost as an aside, 'it's a tiny, stupid little car.'

Therein, I suspect, lies his real gripe. For Mumbai's chauffeur fraternity, the car just isn't big enough to cut it.

Rant over, Babu pulls the keys from his pocket and opens the door of the Maruti Swift. Contorting himself back into the driver's seat, he ignites the engine and pulls out. He over-revs and we rejoin the traffic to the sound of screeching rubber and spitting gravel.

It feels good. Like we're not in the lowest-status vehicle after all.

Babu's boss generously invites me to make full use of his car. So over the succeeding weeks and months, whenever I'm in Mumbai, Babu, the Swift and I end up spending a considerable amount of time together. We make for a compact trio: criss-crossing the city, rushing for appointments, waiting at traffic lights.

Babu seems to enjoy the break from his usual routine. And I enjoy his company. He proves eager to help. As well as driver and tourist guide, he appoints himself my unofficial translator, fixer and general aide.

A trip to Film City provides him with the chance to mix all five roles together. I'd arranged an interview with the director Vipul Shah, via a contact in film production. He'd told me to meet him on set. Mr Shah is shooting a movie with action hero Akshay Kumar and doesn't know when he'll be free. Visibly excited, Babu spends much of the journey on the phone: half the time informing friends of his pending meeting with 'Akshay', and half the time checking (and rechecking with each successive wrong turn) the directions.

We arrive late to find a moody Vipul Shah sitting in the trailer park. His star actor had walked off in a sulk. Filming was cancelled for the day. Not one to be set back, Babu bowls up to my interviewee and shakes his hand energetically. 'Sir, please for you to meet Mr Oliver from Lon-don. He is journalist, sir.' I can see the grim-faced director trying to fathom out exactly who Babu is. Describing him as my driver somehow doesn't seem right. For starters, strictly he isn't my driver. He is someone else's. Secondly, as a general rule in India, drivers stay in their cars or keep out of sight. Babu, on the contrary, is already drawing up three seats so we could all sit together. 'This is my . . . er . . . assistant,' I mutter, gesturing towards Babu, who had already taken a seat and was waiting for the conversation to start. He beams.

The interview is not a great success, what with Babu's nodding presence at my shoulder and his regular grunts of agreement. When we finish up, my new assistant launches into a short speech about what a pleasure it was to meet Mr Shah and how much he enjoyed his films. 'My wife and I are watching *Waqt* many times,' he says. 'A very nice family movie actually, sir. We are laughing very much.' More handshaking follows. I suspect Babu might be about to ask for his autograph and usher him quickly away before he does.

We then go in search of my contact, the production manager. A crew member directs us to the mess tent, where we find him eating. He is sitting alone and invites us to join him. Babu smiles and heads off to the steaming line of hotplates. He returns with the best of the buffet loaded high on his plate. Conversation is slow. Babu is torn between translating and eating. For the most part, the unexpected feast commands his attentions. Not that it matters too much. The little that does reach me seems centred on obtaining photographs of my wife and children. The producer films television adverts as a sideline. A few Europeans on his list could come in handy. He gets up to go. Babu waves him off, emits a satisfied belch and goes up for seconds of the sweet rice dessert.

The trip provides us with a turning point. Until then, I'd ridden on the back seat, just as Indian etiquette has it between the driven and their drivers. Heading back from Film City, I move up front.

It's a simple gesture, but alters our relationship profoundly. No longer do we need to talk through the rear-view mirror. We can speak on a level. I take full advantage of the fact, peppering the ever-loquacious Babu with a constant flow of questions. His answers slowly reveal the world as he sees it.

Life Babu-style, I learn, emerges predominantly in black and white. Neutral colours don't occupy much space on his palette of opinions.

Take India and Pakistan, for example. The quarrelling neighbours are, as this proud Maharashtrian sees it, 'blood and blood'. The friction between the two countries is due entirely to their respective governments. 'Politicans', I should know, 'only care about lining their pockets.' India's northern cousin does have some 'backward practices', he concedes. Making women wear the burkha, keeping 'the girl childrens' uneducated, hanging models for wearing skimpy clothes – all these comprise 'the bullshit' in Babu's view.

When it comes to geopolitics, the British come off little better. They gave India education and trains, but took everything else. It's not a bad synopsis. As for the United States, their money is 'big'. On the downside, 'they always promise, but they do the falsehood behind the promise'. His prime examples are American incursions into Iraq and Afghanistan. Babu echoes the common sentiment in India that arresting Saddam was justifiable, but executing him probably wasn't. 'Everyone has the human rights actually,' he opines. Pakistan's women included.

As for India's role on the world stage, he is ambivalent. He has heard the talk of India becoming the 'next superpower and all'. He would like to believe it were true.

We are sitting over a cheap restaurant lunch of vegetarian kofta as we discuss the issue. A battered television, stained with grime from the street and oil from the kitchen, is running a daily news show. A headline runs along the bottom about a multi-billion-dollar nuclear energy deal with France. Babu points at the screen. 'I am looking at the news.' He has seen 'the India scientists going ahead' as well. Not to mention the troop of state leaders flocking to Delhi. 'India has so many contacts with the foreign countries. Like Russia is supporting for such a long time.' He places particular weight on India's military stockpiles. 'Nuclear

rockets, warships and fighter planes – India has so very many.'
His is a Ben 10 view of political supremacy: the bigger your Omnitrix, the more your clout.

'And economically?' I venture. 'Could India become a global
leader?'

'Absolutely. India is growing. Economic is more.' He talks
about the soaring buildings downtown and all the new cars on the
road.

But then his expression grows morose. Indians do not follow
the rules, he contends. Nor do they plan anything. For these reasons, his homeland 'may not become a superpower actually'.

I push him for some examples.

'Like chewing the paan,' he responds.

'I'm not sure I follow.'

He draws his breath in a search for patience. An Indian will always spit his paan on the floor, he explains, as if it were the most
obvious thing in the world. He'll never use a dustbin. 'He doesn't
think people will see. Or he doesn't care if they do. Everything
in India is like this.' Everything from minor traffic accidents to
massive political corruption: it all comes down to a bending of the
rules.

I sense he is on a roll. I order two teas.

India's population growth represents another clear case of lack
of planning, as far as Babu is concerned. He cites an acquaintance
in the slum who has five daughters. 'He keeps waiting for a son.'
Babu shakes his head, evidently appalled. 'He is a stupid man actually.' Two children, in his opinion, are quite enough. 'With lots
of children, you have a lot of problems. Already I scold. My wife
scolds. Sometimes we give beatings.' More follows about Ashu's
'stubbornness'. After two kids, all 'good Indians' should be steril-
ised, Babu believes. He means loyal Indian women, of course. The
government covers all the costs, right down to the taxi to the hospital. He should know. He made Jyoti go.

A few weeks later, Babu and I stop in at Veg Wonder, a down-
at-heel lunch spot along Worli Seaface Road. By now, long
lunches have become a regular feature of our excursions. Between

one helping of rice and the next, Babu extends his thinking on lack of planning to the realm of personal finances.

'In India, people want to get money. But all they do is work, go home, eat, do shit, and then get up and work again. They don't think why. They don't think about month's salary and savings. People put money in stupid things. So they go and ask for loan, from friends and things.'

I think back to the way Babu had meticulously counted his income and calculated his outgoings. Bar the surround-sound music system, his habits seem frugal. He wears a plastic watch. His diamond ear-studs are transparently fake. Even his motorbike, as he openly confessed, could do with an upgrade.

Babu hasn't always been so careful about money. A mischievous look comes over him as he pushes away his plate, signalling to the hovering waiter that he can eat no more. I sense a confession coming on. My lunch guest does not disappoint.

'Now you are not to be telling Jyoti this, okay,' he says as a preamble. I nod. When he was first married, he continues, he and his friends used to frequent the city's dance bars. In Colaba, mostly. They were well-enough known to have tabs in some. 'We were like owls. We never sleep. All the time to enjoy.'

The tea arrives. Babu doesn't seem to notice. Arms flailing, he is caught up explaining how best to throw money at dance girls. It's an amusing spectacle.

The key is for the notes to be 'fresh', he says, growing increasingly theatrical. That way, they fly straight. As for the best way to throw them, it's all in the wrist. He mimics the action. I look confused. 'You don't get it?' I don't. 'Then you should see gangster movie, *Vaastav*,' he advises me. 'In that movie, it shows how they are doing the throwing.'

I say I will and empty a sachet of sugar into my tea.

As I sip, Babu describes one night in particular. He'd gone with a friend from the slum to a dance bar called Crossroad, close to the meat wholesaler near Metro Cinema. His friend's brother worked in the kitchen on a P&O cruise liner. He'd recently wired some money home. Four hundred UK pounds, 'notes so huge they don't fit into an Indian wallet'. His friend blew the lot buying strangers drinks and throwing it gangster-style at the dancers. '"Stop for your goodness," I am telling him. He's telling me, like, "get lost".' Babu salvaged some loose notes and put them towards his gas bill. The rest disappeared.

Eventually, in the early hours, his friend gets thrown out onto the street. The bar closes and the girls drift home, while the punters head off to sober up on hot, sweet chai. His friend is slumped on the pavement, stamping his feet on the road and cursing himself. '"You are stupid," I am telling him.'

Babu writes off the whole episode with a laugh and a flick of the wrist. 'Anyway, he's Bengali and a drunk.'

The story has a purpose. Babu wants me to know how he has changed. He no longer goes out late or gambles away his money. Not because Crossroads closed down, which it did. ('The government said girls should not dance and not attach money to their bodies. But if girls not dancing, customers not going.') Nor because Jyoti used to give him hell in the morning, which she did too.

He stopped because of what happened to his father.

On 24 September 2007, the water vendor Naruddin Nabi Shaikh was knocked off his bicycle by a speeding motorbike. He was thrown to the floor. The frail fifty-nine-year-old did not – or rather, could not – move a muscle.

A policeman witnessed the incident and instructed the driver of the Pulsar Bajaj motorbike to take the victim immediately to the hospital. Rajput Vir Singh, a muscled Popeye who worked as a bouncer at a Colaba nightclub, did as instructed.

Mr Shaikh arrived bloodied and unconscious. Tests showed that he was suffering from a brain haemorrhage. Soon after, he slipped into a coma. The white coats that examined him put his chances of survival at 'minimal'. His family prepared for the worst. Amazingly, after a four-day vigil at his side, the head of the Shaikh household woke up.

The injured water carrier proved unable to speak. Nor did Mr Shaikh bring his memory back with him from the dead.

Worse was to come. Subsequent tests ('the doctor was all the time scratching his foot with a pen') revealed him to be partially paralysed. Only his head would move with any freedom. The entire right side of his body was rendered entirely immobile. As for his other side, motion was largely restricted to the thumb and middle finger of his left hand. Even then, the fingers worked – to quote his son – 'like a crab'. The water-supply business, needless to say, ceased trading.

One morning, after dropping his boss at work, Babu took me to see his crippled father in Geeta Nagar slum. Father and son are almost neighbours, their respective shanties separated only by a short, narrow causeway between the compound wall of Navy Nagar and the sea. The space is just wide enough for a dirt track.

Babu's father moved there from his birthplace in Jamkhandi, in Karnataka, back in the late 1950s. His brother, Babu's uncle, had found a job and sent for him. Aged twelve, he arrived with a small trunk and an arranged wife. The slum was just spouting its first shoots then. Back then the area used to be scattered with bushes, elderly residents recollect with nostalgia. Back then, they would keep hens and goats. An old British cannon used to stare out to sea on the stone-built tide-breaker. In the early 1960s, Mr Shaikh moved out of his brother's house and built his own bamboo hut. Sectarian issues were simmering. India had already fought one battle with Muslim-dominated Pakistan and a second was about to follow. When it came, Geeta Nagar was shrouded by blackouts, night after night.

Babu was born on the spot of that bamboo hut, as were the majority of his five sisters (the public hospital started charging for beds after the birth of daughter no. 1). His parents live there to this day, although now its walls are of brick and the roof a mix of corrugated iron and blue tarp. A quarter of a century and much lobbying later, Geeta Nagar finally gained access to fresh water. It took a further decade to get electricity.

Before arriving, Babu parks the Maruti on a rocky bulge midway down the walled causeway. 'I need piss,' he says, extricating himself from the car and wandering down to the waterfront.

I wonder if urinating represents some kind of pre-visit ritual for him. The thought doesn't distract me for long because soon a group of three boys wander over and begin peering inquisitively through the car window.

I'm grateful when Babu returns. 'Uncle, uncle,' the boys shout with genuine affection at the long-limbed driver, who is doing up his fly. There's nothing of the 'baldy' jokes here. Each is dressed in a football shirt and, to a boy, aspires to become a professional cricketer in the future.

'Geeta is the name of a woman actually,' Babu says, breaking off to shout at the grubby trio who are messing with his wing-mirror. She was a politician from here, he continues. She's still alive, actually. Babu worries about when she 'gets die', as he puts it. 'They will snatch the place actually and make seven-storey apartments there.'

For the moment, Geeta Nagar is safe. 'This is a lovely place actually,' he says, pointing out to the bay in front of us. Moment-arily calm and creatively decorated with driftwood and plastic, the inky water stretches out in an ample arc. To the left runs the old sea wall, now bereft of armaments and pockmarked by stone-stealing looters. Inland, to the right, a sturdy buttress of reclaimed land stands above the water line. Trimmed with reed beds, it bends round to the elegant, expensive apartments on Kuffe Parade. 'That is the Coastal Regional Zone,' Babu says, re-calling the open creek that preceded the reclamation project. He directs a finger towards the sky-rises across the bay, now creep-ing their way on to the precious plot wrested from the sea. 'These constructions are illegal actually.' He is, most probably, right. Yet I have a hunch Mr Shaikh's lifetime home will be levelled long be-fore a stop order is ever placed on the big-ticket building projects opposite. Babu turns to go.

It is an hour before we reach his parents' house, which is loc-ated at the far end of the slum, almost rubbing up against the Navy wall. The walk through the bustling passageways reminds me of my earlier visit to Babu's home. Geeta Nagar has much the same vibrancy about it; people at every turn, working, shouting,

praying, selling, washing. It is life in the raw, where fights and for-
nication are as open to all as the contents of a postcard.

Babu moved out of Geeta Nagar when he married Jyoti. He did
so because he felt 'claustrophobic', he'd told me previously. Pic-
turing the cramped cul-de-sac that he now calls home, I'd failed
to understand what he'd meant by the term. Now, walking beside him, watching him stop and greet all and sundry, listening
to him talk of childhood friends and long-gone events, the penny
drops. His claustrophobia is not physical; it's emotional, perhaps
even psychological. He is living on top of his life, constantly tread-
ing and re-treading old memories, forbidden from ever properly
starting again. It makes for a composite existence, each day, each
experience compressed against those that came before, another
layer in the persona that is Mohammed 'Babu' 'Baldy' Shaikh.

He might have fled, but he hardly turned prodigal. Every
Sunday, he returns to give his father a scrub and to shave his pallid, grey-stubbled face. During the week, he'll pop round to check
on them as well. If they need medication, he'll buy it. If they need
more 'rations', he'll stock up. 'I'm the lone son of my parents.'
The phrase implies an unquestioned obligation.

When it comes to family responsibility in India, primogeniture
rules. And Babu's inherited burden is not inconsiderable. Apart
from his father's paralysis, his mother has severe diabetes. On one
of our many lunches, Babu had appeared unusually sullen. His
mother, he'd revealed after some prompting, had been rushed to
hospital the previous night. She'd been suffering from acute 'body
pain' for several days and eventually fainted.

For once, Babu was devoid of appetite as he recounted the
episode. He'd paid for a taxi to take her to G. T. Hospital in
Colaba, reasoning that 'it is difficult to get a patient on the motorbike'. On arriving, the doctor had given him short shrift. 'Why
not eating?' he asked. 'Why spend one hundred rupees on taxi to
come to hospital too?' He'd sent them home, mother included,
ordering the patient to purchase an Accu-Chek meter to measure the glucose levels in her blood. The contraption costs just shy
of two thousand rupees. Cash-short as ever, Babu doesn't know

whether 'to buy or not to buy'. His mother's life might depend on it. It is a Shakespearean dilemma – one of many played out in the slums of Colaba every day.

Babu's obligations don't end there. His sister Bano married a drunk who beats her. The two are temporarily separated. Until they 'compromise', Babu has her and her two teenage children to care for as well. His eldest sister recently died of cancer while on a trip to Madhya Pradesh. Babu paid the cost of the taxi that transported her body the two-day journey home.

His two other surviving sisters – Janeb and Fatima (the fifth died shortly after birth) – married well. Their husbands run a stone-necklace business in Crawford Market. 'They are quite rich and have a good lifestyle.' Unfortunately for Babu (and his parents), paternal care passes through the male not female line. The daughters' obligations lie with their husband's parents now; a belated adoption via marriage.

'I have many mouths to feed,' the boy from the slum says as we draw up to the hut where he took his first breath. 'That's why I never miss my duties.'

It brings the notion of 'enterprise' into sharp relief. India's young entrepreneurs strive and struggle to create that highly prized thing called 'value'. Babu works every hour to keep his dependents from starving. Hundreds of millions of industrious Indians are just the same.

Stooping beneath the low door-frame, we enter his parents' home. The air is oven-hot and sprinkled thick with a dust of powdered sugar. His father is sitting cross-legged on a small, elevated bed in front of the door. The bed's positioning is intentional, providing its invalid occupant with a view of the children playing outside. They are his sole entertainment. A wooden bracket stands bolted just above the door, enabling him to reach up with the crab pincer of his left hand and lever himself upright. White-haired and rickets-thin, Babu's father (with his son's help) has attempted to spruce up his woebegone appearance with a smartly trimmed goatee. The old man's eyes brighten a fraction on registering our arrival. I spot kindness in them, or would like to think

I do. I have no way of checking, however, for it is the only gesture of recognition that I can discern. He remains looking forward as we pass.

Babu's mother, Jamila, is also sitting cross-legged, but on the concrete floor. She is chopping cauliflower. Dressed in a pale blue cotton sari with faded pink flowers, she looks crumpled and battle-worn. It's impossible to conceive of Babu's emaciated mother as a child bride, presumably young and hopeful once upon a time. Her salt-and-pepper hair is tied back in a bun. Metal bracelets rattle softly from her stick-like wrists, a close-at-hand reminder of a far-off wedding. She is making papad, picking out Styrofoam-like curls of dhal rice from an old biscuit tin and tossing them into a hot frying pan. The dehydrated food hisses and spits as it hits the sizzling oil, filling the room with a curious smell of fried onions and burning plastic.

The visit proves a dispiriting experience. Jamila offers gap-toothed smiles, yet says nothing. Mr Shaikh merely sits and stares blankly. Babu tries his best to lighten the mood and make me feel at home. He directs me to the room's only chair, sends off the ten-year-old Soyab (who, in the fluid way of Indian relations, is identified as both his sister's son and his cousin's brother) to buy some Thums Up, and generally sees off the silence with his own brand of repartee. The latter focuses mostly on his mother's dwindling health and his father's toilet problems.

Feeling suddenly depressed at the grimness of it all, I look around for a distraction. My gaze settles on the room's only dec-oration. It comes in the shape of a poster depicting a milky-white, rosy-cheeked baby. 'Smile and the world smiles with you,' the caption reads. The fresh-faced image almost seems cruel in its can-died, blueberry-pie optimism. Babu's mother follows my eye. She turns to her son and mutters a short muffled sentence, her first and last. 'My mother says she is happy,' he translates back to me, 'but she is sad in the heart because all her children have gone.' Gulping back my drink, I ask Babu if we might be best to leave his mother to her cooking. I'm not sure how much more I can take.

We exit through the back. The Shaikh residence differs from

Babu's in having two rooms. It is not the exception. The hut opposite even has a second storey, like two Lego bricks affixed one on top of the other. The owner works in the Gulf, Babu explains. 'He died recently.' The way he says it, I imagine the man's ghost still lugging bricks on a construction site in Dubai, carefully saving his money to send as remittance home.

I breathe deeply as we leave the hut through the rear door. The salt air, caustic and ungranulated, clears my head and fills my lungs. I take another gulpful as my eyes adjust to the sunlight. In front is the sea, lapping against the litter-strewn rocks below. Across the water sweeps the curved esplanade of Marine Drive, known as the Queen's Necklace for its twinkling lights after dark.

A footpath of sorts, lined with an open drain, separates the huts from the sea. 'Sometimes it floods,' Babu remarks without any special emphasis, lowering a flat hand to his thigh to show how high the water rises. He points to the stain of a tidemark on his parent's brick-plaster house.

I see that a fishing rod is wedged on the zinc roof between odds and sods rescued from the sea. Fishing, along with swimming, comprises a childhood passion that Babu has taken with him into adulthood. 'I fish just there,' he says, pointing to a rocky outcrop at the water's edge. As if following his finger, a small boy emerges from a nearby shack, clambers down the sloping sea wall, drops his trousers and defecates on the exact same spot. Two elderly men are similarly engaged further along the wave-splashed rampart.

We begin to make our way back to the car. As we turn to leave, a gap-toothed young man just out of his teens joins us. Babu introduces him as Govind and describes him as his 'brother-in-law'. His obvious youth (he must be two decades younger than Babu's youngest sister) makes that doubtful. Perhaps he's the brother, or even the son, of his genuine brother-in-law? Either way, there's an evident affection between the two.

'Govind is into crime and all,' Babu says, gently cuffing the semi-relative on the back of the head. The young man looks at him blankly, his mouth drooping open like a thirsty dog's. It's the expression of a halfwit or a drug user. Which of the two, I can't tell.

Govind is still in eleventh standard. Babu's younger charge somehow owns property. Inherited, quite probably. Walking back through the slum, Babu points out a single-room shack. A woman is scrubbing her child in the far corner of the furniture-less space. Her husband is at work. He checks stock levels in a biscuit factory. The couple pays Govind one thousand five hundred rupees per month for the privilege of the leaking roof and concrete floor. His rental portfolio comprises two other similarly spartan dwellings.

Despite the steady income, Babu worries that he is wasting his youth. He'd like to see him with a career. What about driving? Babu counts several driving protégés in the slum. His preferred means of instruction are unorthodox ('I teach by hitting and slapping'), but all have gone on to secure jobs. Govind is not cut out as a driver, though. Too little concentration, according to Babu. 'Anyway, driver is not a good status job, actually.'

In conspiratorial tones, he leans over and shares his own aspiration for the younger man. 'I'm trying to get him into the police.' Govind grins inanely. It is one of the few legitimate professions to which the young delinquent appears vaguely amenable.

As the months pass, I'd like to think Babu and I become firm friends. Or as firm as our different backgrounds, languages and cultures allow. The more we lunch, the more we confide, as though food and privacy are inversely correlated. He regularly asks me about my wife and children, who are living in a rented flat in Kerala and whom I miss when I'm away. We talk at length about his family too: the progress of Jyoti's diet, Nabi and Ashu's school marks, his parents' ever-failing health. Some of what he shares is personal, such as the fact he's not circumcised (his antipathy to Islam evidently has a history) or that he keeps liquor under his bed (although he claims never to touch it, 'hardly ever actually'). But much of what we discuss sticks to the everyday, like the best way to rid a dog of maggots or which is the best-flavoured lassi (mango, apparently).

I remain fascinated by how Babu views the world around him, especially in a city such as Mumbai, where the divisions between the haves and have-nots are so stark. Doesn't it frustrate him to be surrounded by so much wealth? When he's driving past Anil Mabani's two-billion-dollar skyscraper palace or watching the banking crowd feast on fresh salmon at Olive, doesn't it make him jealous?

Over lunch one day in a greasy Chinese joint along Colaba's main strip, I put the question to him directly.

He places his fork on the table and thinks a moment. Slowly, he works the chicken chow mein around his mouth. (Our lunches are exceptions to his usual veg diet.) He eyes squint ever so slightly with deliberation, as if he's trying to work out if my question is somehow more complex than it appears.

'I am not jealous with them. They are more studied than me.'

It is both an answer and not an answer, a politician's response. Could he expand?

'Maybe they come from a royal family, that's why they have a good house. Maybe they have black money. Who knows?'

The truth of the matter doesn't seem to bother him. He assumes no relation between his own lot and that of Mumbai's moneyed classes. The two – the loaded and lacking – might be living cheek and jowl, but, in this driver's mind at least, they are occupying different orbits.

'Doesn't it make you feel angry?' I press, placing my fork on the table as well.

It suddenly feels as though we're sparring, as if a duel with pronged cutlery is about to kick off.

'No, I don't feel angry,' he replies, part indignant, part confused. 'Why should I?'

It falls to me to wonder whether his puzzlement is genuine or if there's more to his response. 'Because of the unfairness of it all!' I want to shout. 'Because your kids go hungry while theirs grow fat!' But I hold back. If he can't see it, then I can't explain it to him.

Maybe jealousy is too localised an emotion to feel about people so far removed from his own affairs, from the world of Ganesh Murty Nagar? Perhaps envy requires relational proximity to foster? Towards his neighbours – for their new extensions or their foreign remittances – its sting is stronger. But for those across the invisible wall, the visible divide, that separates India's rich from its poor? No, it's senseless, a futile waste of precious energy. It would be like me harbouring a hatred against Neil Armstrong for walking on the moon instead of me. What's the point? The logic makes sense, but something about it – the impassivity, the resignation, the detached acquiescence – still doesn't feel right.

I try another tack: 'What do you think the best thing about being rich is?'

The tension dissipates. He chuckles and picks up his fork again. 'The best thing is – what you call it? – a stylish life. Without doing anything. Just attending phone calls. Not doing big, hard work.' He traps a straggle of stir-fried noodles and searches out a piece of chicken around which to wind them. 'Not like my work. Running in the traffic all day. And police harassment for the parking. And dying in the pollution. I hate those things actually.' I ask if he'd like a job in a big company. He says he would. The trappings of a 'good position' appeal to him particularly. 'I'd like a car and a driver and a good flat along with the maid.' He looks wistful and then a smidgen dejected. 'But that is not possible because my education is low.' He despises 'the maths subject' especially. 'I don't want to kill my mind by giving interest in those things.' He bites down decisively on the noodle-wrapped fork and begins to chew.

Several months pass before I am back in Mumbai. When I return, Babu tells me he has been thinking about our previous conversation. 'About the jobs and all.' We're in the lift going up to his boss's apartment block. I'm staying there temporarily, borrowing his spare room as well as his car. Babu has an hour to kill. I suggest he comes in.

The flat is on the twenty-eighth floor. It is the maid's domain. Babu rarely enters, spending his days in the basement car park instead. He wanders across the room towards the floor-to-ceiling window. Mumbai soars up towards him, India's Manhattan. The double-glazing and altitude combine to seal off the space from the world around it. Free from car horns and chaos, it is like living in a light aircraft: semi-suspended, both literally and figuratively. For Babu, whose home is down to earth in every sense, this is good society living in the flesh.

After a few minutes, he pulls himself away from the window and takes a seat at the large dining table. The piece of furniture, I find myself thinking, would fill half of Babu's house.

'So I've been thinking', he tells me, 'driver is not such a good job.'

He explains his rationale: the 'much less salary', the long hours, the lack of stability (his boss's secondment is due to finish within the year), the risk of accident. He returns to the issue of status. 'A driver is just like a small people. He is just an ordinary man. He is nothing.' He describes how his driver colleagues steal petrol from the tank and use their employers' cars for private work, cruising here and there and 'putting their mind to doing the sex with the madam or maid'.

'Are you thinking about a career change then, Babu?' I enquire, wondering where this is all leading.

He shrugs. He mentions again his lack of education. Inspired by his friend's brother, he'd once thought about applying for a job on a P&O cruise liner. But it would mean being away for ten months a year. He didn't feel he could leave his parents for so long. 'You only have one dad and mum once in life.' He's also thought about trying his hand as a kitchen helper or a cook. He has seen the physique of restaurant employees. 'They have got a good body and big muscles because they have good food to eat inside.' The food is free, he thinks. If he had such a job, he would eat his way through the menu. 'From a young age, I have wanted to be a muscles man.' Realistically, though, he will probably have to become a security guard or a lift operator once his driving days are over. 'Or maybe a gangster.' It's a joke, I think.

He stops tapping. He's been mulling over one idea, he confesses. But he doesn't think it will work.

'Come on, Babu,' I chide him. 'Tell me. What is it?'

He shifts in his seat, uncharacteristically shy. 'Lately, I am thinking very much about the foreigners' guidance actually.'

His voice betrays a lack of confidence. I tell him that I think it sounds like a great idea. His face lights up.

'Yes, I am liking very much one day to help with the tours and all.'

His excitement grows. He knows all the places 'for the sightseeing'. And the hotels need English-speaking drivers.

'So how would you go about it?'

'I would have, like, ten cars. And with them I would have drivers who are speaking English very good. When tourists are arriving in Bombay [Mumbai], we would be taking them for the sightseeing and for the heritage tours and for the shopping. They want to know about that thing. So I want to guide them to each and every spot.'

'Do you have a name for the company?' I ask.

He doesn't, as yet. The name will come when the cars come, he says, as if it were an automotive component. And there lies the rub. He has no money of his own to invest. Even if he did, cars are like elephants. 'I can buy an elephant, but can I pay for his food? He has big stomachs.'

First he would need a 'jak', or contract, with the big hotel chains and the large 'travels' (travel agencies).

'Could you go to the bank and ask for a loan?'

He shakes his head. He has no collateral. 'I am a strong human being of more than six foot. That's all I can say.' I agree, that might not wash with a bank manager. Anyhow, he has 'a little panic in his heart' about borrowing money.

His best option, as he sees it, is to find a private investor. He has a picture of the sort of individual who might help. 'Like, some rich guy or a normal person who has money but doesn't have knowledge about how to use the money.' If that fails, he'll try borrowing someone else's car. That way he could possibly raise enough money to make a down payment for a car of his own. 'Then from one car to two cars to three cars and many cars will come. My wish is there to do.'

The alarm on his phone rings. He should go. His boss needs picking up. It's been good to talk, he tells me, patting his pocket for the car keys. He ambles towards the door and heads back down to the basement.

3

Prahalad's Promise

[bottom of the pyramid]

'Any company that cannot imagine the future won't be around to
enjoy it.'
 C. K. Prahalad, Professor of Business and Management

Mumbai

The coffee comes in a small white disposable cup, hot and steaming. I hold it to my lips and blow. It tastes strong and grainy, and
nearly scalds my tongue. The heat mocks the cup's thin plastic
casing, which bulges and bends in my grip as though squirming
in pain. Fingers burning, I put the drink down hurriedly. A splash
of the dark brown liquid spills onto Nitesh's self-assembly MDF
table.

Nitesh, a branch manager at micro-finance firm Svasti, calls
over the barefoot cleaner. The elderly lady lays aside her short-
handled sweeper's broom, picks out a dirty rag from her bucket
and wipes the spilt coffee away. I thank her, but she shows no
acknowledgment, immediately crouching back down on her
haunches and resuming her sweeping. To the swish-swish-swish of
her grass broom, Nitesh boots up his netbook computer.

We are sitting in Svasti's headquarters in Mumbai's Andheri
East district. Tucked away on the ground floor of a drab apartment block, the office squeezes into a single room. It is decorated
with peeling paint and dark mildew stains. In the entrance stands
a small counter. A tall glass panel with two semi-circular bore-
holes provides a barrier between customer and teller. The rear of
the room is fitted with several desks, each the size of a primary-
school classroom table. An Internet router clings like a slug to
the far wall. It is sprouting black computer wires. Three scratched

motorbike helmets and a couple of well-worn rucksacks lie dumped on a fibreboard desktop. Plastic chairs are stacked high in the corner, their crooked legs slotted just so, as if each were sitting on the knee of the one below.

The room evinces a careful administrative hand, despite the apparent jumble. Lever-arch files teeter from narrow shelving. Neatly written descriptions mark their spines: 'Deepak processing files', 'Collection Docs', 'Santosh: Cancel Files'. On the main wall hangs a white melamine noticeboard. On it, the work rota for the week is laid out in square grids. The far left-hand column reveals the names of Deepak and Santosh within a list of fourteen CRMs ('Customer Relationship Managers', as I later learn). Just enough wall space remains beside it for a small poster. 'Know Your Notes', the title reads in bold capitals. Illustrative graphics below show how to spot fake intaglio printing and counterfeit watermarks.

The universal sing-song sound of Windows booting up brings my attention back to Nitesh. In his late twenties, he is one of Svasti's oldest and longest-serving employees. He reads through a set of PowerPoint slides verbatim. 'Set up in September 2008. First loan dispersed on 9 October 2008. Total loan portfolio Rupees 124 lakhs (c. $US280,000). Default, zero.'

He shows me a map of Andheri East, one of the city's poorer suburbs. An elongated circle with the letter 'A' identifies our current location. Around it is drawn a jagged blue line. The demarcated area measures five square kilometres. Two hundred and thirty eight slums are within its contours. Svasti has identified roughly half as viable markets for its loans, which start at ten thousand rupees a piece.

One of the slides in particular catches my eye. When Nitesh is finished, I ask him to click back to it. The page in question reveals several multi-coloured pie charts. Each delineates a particular characteristic of the loan recipients. All are women. Most have large families, four offspring being the approximate average. Roughly a fifth describe their primary profession as 'housewife', with a slightly smaller percentage working as seamstresses, caterers or domestic help. The formally 'employed' occupy by far the thinnest slice of the pie.

Away from the skyscraper offices that dominate the Mumbai skyline and the 'boom India' storylines, the country's economy remains a largely informal affair. More than nine in ten (ninety-three per cent) of working-age Indians are employed off the books. That translates into roughly three hundred and sixty million working-age adults with no regular salary, no labour rights and none of the benefits that come with a signed contract.

Few are unemployed, however. As Gopinath observed and my time with Babu illustrated, Indians work hard. In many cases, they are compelled to do so. India's industrial sector is not without its sweatshops and near slave-like treatment. No one bar the most unfortunate bonded labourer is technically compelled to work under such conditions. Presumably the alternatives are even more appalling: hunger, homelessness and the continuation of a wretched life.

Plastering the charge of workplace abuse onto the informal sector as a whole would be misleading, however. Small family-owned businesses abound. One-man bands proliferate. The Mumbai slum of Dharavi, said to be Asia's largest, is reckoned to house more than fifteen thousand single-room factories. In a good year, 'Slum Inc' (as one headline writer put it) generates revenues in excess of eight hundred million dollars.

In the past, India's economy has always been a top-down affair. Under the British, the Crown's representatives dominated and directed every step in industrial and trade affairs. Space for private ingenuity was negligible and economic independence nil. Post-Independence, the job of industrial overseer fell to elected government officials. It was the politicians who bequeathed licences, set production targets and delegated the management of state-owned companies. Back then, the idea of slum dwellers striking out for themselves would have been preposterous. According to Nitesh, the loan-maker, that is precisely what is unfolding now.

The branch manager invited me to see for myself. It's collection day. Aniket, a junior salesperson with spiky hair and hips as narrow as a waifish model's, can take me. Nitesh hands me one of the worn helmets and packs me off.

Most of Aniket's week is taken up with forming women into lending groups and registering first-time loans. New to the job, he has a list of ambitious monthly targets. He missed last month's, he tells me. He took ten days off to get married.

Armed with his accounts ledger, he sets off on the office's black Bajaj motorbike. I ride pillion. For a kilometre or two, we weave between the traffic. Then, on reaching a T-junction, Aniket ignores the opportunities to turn left and right and heads straight across the road. On the other side, he mounts the kerb, driving along the pavement, waving pedestrians aside before suddenly ducking down a narrow alleyway.

Fifty yards later, we emerge from the walled walkway into open space. Greenery is rare in this impossibly overpopulated city. Yet for the next twenty minutes we cruise along dirt track and country roads, through woods and empty grasslands, past boys playing cricket and pigs snorting in the mud.

The journey ends in a slum community at the bottom of two neatly bordered rice fields. Unit Seven comprises a hamlet of concrete-box shacks climbing up the slope of a small rise. A woman in a cotton slip is laying a cement step beside the snaking footpath that serves as the slum entrance. The atmosphere is tranquil, almost village-like. The view across the forested valley is uninterrupted. It feels like an experiment in urban resettlement, as though Mumbai's town planners had squared off a corner of unregulated shanty and deposited it wholesale in the countryside.

We walk down the footpath, passing open doorways, inquisitive chickens and children playing the mud. At a modest three-room house, identical to those squashed up against it, we stop and knock. Aniket issues a brief word of welcome to Manjula, the young Tamil lady who opens the door. Then he takes his seat on a tatty sofa and pulls out his accounts book.

His style is perfunctory and pragmatic, his tone not so much impolite as abrupt. He is obviously a regular. Coming every week, the young salesperson sees no reason for chitchat. The women are equally taciturn. They hand over the money, see it counted and leave. As financial transactions go, it all feels very clinical.

Over the next fifteen minutes, four groups of women file in and out of Manjula's cramped front room. Each leaves with their payment slip stamped, another week down on the fifty-month repayment schedule. We repeat the exercise in four similar communities in and around the semi-rural Adarsh Nagar district.

On every occasion, the women are waiting patiently. Each is part of a 'limited liability group' of five, the idea being that each individual member vouches for the others. Once or twice, someone is missing. 'She's gone back to her village,' one member explains. Or, 'Her mother fell suddenly sick.' Aniket doesn't raise an eyebrow. He doesn't need to. The absent person has always left their contribution with another of the five. Not one payment is missed the whole day.

At each stop, I ask about the use of the loan. Nitesh had assured me that the money was borrowed with 'productive purposes' in mind. Svasti had entitled its product 'Pragati' (meaning 'Development' in Hindi) for that reason.

The answers that come back are varied. One woman, Laxshmi, runs a 'lady wear' shop. She buys the underwear at the wholesale market in Malad and sells it back in the slum at a small profit. Another, Gaolachi, buys cheap metallic hairclips, paints a simple floral design on the back and hawks them in batches of a dozen at Goregaon station. Kanti, meanwhile, a widow in her early forties, runs a small corner store out of her house. Half the profit she makes goes into building her stock of washing powder, soap, sweets, biscuits and pre-paid phone cards. The other half goes to repaying the Svasti loan.

Micro-finance in India has come in for heavy criticism of late. Its opponents claim the interest rates are 'usurious' (Svasti charges fifteen per cent, around average for the industry). They point to borrowers in rural states committing suicide. They accuse micro-loan providers of growing rich at the expense of the poor. No doubt, such examples exist. India is a big place and micro-finance a nascent, under-regulated industry. Yet in Andheri, at least, I witnessed no evidence of foul play. Nitesh did not have the air of an unscrupulous money-lender, nor Aniket that of his burly henchman. Likewise, the women claimed to have been liberated by the loans made out to them, not subjugated. The alternatives to micro-credit, it should be said, are credit at exorbitant interest or no credit at all. Each of the women entered the agreement aware of the repayment burden. And all welcomed the extra income it had helped them generate.

Nowhere is this more true than in Gautan Nagar, the slum abutting the gates of Film City. The untidy collection of wood and concrete huts plays home to a community of dalits, untouchables. Aniket refers to the tumbledown township as 'No Electricity City'. A large banner sporting the bespectacled face of Dr Ambedkar, champion of the dalit cause and author of the national constitution, stretches across the approach road. Gautan Nagar's men mostly work as part-time 'setting wallahs', constructing backdrops for the Bollywood movies created in the adjacent studios. Their wives supplement their family incomes as seamstresses, making and repairing costumes for the actors and actresses across the fence. The hillside shacks hum to the sound of sewing machines, many of which are financed through Svasti loans. I peer through a window glazed with chicken wire. A woman is sewing the hem of a skirt. Her foot presses rhythmically on the pedal. 'No power, you see,' Aniket explains.

Gautan Nagar marks our last stop. In the film lot opposite, a Marathi-language movie is being shot. We crawl through a hole in the perimeter fence to take a closer look. The director is barking through a megaphone. 'Action,' he shouts, prompting an actor dressed as a gangster to approach a waiting car. The window is open, the engine idling. The criminal-looking character passes a briefcase to an unseen accomplice in the driving seat. The engine revs and the cars speeds off. 'Cut,' shouts the plump director, who's wearing a sleeveless Puffa jacket despite the heat. 'Let's roll it again. One more time.'

We return to Svasti's cramped branch in Adheri, this time passing the huge government dairy in the woods behind Film City.

Cows moo, not four hundred yards from where Indian block-busters are being put together.

Back at base, Aniket counts his takings for the day. He carefully notes the figure in his account book. 'Rupees 24,150.' The young sales agent is entrusted with a similar amount from two of his colleagues. He sets off on his motorbike to deposit the sum in the bank. I warn him not to misplace the bulging rucksack. He laughs, mimicking the macho walk of the briefcase-carrying gang-ster from the film set.

The young newlywed mounts his bike, this time his own. It's black and flash, a Hero Honda CB2. Babu would approve. He sees the admiring look on my face. 'Brand new,' he chirps. It must be worth a year's salary. I ask how he paid for it. 'A loan, of course,' he replies, shouting over the roar of the twin exhausts. 'From the bank.'

Thiruvananthapuram

From Mumbai, I head south. My experience with Svasti has inspired me. It proves just how far a little capital can go, es-pecially when placed in the hands of the industrious. In their own way, the slum-based enterprises are impressive. They con-tribute to women's financial independence and, ultimately, their self-empowerment. Yet they fall short of being strictly 'entre-preneurial'. A corner shop or market stall doesn't represent a new approach to making money in the way that Air Deccan or InMobi do. Realistically, it needs more than a briefcase full of cash to turn the likes of Laxshmi, Gaolachi or Kanti into the next Captain Gopi or Tewari.

What money can't do, technology – potentially – can. New In-dia abounds with stories of wired-up solutions for the poor. I travel down the coast to Thiruvananthapuram, the capital of Ker-ala, to learn about one such case.

The South Indian Federation of Fisherman Societies occupies an isolated, two-storey building below a road bridge on the edge of town. Surrounded by tropical undergrowth, the building looks to be slowly but happily losing its fight against the rampant vegetation.

I have the name of Sahay, a programme coordinator at the Federation, which I pass to a young lady at reception. She directs me up a rickety wooden staircase to a tiny garret on the second floor. I find my contact on the phone, a bulbous old-style handset clamped to his ear. I take a seat on a metal-framed chair. A rip runs down the length of its faux-leather cushion.

The space has the distinct feel of a neglected government office: admin papers piled high on the desk, paper-bound files held down by paperweights, metal filing cabinets rimmed with dust, an old rusty fan wheezing away, a single huge padlock key.

After a few minutes, he puts down the phone and, with a cheery smile, moves to shake my hand. 'We may speak in Eng-leesh?' he asks, a polite question mark hanging over the last word. We both know that the idea of dropping into the vernacular Malayalam or his native Tamil is improbable. The invitation makes me warm to him right away.

In his early thirties, Sahay is at great pains to appear professional. His black hair is neatly brushed, the side parting so straight and rigid that a pencil could rest in its lacquered groove. An ironed shirt covers a splendidly premature pot-belly. He takes out a brand-new notebook and writes down my name in a careful hand on the first page.

Sahay oversees a pilot scheme that provides the Federation's members with daily fish prices by mobile phone. Before we talk about the project itself, the amiable coordinator feels some background would be instructive. He starts with himself. He originally wanted to be a priest. 'One needs to be very pious,' he says with an impious grin. Revising his calling, he dropped out of the seminary to study social work. By religion, he is Catholic. By caste, Mukkuvar. Many of the fishing communities in India's deep south are similarly low-caste Christian. The fishermen's charity seems a natural home for him.

He shifts the topic to the Federation itself. It was set up by a

Catholic priest for 'the good of the fishermen community'. When? He's not sure of the exact date. He'll check with his supervisor.

Anyway, back whenever it was – say thirty or forty years ago – the charity helped introduce stitch-and-glue plywood boats. What did they use before? Catamarans, he replies. Like . . . ? My image of catamarans is one of sleek-hulled yachts. 'Like canoes,' he says patiently. Later, the Federation spearheaded the move to fibreglass. Other innovations followed. Outboard motors, for instance. The non-profit outfit has exclusive import rights for Suzuki engines, which it sells to its members through a generous credit facility. Then came nylon nets in place of cotton. The latest novelty to hit the shores is a twin-engine trawler with cold storage.

'How is my English? Are you understanding me very well?'

'I am,' I assure him.

Sahay is very concerned about his command of English. He wants to move to Australia but it requires passing a language competency test.

His preliminary comments over, he tells me about the mobile-phone scheme. It's called the 'Market Intelligence System', he says with pride, pronouncing each individual word with clipped precision. The Federation employs data-gatherers in harbours and fish markets up and down the Keralan coast. They then clock the day's prices for different fish species and text them through to the Federation's headquarters.

'Now, let's imagine we are collecting the data,' Sahay tells me, attempting to help me visualise the process. 'Actually picture yourself as the data.' I'm not sure what he means. He makes himself clearer. 'You are such and such a species code, with such and such an origin, at such and such a price. And you arrive, just so, in the computer room over there.'

He leads me out of his office and across the creaking corridor. In front of the computer room's one working terminal sits Aravind, a shy and well-meaning technician. Tapping at the keyboard with ring-adorned fingers, he brings up a data entry webpage. 'So you're an oil sardine. Code "003". Goes in here.' He types the digits into a rectangular box. 'And you're from Munambam. So that's "13". Here.' My price, quality and catch size fill subsequent boxes.

With the press of the 'Return' key, I find myself suddenly shunted into a narrow data column above the Cuttle Fish and Squid and below the Flower Prawns and Poovalan. Aravind checks the digital watch on his wrist. At one o'clock, he warns me, I'll be sliced, spliced and reconfigured, before being dispatched through the ether to thousands of waiting cellphones. Torturous as it sounds, the journey will be worth it, Sahay assures me. I, in my text-message form, will enable South India's fishermen to get the best price for their day's catch.

The two employees prolong the roleplay for a while. As they embellish the pilot programme's dramatic credentials further, I begin to grow more comfortable with my SMS persona. It dawns on me that I suffer several character flaws. For one, I am in English, a language that precious few of SIFFS' members can read or even speak. Secondly, my theatrical range is severely restricted, squeezed as it is into a mere one hundred and sixty letters and symbols. In practice, that limits me to the price of one fish type at one market.

Worst of all, I am a figment of my own imagination. The Federation's funding ran out last month. Sahay is waiting for a cheque to come through from the Marine Products Export Development Authority. Until it does, the Market Intelligence System is officially offline.

Remembering some of his earlier professionalism, Sahay adopts an official tone. Obviously if other donors were to come forward, the Federation can easily change the languages and improve the programme. 'Did you get that? You'll write that down, won't you? With more money, it'll be a tip-top programme.'

The next morning, at Sahay's advice, I travel by train towards Kanyakumari, positioned at India's southernmost tip. The programme coordinator had given me the address of the Federation's local office there.

On arriving, I make my way by foot down a steep road that leads towards the sea. At the bottom, beside a small flotilla of lolling fishing boats, stands a long queue of Indian tourists. A ferry awaits them, its engine puttering. On a rocky outcrop just off the shore, a forty-metre stone statue of a bearded yogi surges out of the water. The Tamil saint Thiruvallur is giving a three-fingered salute.

On another rocky islet behind, presiding over the meeting of the Arabian Sea, the Indian Ocean and the Gulf of Mannar, sits an expansive memorial building. The popular tourist attraction recalls the enlightenment of another holy man, Swami Vivekananda. The ascetic's nirvana moment had come to him on the rock while meditating about India's past, present and future.

I silently ask for a fraction of his insight as I turn left, away from the queue, towards Sahaya Martha Street.

The narrow road leads down through a poor seafarers' community. The fishermen's cottages are small and quaint and painted in soothing colours that soak up the sun. At the far end, the twin bell-towers of the whitewashed church of Our Lady of Ransom jut boldly into the aqueous sky. For a moment, I feel as though I've taken a wrong turn and ended up on the Amalfi Coast.

I enquire after the Federation's office. No one knows for sure. It's moved, one resident informs me. It's closed for the off-season, says another. Never heard of it, says a third, who invites me in for tea.

Taking him to be the most honest of the three, I join him. His name is Marcelin. He's spent more than half his life at sea. His middle-aged face is weather-burnt and as tranquil, as the ocean deep.

I ask him about his work. He fishes at night, generally selling his catch at the shoreside market by his house. Business has improved since he acquired an outboard motor a decade or so ago.

'Suzuki?' I enquire.

'Lombardini.'

I spot a basic Nokia phone on the low brick wall beside his cup of tea. I tell him about the SMS service run by the Federation. He looks at me askance. He doesn't send text messages. Doesn't know how to. What does he use his phone for then? His wife calls him when he's out fishing. She wants to check that he's safe and find out when he'll be home. 'That's all?' No, if he has a good night and returns with his nets bulging, he telephones his contacts in Chinna Muttom, Thoothoor and other nearby harbours. If the price is better, he goes there. Other fishermen phone inland to the wholesale market in Nagacoil. Marcelin would do so as well but he doesn't own an icebox to keep his fish fresh.

The chance meeting renews my spirits. I'd left Thiruvananthapuram slightly sceptical. The Federation's messaging scheme was well intentioned. It was – when fully funded and operational – no doubt a useful resource too, even with its linguistic and content limitations. Yet, like so many charitable projects, it struck me as an interim step, a product of Intermediate India, stuck somewhere between the paternalism of the past and the individual empowerment of the future.

Several months later, I'd visit another pro-poor technology scheme in Tamil Nadu. On this occasion, it was run not by a charity but by a multinational company. ITC, formerly the British-owned Imperial Tobacco and now an Indian version of the same (just bigger), was equipping farming communities with Internet hubs or 'e-choupals' ('electronic gathering places'). The firm invited me to Sundra Natapu, a rain-starved village close to the temple town of Madurai, where I'd watch an elderly farmer proudly log on to a computer terminal in a new annexe of his home. With the idols of Tirupati, Lakshmi and Lord Murugan looking on curiously from the household shrine, the old man clicked through to daily crop prices, upcoming weather patterns and advice on modern farming techniques. The 'useful links' tab took the farmer through to a sole web page, the technical papers section of the Tamil Nadu Agricultural University website. No other websites were accessible.

Such a restriction felt like dangling a carrot, offering something without really offering it. It was natural for the farmer to adapt the system to his own ends, as the DVD on top of the hard drive would prove. 'Games,' it read, in big, black felt pen.

Marcelin had done likewise. With the provision of a satellite signal, a mobile handset and a little nous, he'd succeeded in leapfrogging from Old to New in a single jump.

I head back up the other coast to Hyderabad, leaving the three seas and their merging, swirling blue-black-green waters behind me.

Cholleru, Andhra Pradesh

'Come out from your homes, come out. Quality products at lower prices.'

The old man's low-pitched voice rumbles down the rain-parched village high street, enveloped in dust balls as it trundles past low-hung doorways. A dawdling black starling on the eaves of a tiled roof takes fright and flies off. From around the corner of a narrow passageway, a mongrel peers out. His whiskery nose twitches in the air. Such hue and cry in the late morning has him curious.

'Discount, discounts, come and see for yourselves. Such bar-gains.'

The commercial incantations are the only noise in the other-wise silent village of Cholleru. The day is blisteringly hot. Some men are out at work. Most are lazing in dark, cool corners of their homes. A few older men have collected under a neem tree in the centre of the village. Their eyes droop with heat and years.

The herald's cries shake the village slowly to life, just as the cockerel did that morning and every morning since the beginning of time. Faces appear in curtainless windows. Doors creak open. People step out onto the street. Before leaving, they collect their hard-earned cash from a locked kitchen drawer or a rusty tin and tuck it discreetly in the folds of their shirt or sari.

They head towards the slogan-shouting town crier and the yel-low Piaggio Apé truck parked behind him.

At the sight of the emerging crowd, a toothless grin fills the old man's white stubble face. He beats a kettle-drum hanging from his neck with a final burst of vigour. Then, like a dancing bear after a round of tricks, he folds his legs beneath him and seats his bony backside on the earthen road. Below his white lungi, two knobbly knees protrude like gnarled knots on a fraying rope. He watches the growing queue behind the truck with detached pleasure.

The vehicle at the centre of the scrum is less a truck than a motorised cart. Fitted with a small engine and the cabin of an autorickshaw, the three-wheeler carries behind it a small open-topped trailer. The sides of the trailer are fitted with horizontal metal bars, attached to which are two advertisement banners: one for a water purifier called PureIt and another for Pond's moisturiser. The trailer itself is full of cardboard boxes, each packed to the brim with home and personal-care products: dishwashing powders, soaps, detergents, toothpastes, shampoos, talcum powders, body lotions, face creams, tea bags, salt, wheat flour.

At the rear of the cart, forty-five-year-old Srilatha is a flurry of activity. Hands waving and tongue wagging, she is busy explaining her products, clarifying prices, taking orders and, as quickly and politely as she can, divesting the villagers of their money.

'Now, have you tried the new Vim? Ooh, it's so much better than the other stuff . . . Yes, yes, yes, it's the same price. Well, just a teeny bit more, but you'll notice the difference . . . yes, the shampoo deal still stands . . . no, no credit, I'm afraid.'

Sale done, Srilatha moves onto the next customer. And so on, until the queue begins to dwindle. The villagers wait their turn patiently. The Piaggio Apé is a new entrant to village life. They treat it, and by extension its proprietor, with shy respect. After their purchase, each backs away as if they've just been privy to a private audience or special honour.

The orderliness of the shopping experience is temporarily broken by a tall middle-aged woman dressed in a thinning red sari. She is irate. 'What do you mean I have to pay? This is absurd. I don't have any money. Aren't you from the government?'

Srilatha and the lady go back and forth on a similar tack until it is eventually understood that the goods are for sale and not part of some pre-election, vote-buying exercise. Reluctantly, the woman hands back her plastic-wrapped consignment of three Rexona soap bars and bag of Active Wheel Easy Wash.

Helping Srilatha is Ravi Kumar, a friendly and industrious local man in his late twenties. He is keen to impress. Ravi is a Regional Sales Promoter. His boss, Guruvaiah, is watching from the sidelines. Ravi takes it upon himself to distribute ten free sachets of Clinic Plus shampoo to every customer who spends more than one hundred rupees. For those who fall short, he notes down their name and the amount they spend. 'Don't worry, the offer still stands. When your total hits one hundred, you'll get the shampoo.' A joking remark and a generous smile from Ravi then follow. The customers smile back. 'Till next time then,' they tell him. Like Srilatha, he is an adroit salesman.

A short, thin pensioner with withered hands purchases goods worth one hundred and fifty-two rupees. Ravi pounces on the infirm gentleman and insists I take their photograph together. With little choice, the man obliges. The camera records the villager's tremulous stare beside Ravi's beaming grin. 'Happy customer,' the salesman enthuses, patting the man on the back. The man retires without a word, a bit part in what feels like a badly acted television advertisement.

But this is real. Srilatha's note-taking proves as much. Armed with a stubby HB pencil, she diligently records each sale in a thin-lined ledger. On to a second sheet of paper go the names of all those who buy a fifty-gram pack of Pond's talcum powder. Each purchaser obtains a free sachet of shampoo for their efforts. As for Srilatha, she's set to earn a one-hundred-and-fifty-rupee bonus for every hundred talcum powders she sells. Paid in product, not cash.

After forty-five minutes or so, Srilatha thanks the last of her customers. Only a hunchbacked beggar holding a thick walking stick is left. Ravi waves the aged cripple away. He does so with minimal aggression. His boss, after all, is still observing. Two or three of Srilatha's customers are in debate with a savvy seed merchant who's taken advantage of the brouhaha to set up shop on the roadside opposite. Soon, they too move on, following everyone else in heading home. The road is empty again bar the dozing geriatrics under the neem tree.

Srilatha signals to her ad-man with the drum. He unbuckles his knees and picks up his drum. The Piaggio Apé heads up the high street and down a side road. The old man's cries drift across the tiled roofs until they are frazzled into silence by the midday heat.

Guruvaiah ushers me in the opposite direction. I follow. The cheery sales chief is enjoying his day out from the offices of Hindustan Unilever, the local subsidiary of the Anglo-Dutch consumer-goods giant. He's dressed down, which means his black flat-soled work shoes have been replaced by a spotless pair of trainers in production-line white.

Bouncing off down Cholleru's main street, he suddenly stops outside a 'mom and pop shop' and beckons me over. There is no sign above the door and little to differentiate it from the three similar stores in the village. The shop comprises a single poorly illuminated room. The products are lined up haphazardly on shelves along the walls. Long strips of sachets hang from a string across the room. The effect creates a plastic lattice-blind of creams and shampoos. Customers aren't invited in. Instead, they stand at a large open window that looks out into the street and point to what they want. It's a laborious way to shop.

Manning the nameless store is Praveen, a big-boned adolescent with Billy Bunter glasses and an obliging smile. He is filling in for his parents during his school vacations. He aspires to be a chartered accountant, he tells Guruvaiah, who'd asked what his plans were on finishing high school.

In the hour's drive from Hyderabad railway station, Guruvaiah had described the 'sea change' afoot in India's rural heartlands. He credited television commercials and better road connectivity for the transformation. Disposable incomes are going up. Education is improving. With around seven in ten Indians living in rural areas, it is, as Guruvaiah had pointed out, 'a massive untapped market'.

The Fortune at the Bottom of the Pyramid. Guruvaiah had referenced the term half a dozen times. It's a buzz-phrase that crops up sooner or later in the spiel of all marketing folk. As a concept, it's very Indian, right down to C. K. Prahalad, the Tamil management guru who coined it.

The Unilever rep had used the drive to explain the essentials of the theory. The Indian consumer market can be broken down into three, he'd said, drawing a triangular diagram to help illustrate. At the top sit the rich, a tiny dot of icing on a gigantic cake. Next down runs a slightly wider band depicting the growing minority on middle incomes. What had made Guruvaiah's eyes gleam was the thick layer of sponge at the base: India's impoverished.

Statistics differ on just how many poor there are in India. The World Bank puts the cut-off point at an income of less than two dollars per day. Below that and you're officially 'indigent'. By that marker, around three hundred and fifty million Indians qualify. Until recently, the country's mega-brands have ignored them, pitching their wares instead to the wealthier categories above. The trick is to treat the poor not as individual consumers but as a collective. That was C. K. Prahalad's insight. Looked at in this way, the joint spending power of the poor suddenly morphs into a potential treasure trove.

Guruvaiah sizes up Praveen's store like a commander scoping the terrain of an upcoming battle. For him, as for his company bosses, every rural sales point marks a staging-post in the fight for the bottom of the pyramid.

He asks Praveen to pass him a shrunken-sized bar of Eta Detergent Cake, a non-Unilever brand. The boy hands it over. Guruvaiah turns the blue-wrapped product over, examining it up for shape, smell and packaging. He could be a gem dealer choosing between three precious sapphires. 'How much do you make on this?' he asks, noting the six-rupee price label. One rupee twenty-five paise, the future accountant responds. Guruvaiah exhales and cocks his head, a sign that he's impressed. They talk about buyer margins on Unilever's other competitor brands. It's information that Praveen freely shares, and which the sales exec gratefully stores away for his next marketing meeting.

One of the features of Praveen's stock that strikes me as curious is product size. Large packs are entirely absent. For the rural mar-

ket, small is beautiful. Proof comes in the form of the humble
sachet. Unilever was the first to dream up the idea of miniature
packaging, geared specifically for customers on the breadline. Ex-
periments with mini-packs of shampoos and soaps came first.
Sales rocketed. Now, everything from toothpaste and cigarettes to
coffee and tea bags comes in little and large.

Guruvaiah counts off the sachets above Praveen's head. Seven
of the twenty-six carry the Unilever symbol. It's a reasonable percentage. All the same, Guruvaiah wants to know how fast his
company's products are shifting.

'Did you place an order last week?' he questions Praveen.

'No,' interjects Ravi, who has been standing on his boss's
shoulder all the while waiting for an opportunity to make himself
useful.

Praveen concurs. The sales chief looks from one to the other,
seemingly unsure whether to blame his underling for missing an
order or the bespectacled student for not placing one.

He picks on Praveen. 'Why not?'

His tone is non-confrontational. He appears genuinely quizzical as to why the citizens of Cholleru shouldn't want more Lux
soap or Red Label tea.

'We need to sell the stock we already have first,' Praveen responds.

'But why didn't you sell enough of the existing stock?' Guruvaiah presses. 'Were you closed? Was there a family wedding?'

'No, we just didn't sell it. We sell if the customers ask for it.
What else can we do? We can't give it away, or force them to buy.'

The large-framed shopkeeper shrugs his shoulders. His logic is
unerring and his temper even. He'll make a good accountant.

Not wanting to look foolish, Guruvaiah turns to Ravi and
seeks to present the situation as a learning opportunity for the
eager young Regional Sales Promoter.

'Now Ravi,' he says in his best instructor's voice. 'Ask yourself:
last time, did they buy heavily from us? Did they overstock? Or
do they buy just once a month but in large quantities? These are
questions that require right thinking.'

Ravi racks his brain for the answer that will best please his boss. He hesitates. His chances of being put forward for promotion revolve on moments like these. By the time he's settled on a response, Guruvaiah has turned on the heel of his spanking new trainers and left. He is heading away down the residential high street. Again, we set off in pursuit.

Cholleru is typical of small villages across rural India. The mud-brick houses are squat and sturdy and spruced up with a lick of paint. An open-drainage ditch runs outside the front doors. There are no gardens. Goats, cows and chickens rummage in part-sheltered lots beside bedrooms and kitchens. Uneven rooftops create a meandering line away into the distance, flowing gently up and down like the notated musical score of a baby's lullaby. Above, wires carry power from one crooked electricity pole to another. Hovering over everything is a cloudless azure sky, arms thrown open wide and crowned by a blazing sun.

We turn a corner and head down a side road, looping back on ourselves along a narrower parallel street. Waiting on the doorstep of a well-built three-roomed house is Srilatha. She is on her lunch break and ushers us inside for refreshment.

Guruvaiah invites me to take a peek at Srilatha's stockroom. The box-shaped storage space comprises a purpose built annexe next to the entrance lobby. The door is made of wood and stapled with crumpled metal advertising hoardings. Metal-framed brackets stretch from floor to ceiling. On their shelves, laid out in regimented multi-pack lines, is the company's high-grade arsenal: a military array of powders, tablets, bars and liquids ready to go forth and conquer.

Guruvaiah picks up a plastic carton of Vim Drop Dishwash Extra Gel from the nearest shelf. He holds it up in front of him, admiringly. 'First it was a powder, then a tablet and now it's a liquid.' One drop cleans between fifteen and twenty plates. So it's more economical for the consumer. He reaches for another product, a 200 ml bottle of Domex. Before, the flagship floor and toilet cleaner only came in bottles twice the size, he explains. 'This is a new promotional range.' The company has changed the colour too. A beam of genuine glee crosses his face. 'The new version comes in penetration pink.'

Enclosed within an emporium of his company's household brands, Guruvaiah is in his element. For fifteen minutes, he talks to me about 'product verticals' and discount schemes, about temporary price reductions and freebie offers. 'There's a honeymoon offer on Rexona at the moment,' he says at one stage, pointing to a stack of the market-leading soap brand. The job lot comes with a free ballpoint pen.

'And as for quality . . .'

He takes a step further into the cramped stockroom, running his hand over a shelf of packaged detergents as if they were gold-bullion bars whose intrinsic value was self-evident. 'Domex.' The word leaves his lips in the hushed voice of the reverent. Unlike Phenol, the main competitor, Domex removes stains as well as killing germs. 'Phenol has a pungent smell too, which Domex . . .'

Srilatha peeks around the door, breaking off Guruvaiah's description of the detergent's winning odour. 'Tea's ready.'

Gratefully, I retreat from the Aladdin's cave of personal-care products and take a seat in the entrance room.

I motion my appreciation to our host for the tea. She smiles appreciatively. 'It's Taj Mahal.' The words serve as music to Guruvaiah's ears. 'Premium, you know,' he says with a knowing nod, before taking a long, luxuriant sip himself. 'Aaaaah.' I am back in the television advertisement again.

Prahalad's theory has one fatal flaw. The Last Mile. The logistical muscle of a company as large as Unilever now puts regional towns within its reach. All those trains at its disposal, all those trucks, all those warehouses. India's many thousand villages are another matter. Situated down bumpy roads and dusty footpaths, they lie beyond standard transport hubs and distribution networks.

That's where Srilatha comes in.

She and thousands like her are the Avon Ladies of rural India. Armed to the hilt by the Anglo-Dutch consumer giant, they go door to door, hawking the companies' wares. It's the British and Dutch East India Companies merged and miniaturised for modern times.

Guruvaiah calls the vending conscripts 'direct-to-consumer sales distributors' when he remembers, and 'Shakti Ammas' when he does not ('Shakti', or 'empowerment', being the name of the programme, and 'Amma' being Hindi for 'Mother'). The company recruits them from women's self-help groups, which operate in one form or another in almost every village and hamlet across the country. To gain the women's buy-in, Unilever gives them a cut on every sale.

On cue, Srilatha picks up my empty cup and replaces it with a hard-backed accounts register. Her full profile and that of her catchment area is detailed on the front page. Guruvaiah encourages me to look over it.

Name of Shakti Dealer: Kadem Srilatha
No. of family members: 4
Name of village: From Cholleru
Name of Block: Bhaugiri
Name of District: Nalgonda
Name of self-help group: Sri Pragathu Mahila group
No. of group members: 30
No. of groups in the village: 33
Village population: 3,000
No. of households: 1,000
No. of outlets in village: 05
No. of schools in village: 2
Distance from RD point: 86 km
Name of Supply RD: Santhoshimatha Agencies
Phone number of RD: 9885886175
Phone number of RSP: 99493 10223

'That's Regional Distributor,' Ravi says, pointing to the letters 'RD'. 'And RSP. That's me,' he adds for clarification. 'Regional Sales Promoter.'

Guruvaiah beckons Srilatha to take me through the remainder

of the ledger. She bustles forward, her wide hips and rose-patterned sari combining to necessitate short steps. She runs her finger down a narrow column of carefully handwritten numbers, her purchase summary for the last six months.

On the next page are details of Srilatha's Homes Sales Tracker. Listed one below the other are the names of her individual household customers. One hundred and seventy of them in total. Diligent pencil marks chart her weekly visits and her clients' expenditure: '26.00Rs', '17.50Rs', '56.00Rs', and so on. Larger numbers are recorded beside the two retail outlets that she supplies in Cholleru. Neither belongs to Praveen.

The quantity of data must be keeping a team of marketing analysts very busy back at Unilever headquarters. The numbers also reveal the sheer scale of the operation. Guruvaiah's patch alone covers eight districts, with close to one and a half thousand Shakti Ammas. Their total turnover hovers around sixteen million rupees every month. And for each Shakti Amma, Unilever has the name, date and point of sale for every sachet, bottle and packet sold. Calculate that for thousands of saleswomen in tens of thousands of villages and the Bottom of Prahalad's Pyramid suddenly looks a very profitable place to be.

Profitable for Hindustan Unilever, for sure. But for the Shakti Amma too? Looking back at Srilatha's sales register, I ask about her profit on each sale. She is about to explain when Guruvaiah cuts in. 'For Home and Personal Care, we give eight per cent on detergents and ten per cent on personal products. For Food and Beverage, there's a three per cent discount. So in total, for stock worth forty thousand rupees, say . . .' He pulls out his mobile phone and types the numbers into the calculator function. '. . . three thousand two hundred rupees per month.' This is, by Guruvaiah's estimation, 'very big money' for a housewife sitting in a small village. A touch crestfallen at the interruption, Srilatha merely nods her agreement.

Her husband, Srinwas, an employee in the local explosive factory, enters the lobby area from the main room of the house. He has a placid face and soft, pale eyes. His rounded belly and crisp ironed clothes speak of a contented life. He is holding a piece of paper. It is his daughter's report card from her English-medium school, paid for from his wife's earnings. He hands it to me. 'Score: 552/600.' The happy couple shares a proud glance.

The Unilever rep insists the strategy is a 'win-win'. It's a phrase that I've heard repeatedly over the years in my day job covering corporate-responsibility issues. As with many clichés, the original idea behind the phrase is sound enough. In this case, it's not just sound, but attractive too: the idea that companies can go about making their profits, while making the world a better place. Social Capitalism.

Only more often than not, there's a catch. In the case of ITC and its e-choupals, it's straightforward. In exchange for helping the farmers, the company gets first dibs on their harvests. In this instance, it's more discreet. The Shakti programme ultimately aims to flood the dusty roads of Cholleru with consumer goods. What next? There lies the catch. Relentless advertising. A rush to buy. The need to have. And all for what? So that shareholders many thousands of miles away can continue to collect a healthy dividend?

Guruvaiah sees things differently. Shakti is the star in Unilever's Corporate Social Responsibility crown. This isn't cigarettes or fast-food pap that they're foisting on India's rural poor. It's daily 'essentials'. Toothbrushes, instead of neem sticks. Shampoo, rather than carbolic soap. Disinfectant, not sponge and water. People are now healthier and cleaner, their homes germ-free and perfumed. In fact, studies show that diarrhoeal deaths have dropped thanks to the use of Lifebuoy soap, Guruvaiah points out. How many? 'Lots,' he says.

Nor are the products being 'forced' upon the buyer, he adds. It's simple supply and demand. Yes, villagers might receive complimentary dental care, paid for by Unilever. Yes, they might be sent away afterwards with a free tube of Close Up toothpaste. But, no, they are under no obligation to buy. And, anyway, in my country, I have the choice to purchase from a wide range of products, do I not? Yes. So why shouldn't the citizens of Cholleru? Do they deserve less?

Srilatha rises from her seat. She has her afternoon rounds to begin. Guruvaiah suggests we join her, 'to gauge consumer demand' for myself.

And so, a few minutes later, we are calling on Satyamma and Suyalu. An elderly couple, they live on the neighbouring street. Suyalu had spent his working days scrambling up and down coconut trees to make toddy, a country liquor popular across southern India. Now frail and old, he can barely lift himself out of his armchair. His wife ushers us in.

The bare, one-room house is starved of light and furniture. A picture of Sydney harbour hangs above the back wall. Below, a Videocom television stands on a rickety table. An old-fashioned air cooler the size of a small cupboard chugs rhythmically in a corner. Srilatha lays out her wares on the single bed for want of a table. Satyamma's thin, arthritic fingers pick out an assortment of items: toothpaste, talc, detergent, soap, shampoo, tea bags. It's just enough to push her over the one-hundred-rupee mark. Ravi duly throws in the ten free sachets of Colour Plus.

'Are you happy with the products?' I ask, suddenly aware that it's the kind of set question Guruvaiah would ask.

The old lady crooks her head. She taps her left ear. Srilatha repeats the question into her other, good ear. The words register and her crinkled forehead scrunches into a crinoline frown. She picks up a Vim dishwashing bar. 'Before,' she says emphatically, 'we washed our dishes with ash.' Enough said. Politely, she ushers us out.

It's difficult to argue with such logic. I'm not one to eulogise rural life, to fossilise a community in the name of protecting their cultural authenticity. It is their choice what to take and what to leave. Yet, I wonder where it will all stop. Are Barbie Dolls an 'essential'? Or SUVs? Or shopping centres? They are to some. Are they to India's villagers? Not now. But they could be soon.

Mahatma Gandhi would have railed against such a future. For India's Great Soul, the rustic village personified the non-materialistic, harmonious world of which his teachings and dreams were filled. Yet the course seems set. Rural India marks the last retail frontier, a succulent mango ripe for the eating. The bottom of India's pyramid is simply too lucrative for marketers to leave it in peace. US consumer goods behemoth Procter & Gamble is, Guruvaiah informs me conspiratorially, already hatching its own version of Shakti. Several Indian firms are already a step ahead. The poor man's Nano car from Tata Motors marks one such example. Godrej Consumer Products is flogging a mini-fridge for the same market niche. The list is growing fast.

We return briefly to Srilatha's front room. Immediately, Ravi and Guruvaiah begin thumbing through her accounts ledger. Both recognise that sales of food and beverage goods are low. They discuss the matter, but conclude little can be done. Rural consumers still prefer to shop for their staples at the local market. There is a lurking suspicion of branded foodstuffs. Plus the price tag turns people off. Unilever's signature wheat powder, which Indians use ubiquitously for chapatti and rotis, costs twice as much as the market-stall equivalent. The Anglo-Dutch consumer giant spends more on advertising than any other company in India. But consumers remain inscrutably discerning, the poor more than anyone. This very Indian attribute comforts me. As the tide of consumerism laps the shores of Cholleru, it could be the one factor that keeps it from drowning.

Appearing once again from the back room, Srinwas approaches my chair. He is carrying an old shoe box. Would I like to see some reading glasses? Srinwas too tries to supplement his income. A charitable outfit providing low-cost spectacles visited the village the previous year. The explosives worker offered his services as their local distributor. I take a pair. They would make a good present for my mother. 'How old is she?' Sixty-three, I tell him. 'No, too old, I'm afraid. Over fifty and they won't do any good.' He takes the glasses back.

Is he naturally honest, I wonder? Or is it that I'm a guest in his house? Or that he instinctively reacts to what's evidently a bad deal? Whatever the case, he sacrifices the sale and I am left grateful and impressed. And also relieved that it is his wife, and not him, who is the main salesperson of the household.

His sale opportunity gone, Srinwas offers me a cup of tea. 'No thanks,' I say. 'Juice?' No really, I insist. 'Water?' He's persistent, though, I'll give him that. 'It's PureIt filtered.' Okay, then, just one glass.

Entrepreneurship, industriousness and enterprise are not ends in themselves. They feed off the promise of a return: the creation of a successful business, a leg up the ladder, the prospect of a better life. Two decades on, India's economic reforms are gradually making good that promise. Opportunities are emerging. Dreams are rising. India is entering an Age of Aspiration.

Part II

Aspiration

4

Actor Prepares

'If there is one place on the face of earth where all the dreams of living men have found a home from the very earliest days when man began the dream of existence, it is India.'
Romain Rolland

Mumbai

Naval greets me as I alight from a rickshaw off Ram Mandir Road in Goregaon. It is just after lunch. The sun is high and the neighbourhood still. We are at the end of Mumbai's metropolitan train line, deep into the interminable suburbs of India's most populous city.

An urban dairy spills onto the roadside. The pastoral fragrance of mud and cow dung sweetens the more objectionable excretive odours of this sweating, overstuffed metropolis.

'Follow me,' the young man says, guiding me along a muddy road between two unfinished apartment blocks. He won't say anything more until we reach his room, as if he's scared his words might be snatched on the breeze and lost to him. The road opens into a muddy scrubland populated by hulking, multi-storey creations of concrete and cement.

This is the Projects. It is unfathomably ugly.

I follow Naval as he picks his way around the muddy edge of the social-housing compound. Ahead, three boys play cricket with a bald tennis ball and a strip of balsa wood prised from a packing crate. Behind the bowler's arm, at the clearing's perimeter line, lies a roadside market. A man is selling scrawny chickens cooped three to a cage. I look up at the rain-stained building above him. The paintwork runs black like smudged mascara under all the windows, as if the sills themselves are weeping. Each tiny flat has a balcony enmeshed behind wire. Clothes hang pegged to the metal grilles. Their bright colours help differentiate the flat owners from the market vendor's chicken. The difference is primarily aesthetic. In terms of relative space, a fight still exists as to who is better off – man or bird.

Behind the first building loom another two identical monsters. Square-jawed and immovable, they spend their days glaring angrily at one another across a dark, sunless corridor of no man's land. We cross beneath, running the gauntlet of food scraps and dirty water cascading down from upper windows.

The first of the two housing blocks, 'No. 15', has no door. Naval steps off the stepping-stone pavement, which wobbles in the mud, and he ducks through a rectangular opening. The acrid stench of urine makes my eyes sting. Mixed with damp in an unventilated space and cooked through the Mumbai summer, it turns positively poisonous. I clasp my hand over my nose, an involuntary reaction of which I'm immediately embarrassed. I keep it there all the same.

Unperturbed by the smell, Naval approaches the lift door beside the stairwell. A pair of unearthed wires protrudes through a round hole where the 'Up' button used to be. Naval tries fusing them together. The naked ends hiss on contact, like the spiteful bickering of two fractious cobras. He raises his gaze, waiting for a mechanical juddering somewhere up the lift shaft. Silence.

Shrugging his shoulders, he turns to the stairs and we begin the long plod up to the seventh floor. The steps are caked with dirt and discarded sweet wrappers. A surface layer of flattened cigarette stubs creates the impression of a mottled carpet. Running up each corner of the stairwell is the splattered red stain of paan spit. It sticks to the wall like tar, dark and viscous as ox blood. Even the piss of the late-night drunks won't wash it off or water it down.

Each floor brings its own smells and noises. Fish curry. Arguments. Fried pakoras. A plaintive lullaby. Garlic and ginger. A radio. Children playing. Steaming pilaf. A TV music channel. A kettle on the boil. It feels as if we're heading into the innards of a living organism, like an Indian version of *James and the Giant Peach*. Only Block 15 is no ripened fruit. It's a rotting carcass.

'A biscuit?' Naval asks, breaking his silence as we enter his room.

I had met Naval earlier in the week. A student at the prestigious Actor Prepares training academy, he is one of tens of thousands of star-blind youngsters who flock to Mumbai with the dream of becoming the next megastar.

In India, Bollywood is bigger than God. Rich, beautiful and sprinkled in stardust, its modern-day heroes are omnipotent and omnipresent. Their lifestyles feed dreams. Their allegiances win elections. And their latest hairstyles shift shampoos. In short, they are marketing manna, the perfect commodity for aspirational New India. Every youngster – even the most strait-laced – secretly wishes they could be them.

The idea of actually learning to be an actor is comparatively new to India. The entry tickets to Bollywood success have traditionally been looks (macho for men, curvy for women) and contacts (it helps if one, or preferably both, of your parents are recognised film stars already). The gossips would add a third: 'the casting couch', a not-so-subtle euphemism for sleeping your way to the top. That is all changing – or so Bollywood's PR machine would have you believe. India's tinseltown, they say, is becoming more democratic. With the spirit of the times, it is opening its arms to nobodies with genuine talent. On the back of such promises, professional acting schools are cropping up all over town. Cinema acting is a trade that can be learned, the academies insist; not a vocation to be inherited. In India's fame-crazed youth, they have an audience only too ready to listen.

The evening class that I attended had been a no-nonsense affair. Two hours of Camera Work 101. Suraj Vyas, a jobbing thespian of imperial bulk, had taken the class through the basics of panning, tilting, low angles, high angles ('always use this for the gods'), tight-closes and close-ups. He picked Naval as his guinea pig. Trapped in the frame of the teacher's digital video camera, Naval's pained face was transposed onto the classroom monitor. Massively enlarged in the process, he looked every multi-pixel bit like a bill-board passport photograph.

'This is my friend Mr Sony. Most of you are terrified of me, right?' the commanding voice of Mr Vyas boomed.

The class sniggered. Naval shrivelled.

As the Actor Prepares instructor waxed on about the need to be 'comfortable with yourself' and 'naked before the camera', I studied Naval on the monitor. The longer the camera rested on him, the more he wilted. His narrow shoulders hunched an inch, and then another. His jaw slackened. A glistening pinball of sweat appeared on his forehead. He looked anything but comfortable.

The corpulent Mr Vyas, in contrast, seemed to derive a masochistic pleasure from his student's squirming. 'Why are people scared of the camera? It's not because you think you look bad. It's because you think that other people think you look bad.' To his credit, Naval didn't look bad. As faces went, his was regular and unremarkable. Fulsome lips cloaked an assembly line of healthy white teeth. Thick eyebrows framed two oval, syrup-brown eyes. Unblemished, sculpted and in symmetry, it was the weaker for all three.

Eventually, the man behind the camera snapped the lens shut. 'This friend of mine, Mr Sony, is inspired by Gandhi. Why?' (Mr Vyas was a master of the rhetorical question, every motivational speaker's favourite trick.) 'He doesn't lie. He will show you only what you show him.' His audience lapped up the concluding piece of pop philosophy. All bar Naval, who was glugging air in pint-sized gulps. Free from the camera's asphyxiating grasp, unconcealed relief washed over him. Would that it were nonchalance.

At the end of the class, a short, stocky student wandered up to me. His biceps bulged against his shirtsleeves. I took notes as we spoke. He told me his name was Srinvas. He was twenty-seven. A gym instructor from Bengaluru. Any acting experience? A few print ads. Dabbled in student theatre. How's he paying the course fees? Personal savings.

His classmates observed me writing. Was I a journalist? Would

I be writing an article? Yes and no, I replied in truthful sequence, hoping a touch of ambiguity might dilute their lust for publicity of any kind. It didn't. Immediately, I had a queue of hopefuls wanting to give me their details. First up was Ajesh, twenty-one. Lived with parents in Mumbai. Father, a Marathi theatre actor. Acting ran in his blood. Then Ravi, twenty-eight, from Meerut in Uttar Pradesh. Lawyer. Tejas, also twenty-eight, a network administrator for The Corporation of India. Next up Santyam, twenty-nine, from Gujarat. Owned an HR consultancy offering soft-skills training for outsourcing firms. Short films and adverts, so far. Just landed a role in a low-budget feature film with a first-time director. He's to be a pimp who tricks rural girls into prostitution. He was there to pick up experience.

Feeling like the school's registrar on Day One, I kept on scribbling. Name, age, home, hopes. It was a barren formula with little rhyme and no reason.

'Naval,' a halting voice said. 'Twenty-five years. Resident of New Delhi.' There was something in his thin, fragile tone that caused me to lift my eyes from the page. Hidden beneath its apparent temerity, difficult to detect yet discernable, lay a stoic determination. Spunk, my Raj-era grandmother would have called it. I looked up to see the young man from the close-up.

Naval blinked. For a millisecond, licks of brilliant orange flared in his eyes, a Catherine wheel of sparks lighting those dark pools of molten brown.

I was intrigued. Would he have time to talk another day, I asked.

And so I find myself in the Projects.

Surrounded by the outside world, Naval somehow looks smaller. In the classroom, on the screen, all the drama-school students are giants of a kind. Even someone as slight of build as Naval. Yet here in Block 15 he is dwarfed by reality, a small fish cast out into a pestilent ocean.

I take my shoes off and follow him into the one-room apartment.

The space measures about fifteen square feet. It owes its decoration to the original builders. Four walls of crumbling plaster. In the corner opposite the door stands a set of low concrete shelves. They comprise the kitchen. There is no cooker and no fridge, just a single tap and a plastic washing-up bowl for a sink. A large plastic barrel like a compost bin is wedged against the wall. A bucket for ladling is perched on top. Next to the kitchen are two cubicles with squat toilets. The additional lavatory seems excessive given the space.

The room is entirely devoid of furniture for sitting, resting, working or eating. The only concessions to comfort are two straw reed mats that lie like lonely beach towels on the floor. Pride of place is given to the television, which is propped up off the floor on two brick-shaped speakers. The cardboard box in which the speakers came sits beside them, as if the purchaser is scared of breaking the bond between product and packaging. The box is not redundant, however. It is spewing dirty socks.

Naval invites me to sit. I find a spot on the tiled floor with my back against a bare wall. My British muscles aren't supple enough to adopt the cross-legged lotus position into which Indian limbs seem to fall so effortlessly. I slump down a fraction to avoid banging my head against a scraggy scar of flaking concrete. A botched wiring job runs the entire circumference of the one-room apartment and acts as an accidental skirting board.

Naval approaches and sits opposite me. A washing line stretches across the room above him. He brushes aside a shirt cuff that is obscuring his line of sight.

He slides across a plate of brown, sugar-sprinkled biscuits. I take one. It tastes stale. Looking for a distraction as I work the glutinous sludge around my mouth, I ask where his belongings are. He points to the corner. Two small suitcases made from re-inforced plastic are parked side by side. They look dejected and lonely, like orphaned baggage abandoned on an airport carousel. One has two pairs of folded trousers and a shirt resting on its travel-worn casing. The other is furnished with a couple of thick blankets and two cushions. He points to the first.

'I have two shirts only,' he says, tugging at his salmon-pink T-shirt. 'This one, and one more. The other is too big, so not so very good.'

The door opens. A young man in jeans walks in. He is surprised to see us. 'Namaste,' I say in what I hope sounds like a friendly voice. Naval brokers a quick introduction and the two share a few perfunctory words. He leaves immediately, creeping out with the exaggerated caution of a mime artist. I cannot conceive what Naval must have told him.

'That is Mr Shilabhadra,' he explains. 'A very good man, a very nice man.'

A year Naval's senior, Mr Shilabhadra is his live-in landlord. The acting student rents a corner of the floor at one thousand five hundred rupees per month. Mr Shilabhadra is an actor himself, albeit out of work. He has two other tenants. One is a camera assistant. Naval doesn't know what the other does. He keeps, as Naval puts it, 'antisocial hours'.

I ask how he came to find the place. The answer is convoluted. His narrative is constantly stopping and starting. At one moment, the words are spilling out in a verbal cheese-grating of manic sentences. The next, he is having to drag out each laboured word.

This is the order of events as I understand them. It begins with his arrival in Mumbai. He came from Delhi by train, though to which station he can't be sure. He then went directly to the Actor Prepares office. He got there by suburban train, bus and on foot. In which order, he can't quite remember. He had his suitcase with him. That much he knows because it kept knocking painfully against his calf as he walked. The month-long course was already into its second week. The administrators let him enrol all the same. They accepted the duress of his journey in lieu of an entrance audition.

He had two phone numbers in the city. Both were given to him by a Mr Dev, an acquaintance from Delhi whom he met in a train station. Or was it the metro? The first number belonged to a Mr Sharma. He answered Naval's call on the first try. Any friend of Mr Dev is a friend of his, the voice said. Come stay. Hold on for a text message with the address. Naval duly waited. The SMS never came. Despite repeated attempts on Naval's part, Mr Sharma never answered his phone again.

'I feel nervous now. I have no knowledge about persons in Mumbai,' Naval recounts, impersonating his own anguish with an effortless empathy that would have won Mr Vyas's applause.

Naval tried Telephone No. 2. This time he met with more success. Mr Shilabhadra said he could stay two nights.

'When was that?' I ask.

Naval thinks a while, counting out the time on his fingers. 'Ten days ago.'

At the sound of his name, the aforementioned landlord returns. He is carrying two cups of tea in large plastic thimbles. He smiles generously, passes us both a cup and exits. He's gone before I have time to mime my thanks.

For a month-long course, it seems remiss of Naval to turn up a full week late. I enquire what caused his delay. A more polished version unfolds. It is a story, I suspect, that he has been rehearsing. For retelling when he's famous, perhaps.

I must understand. Time was always tight. He had only learned about Actor Prepares a fortnight before the course started. Who told him about it? He stumbled on it while surfing the Web. His real passion is to become a director. He figures acting might provide a back-door in. So he started searching around for acting schools. A Google search brought up Anupam Kher's academy. He saw that it ran a full-time course over three months. It sounded perfect. Then he clicked on the fees and his heart sank. The full-time course was way beyond his budget. As he browsed, however, he noticed that the school ran evening classes. The course lasted just a month. The cost, fifteen thousand rupees. It would hurt his pocket, yet it lay within the realms of the possible.

'I bought a chai wallah stall,' he says, laughing ruefully and raising his thimble in an ironic toast to the idea.

The experiment fell flat. Naval's childlike hopes of raising some fast cash did not materialise. For one, the other tea vendors proved vicious competitors. No sooner did he set up shop, than a kettle-waving pedlar would appear with foul curses and dismal threats. Naval ended each day like one of his soggy tea bags, drained of energy and squashed underfoot. The police turned out to be even more unpleasant. They'd bark insults at him and threaten him with their wooden lattis. One even cuffed him around the ear. Naval's tea-peddling exercise lasted four days before he decided to pack it in and sell back the equipment.

By now, the course start-date was almost upon him. His prospects of attending were dwindling by the moment. The aspiring director was over one thousand four hundred kilometres away and flat broke. The time had come for radical action. Naval owned only one asset of any value, an HP Compaq laptop. His father had bought it for him from Nehru Place in Delhi, a giddying flea market of illegal software and cheap electronics. The computer cost 26,700 rupees and was bought to assist him in his studies. Naval decided it had to go. It took him a couple of days to find a buyer, and then a couple more days for the buyer to find the money. As soon as Naval had the cash in hand, he grabbed his suitcase and jumped ticketless onto the first train to Mumbai.

'Look,' he says, leaning over towards his small cache of possessions. 'I still have the bag for the power cable.'

He shows me a black, zipped pouch. The faded imprint of the 'HP' logo is still visible on the side. He uses it to store his valuables, he explains. I can't but notice that it looks awfully empty.

I presume it is his first time in Mumbai. Quite the opposite, he replies. 'Oh yes, I have been many times. Maybe five or six. I forget exactly.' The answer surprises me. He had no family or friends here, only the telephone numbers passed on by the mysterious Mr Dev. Why on earth would he have visited so frequently?

'I came to meet Salman Khan,' he tells me, his face as straight as a masked divinity from a folk rendition of the Ramayana. 'You have heard of Mr Salman, no?'

I had. With blockbuster hits such as *Tere Name* and *Dabangg*, he is one of the most sought-after actors in Bollywood. London's Madame Tussauds has even immortalised him in wax.

'He is an emotional person, Mr Salman,' Naval continues, his use of the honorific prefix passing on a quasi-regal feel to its subject. 'His mind is very nice. Mr Salman appears very angry on the screen, but he has a soft heart. He is a very simple, full of sympathy guy.'

Naval speaks as if he knows the front man of Hindi cinema. However, it rapidly becomes clear that he's just a faceless fan, one of millions. His bond is with the actor's on-screen persona, not the man sitting down to breakfast in Flat No. 3, Galaxy Apartments, Bandra.

The give-away comes as Naval recounts his visit to the above residence. He'd tracked down the address on the Internet. It was seven o'clock in the morning. The gruff security guard at the gate asked his name and his purpose. 'Naval Dwivedi. To see Mr Salman,' he told him honestly. Did he have an appointment? No. Was he an acquaintance of Mr Salman? Not strictly. Then he was sorry, it would not be possible. Naval should send a letter. 'Actually this guard feels irritated to me. He says angrily, "go".' When Naval stood his ground, the guard pushed him in the chest and threatened to beat him up. The aspiring director beat a reluctant retreat.

My mouth lolls open in disbelief. Could anyone really be so naive? Did he really think an unannounced visit to a Bollywood celebrity would play out differently? Naval's description of the incident suggests he remains to this day incredulous at the guard's reaction.

I try phrasing my doubt with an eye to Naval's feelings. 'Would email not have been easier? Or the post, as the guard recommended?'

He did write a letter, Naval says. 'Salman sir,' it read. 'I want heartily to meet to you please. My contact number is . . .' A ten-digit mobile number follows. He is still waiting on a reply.

Despite the helping hand of Google, Naval has no trust in email or the Internet. 'What's to stop his people stealing my script?'

So then I ask him more directly. Had it not entered his head that the guard might bar his way? If it did, he hadn't let it tarry long. Naval's quest has a large dose of the pilgrimage about it. He is riding towards his destiny, an Indian Don Quixote tilting at his own private windmills. An adherent of God, Ram, Jesus and Krishna, he doesn't just believe in miracles. He expects them. Sprawling under the abusive invective of the security man presented one such moment: 'I felt very nervous. I pray to God. "Oh, God, why am I here? What I do? Why no help me, my God?"' Again, he was left waiting for a reply.

I find myself wondering how he had originally envisioned his meeting with Mr Salman. His fertile imagination, I feel sure, would not have rested as the Mumbai Rajdhani Express trundled half the length of the country towards India's Tinseltown.

The hunch proves true. He'd prepared a little speech. Could he share it? Of course: 'I am saying, "Mr Salman, I have script about dowry. I have very nice script about driving this system out. It's a cancer. My Indian brothers hate dowry."'

Naval continues sitting there, stock-still, one leg folded snugly over the other like a knot in a shawl. His thoughts too remain fixed, focusing in on the divine. 'God say to me, he say, "I have your heart."' Such is his faith that he can put the security man's hostile reception easily behind him. In the scheme of things, it marks nothing but a minor setback. God was, he decided, testing his resolve. Three more times (or was it four?), he returned. He'd hop on the train, sleep on the platform and hike out to Galaxy Apartments. With each visit, the guard bristled that bit more. By the fourth time, Naval didn't even approach the gate. He just watched from afar, eating bread pakoras and watching for his thunderbolt from the sky. Once more, Naval had to learn what it was to wait.

'I no see him. I have fear,' he admits, reflecting on his failed sorties out to Bandra. 'Still I have only ever seen him in the movies.'

Then, as if finishing one scene and immediately jumping ahead to the next, he reveals a new twist in his story: 'I belong to Mizapur, in Uttar Pradesh. It's not very much developed.'

'I thought you were from Delhi?'

On reflection, this was foolish. Delhi, as with all India's mega-cities, is an agglomeration of immigrants. Around half the population come from somewhere else. Economic hardship and the hope of a job draw most. For Naval, it was the promise of further studies. His father had enrolled him on an MBA course at the august-sounding All India Management Association. In reality, the Association is not an institution of the bricks and mortar kind. Instead, AIMA (as the Association refers to itself) is a publicly run catch-all for thousands of second- and third-rate business-education providers. Even if it did have an impressive campus, Naval would never see it. His course was conducted via correspondence. Why this necessitated a move to the capital I didn't quite understand. Perhaps Delhi's postal service was more reliable than that of Mizapur?

Either way, Naval didn't trouble the postman too much. After a couple of assignments, he decided the world of business wasn't for him. He dropped out. Swapping his corporate-strategy books for script paper, he began penning his screenplay.

'Did you tell your father?' I enquire, half fearing his response.

'No,' he answers, confirming the worst. He looks at me as if I must have lost my mind. 'My father is very strict. He heaps on pressure like a gas cylinder. My family has a very limited concept about job. You must be engineer, scientist, teacher or civil servant.'

It is a story I had heard across India and would continue to hear again. It is the perennial dilemma: the parents' understandable desire to see their children 'well set' versus their offspring's youthful impulses to follow the hearts. The saddest fact about the tussle is that it leaves no victors.

'Now my father thinks I have completed the course because that is what I told him. I tell him that I have part-time job and that I am going for interviews with banks and manufacturers and all.'

For all his recklessness, I suddenly feel a surge of admiration for this young man from Uttar Pradesh. He has risked everything on a dream. How much easier would it have been just to go along with his parents' wishes? To do the job he was told to do, to marry the girl he was instructed to marry, to hide his unhappiness, to swallow his frustration?

I find myself wondering if I would have the courage to do the same. The romantic side of me would like to think so. Brave new worlds, *carpe diem* and all that. Even before the phrases fully take shape, I can sense my more realistic alter ego smirking. 'Lily-livered,' it goads. Sitting there, immersed in someone else's tale, I guess I'm glad I never had to decide. Or never, at least, in such a stark, all-or-nothing manner as Naval.

Naval doesn't see it that way. Maybe it's the adrenalin of studying at Anupam Kher's school, of the feeling that his journey is finally reaching its climax. His breakthrough is waiting around the corner, a crouching cat ready to pounce on its prey.

Whatever the reason, he views the irrevocable family split as a natural phenomenon, as prefigured as Rama's departure from the throne of Kosala into his forest exile.

Naval's universe is different from that of his father. A plunging Himalayan pass divides the two. The young acting student is caught up in the whirlwind of aspirational India. He has been shown a new world. It only requires his feet to follow. In a sense, chasing his dream is not a choice. It is a question of internal geography, of orienting himself towards his proper course. The MBA student, slotting his homework in the post, no more opted to jump the Mumbai train than a pet fish might choose to swim in circles.

'I am a high visioner,' Naval tells me with utmost seriousness. 'Always, I am asking "why?"' To clarify his point, he touches his hair with a look of childlike curiosity. 'Why black, and not white?'

His father, on the other hand, is the polar opposite: 'He doesn't let me watch television. Mentally' – Naval taps the side of his head with his index finger – 'he thinks TV serials and film are corrupt. He has very limited views.'

My admiration for his decision doesn't preclude a degree of concern for his current predicament. What will he do when the course ends? How will he feed himself? What will his father do when he finds out Naval is a struggling actor in Mumbai and not a junior manager on some nameless industrial estate in Delhi?

The questions trip out one after another. I immediately feel guilty for asking them.

'I'm sorry, I don't mean to sound like your father,' I say, in a belated attempt to dispel some of the negative energy that I've let loose.

Naval merely smiles. 'I have thought it all through.'

Then he begins to rock slightly. Forward, back. Forward, back. Like a psychiatric patient building up to a fit. The action discomforts me. Throughout, his lips are moving, as if mumbling silent stanzas of an ancient mantra. I sense that he's talking to himself, or to his shadow double. What it is that Nawal is wrestling with, I've no idea.

He eventually stops rocking. His face has a calm, resolute expression. When he speaks, it's with cold assertiveness. I've not heard him use such a tone before, yet it feels familiar. Then I realise. It's been there all along – a quiet, shatter-proof confidence buried deep inside him.

'I try and think good ambitions. I am inspired by Abraham Lincoln and Dr A. P. J. Adbul Kalam [a former national President, who became known as the Missile Man of India because of his support for ballistic weaponry]. Film is my passion. Please understand this. In North India, dowry is big problem. My neighbour, she died. She was twelve years old. She loved to me so much. I feel what we doing in society. Why? Is this right or wrong? My heart and soul says it is very wrong. It is not good culture. I hate this.'

Yet again, Naval's version of events leaves me slightly nonplussed. Was his neighbour killed in a dowry dispute? The thought is horrifying. I want to ask him more, but he has said all that he desires to say. He is staring straight at me. No, through me. His eyes, two wells of curtained nightfall, have grown dark and intense.

I hold my pen prone over the page, indicating for him to continue.

He needs no prompting. It's as if the words emerge from out of him in a physical, almost molecular sense, like tattoos on his skin.

'After the course, I plan to stay here. My mind showed that I could not have success in Delhi. I will stay the maximum time. I believe God will help me if I will do good. I am going alone, alone, but I feel near God. All around me. We are buried in the earth. No again chance give from God.'

His last phrase takes me back to the evening class earlier in the week. 'Make as many mistakes as you want here. Do your worst,' Mr Vyas had said as he dismissed his class. 'But don't make mistakes out there. You won't get a second chance.' I'd heard the words as a caution. Naval, I suspect, had interpreted them as a promise. An opportunity would come knocking for all of them. One chance: sure, sealed, guaranteed.

He breathes deep, steeling his resolve.

'Will I go home, you ask? No, never.' His bottom lip quivers at the enormity of the statement. And then he mutters: 'Well, maybe I go back when I am a famous director. I will have success when I go there. And when I go, I will open an academy in my village.'

The glow in his eyes begins to dim. He suddenly looks worn. We switch topics to more immediate matters. He is working on a new script, he tells me. He cannot tell me much about it. The topic centres on preparing for the Indian Administrative Service. It's not a comedy, he assures me. 'It is very serious.'

As for money, he has one thousand rupees left. It will not last him long. But then he knows his path is not an easy one. He believes he will suffer. He also believes in God and 'self-spirit'. For a second, the shine returns to his eyes. 'God tells me, "You are winner. You will win your target and goals."'

It sounds like a business management version of the Upanishads. There is no doubt that Naval believes every word. With the end of the course beckoning and no job on the horizon, it's as well that he has trust in the divine.

I lay down my pen and take another biscuit. For a couple of minutes we do nothing but munch and clean the resulting wallpaper paste from our gums. I ask if we could meet again after the course has finished. Sure, he replies. 'I should have time.'

I pick up my bag, stretch the aches out of my back and see myself out. I venture towards the stairs and the urine, my nose bracing for the onslaught.

Over the coming weeks, I venture back to Actor Prepares several times. The school occupies the top three floors of the Film Institute Welfare Trust. The weather-beaten building is hidden from the road, set back behind a conference hall.

One time I arrive late and find the narrow access road laid with a red carpet. At the end stands the silken arch of a colourful marquee. An energetic wedding band is working up a sweat beneath the gilded canopy. Beside them, a welcome committee busies itself fixing a collective smile into place. Every so often, a camera bulb flashes. Suddenly the scene becomes suspended in an explosive blast of blinding white. I watch the students file past to the school beyond. Few could resist an impromptu strut, imagining themselves as the feted debutants at the annual International Indian Film Academy awards. This was their fifteen yards of fame. Then the bridal car draws up and their dream disappears into the hall with the trumpeters.

Inside the Welfare building, the hallways fill with the divergent sounds of Hindi dance music and voice-projection exercises. Young people, all of them athletic and buoyant, hop joyfully down the corridors. It reminds me of the opening sequence of *Fame*, the hit US television series from the 1980s. I half-expect people to start launching themselves into an aerial swirls and proclaiming they want to live for ever. No one does.

Instead, I occupy myself popping into the various classrooms. In one, I happen upon gym-clad bodies contorting themselves to the beat of A. R. Rahman's chart-topping soundtracks. In another, faces twist and crocodile tears fall as the students work through the navarasa, nine primary emotions. In yet another, I see Mr Vyas putting his class through their paces with the all-seeing, ever-taxing Mr Sony.

I head upstairs to meet with Hernan, the school's marketing

manager. An orderly, goateed man, he is hidden away at a cubby-hole desk. Newspapers pile up beside him. A set of postcard-size photos, an inch or so thick, sits in front of him. He is leafing through them slowly. The school runs a small talent agency, which it falls to Hernan to manage. His most sought-after graduates glare out from larger prints on a cork pinboard behind him. Each is holding a deadpan, rock-star pose. Their names are splashed across the corner of their photographs in white print: Mohit Israni, Parvenn Yadav, Puja Ballutia, Rima Lamba. There is a slot for their age, as well as hair and eye colour. Height details are not so mandatory, with the shorter candidates choosing to omit specifics. As for the lighting, make-up and costumes, all are bold and gaudy. In Bollywood, bling sells. Not bashfulness.

I mention to Hernan my meeting with Naval and ask if he can introduce me to some recent graduates. I'm interested to know what lies in store for the high-visioner from the hinterlands.

Hernan makes a few calls and later in the week I'm invited back to the same studio in which Naval had previously withered before the camera. The room is empty. A dozen theatre lights are trained onto the low-rise stage, where two chairs and a small table sit like pensioners at a picnic. I take a seat in one and wonder if this is how it feels to be a chat-show host.

I am due to meet Arya Banerjee, who Hernan describes as an up-and-coming actress. Other than this salient fact, I know nothing about her. Only that it's the end of a long day and she's late. I kill ten minutes jotting down some questions, and another five toying with my camera and voice recorder. The next forty minutes are kept busy trying to stem my growing impatience.

When the door eventually opens and Arya wafts in, my mood has grown sour and surly. She apologises and smiles a melting smile. A standard excuse about the traffic follows. 'Of course,' I hear myself mumbling, my hard-won ill temper evaporating in a blink. 'Totally understand. Absolutely no problem.' I'm such a sop, my harsher half is saying. Not that I can really hear him. The ringing in my ears is too thunderous.

To put it crudely, Arya is hot. Steamingly, sizzlingly, blisteringly hot, she is all feline curves and silky, sculpted limbs. The whole svelte package is squeezed into a classy black evening dress that ends mid-thigh and clings to her body with the enviable tightness of cellophane. Gold brocade drips from each shoulder. A fragile silver watch hangs loosely from a delicate wrist. Beneath, two long lustrous legs fold out towards me. One black high-heeled toe points provocatively up towards the heavens, a Michelangelo digit communing directly with the divine. I hear her speak, but find myself too distracted to take in the words. Eyes of almond chocolates and lips like cherry plums, she has the kind of face that for centuries has driven men to art or war.

My reaction is less heroic and manifests itself in an attack of nerves. I feel acutely aware of my own unkempt appearance. I try writing and notice that my palms are wet with sweat. My voice is wavering. For some reason, my tongue has grown leaden. What's happening? I have the odd sensation that someone has swapped the tables; that it is me on tape and not her.

The next day, I rather reluctantly play back the recording of our conversation. The interview is not as inane as I'd initially feared. The questions I'd jotted down had helped me keep the discussion more or less on track. All the same, my voice sounds strangely tremulous, like an upset child on the point of tears. Arya, on the other hand, is composure itself. Her accent has the horsey twang of British aristocracy, a mirror of the posh London education she received as a young child.

As the recording runs, I try and glean some pertinent lessons for Naval. These will, as my memory now vaguely confirms, be scant. The two young actors could not be more different. Born and raised in the cultured confines of Kolkata, Arya is the daughter of a renowned (though long-deceased) sitar player. After a degree in classical music and a stint as a model, she joined Anupam Kher's acting school. 'To learn the craft,' as she puts it. She didn't have long to practise. Even before the course had finished, she'd bagged her first break. Her debut role in director Dibakar Banerjee's provocatively entitled *Love, Sex aur Dhokha* won her the critics' praise – and the paparazzi's lenses. Jettisoned onto the Bollywood map, she talks of the difficulties of success (long hours, constant travel, sycophantic acquaintances) and the secret buzz of seeing her photo in the morning paper. 'No one admits it, but we all look.'

With the interview nearing an end, Arya begins addressing the changes in Hindi cinema: how the actors are improving, how the scripts are becoming more international, and how she (as 'part of the new generation of Indian') wants to see realistic films and 'not just farmers and people below the poverty line'.

Then my voice breaks in. Prompted by thoughts of Naval, I hear myself asking about the other students in her class.

A cadence of clipped Kensington consonants and extended Chelsea vowels responds. Most came from smaller towns and 'weren't terribly well-educated', the ex-model hums. Not that background represents as big a barrier as before. Screen presence and talent are 'background enough' for young actors to get their chance. I push a little further. Her fellow students? What's become of them? No, about her batch, she wouldn't be able to say exactly.

Next, I heard myself asking her advice for the school's current group of hopefuls. The question had been meant as a personal request for Naval. I fully intended to pass on to him the response. 'Arya Banerjee says you should . . .'

Now, I'm not so sure. The advice might work for a beautiful girl of artistic pedigree. But is it wise to advise Naval never to give up on his dreams? Is it fair to tell him that it's only his aspirations that keep him alive?

I'd mulled over the dilemma as my conversation with Arya wound up. The request for advice has obviously left her in a philosophical frame of mind. She won't be good-looking for ever, she admits. Glamour won't always be on her side. 'Hopefully that's a long way off though.' The thought disappears into the sweet melody of a girlish chuckle.

Then the upper-class voice in the sultry dress is suggesting we call it a day. She has an evening event. It's across town. The traffic, as we both know, is terrible.

Hernan gives me a knowing look when I next pass through his

office. My hunt for other graduates need go no further, he presumes. Is he right? I guess he is. I'd like to meet with some of those that haven't yet made it, those that are still lugging themselves around town from audition to audition. I'd like to know what advice they might have for Naval. Yet I suspect that he would rather I stick to the success stories. As Chief Talent Scout, I doubt he's even kept the contact numbers of the also-rans.

'So when would you be available to see Mr Kher?' he asks. 'He has availability next Tuesday morning.'

'Uhhh, sure, Tuesday should be fine,' I respond, temporarily wrong-footed.

I'd been pestering Hernan for weeks to speak with the academy's founder and general advocate at large. But the one-man publicity machine was forever travelling or busy on set or otherwise tied up.

As a stopgap, Hernan had kindly arranged a seat for me at Mr Kher's autobiographical play entitled *Kucch Bitto Sakta Hai* ('He will do anything to succeed – even fail'). I'd resolved that a back-row seat at Juhu's Privthi Theatre might be as close as I could hope to get to B-Town's character actor extraordinaire. Unfortunately, bad traffic – predictably – caused me to miss the first half. By the second act, most of Mr Kher's failures already lay in the past. So I sat and watched him play out cameos from his career and project snapshots from his films.

Entering his office the following Tuesday, I'm ushered into a waiting room. A pretty girl in her early twenties, dressed in trousers and floral blouse, is waiting on a bench. Her mother sits beside her, holding her hand. The school is auditioning for its next intake. Across the room sits another prospective student. Clothed in a figure-hugging T-shirt with his hair slicked back, the gym-sharp adolescent is concentrating on filling out his application form. Next to him, three glum fish are looking out from a green tank. They too, I suspect, are dreaming of being someone else.

When Mr Kher's secretary directs me through to his office, I find that I recognise the balding actor at once. Not because of the posters and cuttings pasted throughout the building. These are flat and lifeless. I mean, I recognise him, the person not the face. It's Mr Bhamra, without the turban. From *Bend it Like Beckham*. The strict (but ultimately soft-hearted) Punjabi Sikh who lives huddled under the Heathrow flight path, barricading himself and his family against the cultural onslaught of modern Britain. Yes, it's him. I'm sure of it.

For a second, I stand there stunned. The school's principal reaches out to shake my hand. Robotically, I offer mine in response. Inside, however, a small epiphany is unfolding. I suddenly understand Nawal's personal connection with Salman Khan. Well, an inkling of it at any rate. Before, Naval's sense of intimacy with his on-screen idol had struck me as touching but ultimately fatuous. I'd stacked it up as further evidence of the young man's febrile state of mind. Now, I find myself wanting to tell Mr Kher to forget the racists who barred him from the local cricket club. I bite back the words. It is, I realise, a ludicrous impulse. All the same, it dawns on me that I have underestimated the chimerical power of the silver screen.

I probably owe Naval an apology. That will have to wait. A more pressing concern is upon me. My voice: I must keep it from quavering.

'So, where do you want to start?' Mr Kher asks.

He is seated behind his desk, surrounded by walls of books on art, cinema and literature. His manner is relaxed and disarmingly friendly. Any nerves I have on meeting Mr Bhamra are thankfully put to rest.

'How about from the beginning?' I suggest, seizing at the opportunity to make up for my late arrival at his one-man show.

The tale that unfolds over the next hour or so has an uncanny ring to it. As a film synopsis, it would read something like this:

Baby Kher, born into a lower-middle-class family from Shimla, the hill-station capital of Himachal Pradesh. 'Queen of Hills', the Britishers called it. The town in the skies has four cinema halls. Our youthful protagonist spends much of his early days dodging between one or other of them. He watches classics on repeat like *Pyaasa* and *Mughal-e-Azam*, and dreams of one day 'becoming somebody'. His father, the villain of the piece, harbours 'rigid ambitions' for him to follow his footsteps into government service. The teenage Kher ignores him. Instead, he robs money from his mother's shrine and secretly steals away to the city of Chandigarh. There he auditions for drama school. His acceptance is confirmed later by post. The letter reveals the source of the theft, as well as news of a scholarship. The standard paternal histrionics ensue. (It's Mr Bhamra again, railing against his daughter's wish to play football.) He packs his bags all the same. So the journey to becoming a trained actor commences.

On graduation, he teaches for a while in the same Chandigarh acting school. Three years at the National School of Drama in Delhi follow. Again, only a timely stipend makes it possible for the cash-strapped kid from Shimla to pursue his ambition. After a brief job as a lecturer in drama in Lucknow, he makes the inevitable journey to Mumbai in search of fame. He alights at Mumbai Central railway station on 13 June 1981. It's a Saturday. The trained actor would like to say the day marks the turning point in his life. It both does and it doesn't. His arrival in Bollywood teaches him one vital lesson: his status as a qualified actor is worth zilch. 'Half the people in this city couldn't even pronounce National School of Drama.' He is prematurely balding, not especially handsome and rather thin. And yet he wants to be a Bollywood actor. 'It was unheard of.'

Undeterred, the ambitious twenty-something starts roaming town in the hunt for his break. The search will take him nearly three years. The interim, as he calls it, comprises his 'disastrous period'. Homeless, he crashes on friends' couches and dosses down on railway benches. He knocks on doors, attends auditions and stands for hour after hour outside producers' houses. He tries theatre. He borrows money. Days go by when he eats nothing. Throughout it all, he refuses to give up. He has nowhere else to go, he tells himself. Nor, as he sees it, is there anything else he can do. He is meant to be an actor. He has moments of doubt, of course. On many occasions, he is 'completely shattered or depressed'. What keeps him going is the 'one chance' he sees coming his way. That, and a phrase of his grandfather's. 'If you work hard and you're honest,' he used to say, 'then you'll always get what you want.' He doesn't want to prove the old man wrong.

As with all good Bollywood stories, the hardship does not last for ever. Director Mahesh Bhatt is looking for someone to play a mardy, stubborn old man. For once being bald plays to the young actor's advantage. Bhatt calls him to his house. 'I've heard you're good,' the director tells him. 'You heard wrong,' our bolshie hero responds. 'I'm not good. I'm brilliant.' It isn't arrogance speaking, he'd later claim. The words were spawned from the depths of rage and desperation. The answer singles him out all the same. He gets the role. *Saaransh* comes out on 25 May 1984. It's a Friday. This time the date really does change his life. The film wins India's nomination to the Oscars. Mr Kher's career is made. Cue Act Two.

'Yes,' the veteran actor says, breaking off his tale and picking up the phone for the fifth or sixth time. 'Let me just have a look . . . yes, around mid-June should be fine . . . that's right, we're shooting in the Lake District . . . okay, thanks, I'll await your mail then.'

He turns to me with a bemused look. Have I ever heard of the television show, *Peschardt's People*?

'Sure, Michael Peschardt. It's a documentary show. Goes out on BBC World. Why? Does he want to interview you?'

The acting-school head looks quietly chuffed with my response, but waves off my question with undisguised modesty. In the way only successful people can, Mr Kher considers his personal story a template for wider truths. Placing his hands behind his head, he begins perusing it for salient lessons.

After an acting career of nearly three decades, 'one' (the impersonal third person – always a giveaway sign of the grandee preparing to pontificate) gets a sense of where the world is going. His world, that is. The world of Bollywood. And his verdict? 'It's all change.' Globalisation, modernisation, economic growth, an onslaught of satellite channels ('Star Movies, Warner Brothers,

AXN, Hallmark, HBO') – all, he regally observes, have dealt Hindi formula cinema a death blow.

In Old India, entertainment meant either watching movies or making babies. Then shops came. Malls came. Bars came. Cinema no longer occupies Number One spot. And when people do pay to see a film, they want something new, fresh, exciting. That, Mr Kher asserts, is why so many big movies are flopping. They've not caught up with the aspirations of their changing audience.

I ask what that means for the students at his school. 'What does it *mean*? It means they stand a chance of getting a job.' His manner is matter-of-fact. Directors are looking for actors that fit the role they have envisioned, not just a pretty face. In three years, he predicts, every actor in Bollywood will have had some professional training or other.

I think of Naval. Three years feels like a long time away. Mr Kher managed to pull it off. I wasn't sure if his evening-class student had the stamina to do the same.

'How many of your graduates actually land an acting job, then?' I ask, willing to be persuaded that Naval's odds are better than I surmise.

'About forty per cent,' he concedes. 'But, as I say, it's going up all the time.'

The veteran actor sits further back in his chair, moving his hands from his head to his paunch. He sounds every bit the elder statesman.

From the harsh city of his youth, Mumbai has transformed itself into a melting pot of opportunity. The city, he says, 'has a big heart'. It gives everyone one chance. Everyone and anyone. Whether you're a writer, whether you're a hawker, whether you're a businessman. 'The point is whether you are prepared when you get that first chance.'

Embarking on a career is certainly easier today than in his day, he continues. Back then, there were no casting firms or talent agencies or acting schools. Reality shows such as *Indian Idol* and *Acting Ki Funshaala* didn't exist. Today, you will be picked up.

'But', he reiterates, adamant for me not to miss his point, 'you have to be good.' Which is where his acting school comes in.

'Today's Indian youth is much more irreverent and much more straightforward than before . . .'

A leotard and leggings waltz in, disturbing his flow. The workout two-piece houses a slimline body belonging to the school's dance teacher. She feels sick. He's sorry to hear that. She should go home, get some rest. The dance attire floats back the same way it came in.

'Where were we?'

'The youth of today,' I respond.

'Ah yes, the youth of today. The present generation has nothing to do with the Independence struggle. They have none of the guilt of their parents. They are only interested in what they themselves can achieve. They are ready to adapt. They are ready to take risks. They are ready to go for it. They are ready to fail.'

Confidence. That, Mr Kher believes, is what differentiates the acting students now from those of his era. The current generation has enormous self-belief. It comes from greater access to knowledge, he thinks. It's there and it's 'very, very real'.

He's right, of course. Arya has it in bucket loads. The bionic boys and garrulous girls from the classrooms have it as well. So too does Naval, albeit less obvious to the naked eye. I'd missed it at first. It lay so deep that even Mr Sony, in his roving search for truth, had failed to unearth it. But it lay there simmering, sure as day.

I wonder whether I should ask Mr Kher about Naval. I'm keen to know how realistic he thinks his prospects are. Then I check myself. I'm suddenly aware of what he'll say. His story is just the same, the acting-school's director will tell me. Naval just happens to be at the start of his journey, not the end. His script is still being written. But his one chance will come. He must jump at it when it does, that's all. That requires preparation. And patience.

Patience is something Naval has in spades. Although patience is not free. The young man must eat. It's four weeks since his evening course finished. I decide to head back to the Projects to find out how he is getting on.

We meet at the stretch of Ram Mandir Road and make the same silent walk to his flat.

Naval is wearing thick, tight jeans despite the suffocating heat. Covering his upper body is a close-fitting purple shirt with vertical black stripes. The polyester garment has white rectangular cufflinks for buttons, each embossed with a small black star. A white bunny rabbit nibbles at his breast pocket. The word 'Play-boy' is stitched crookedly beneath. As dress sense goes, it's the very latest in pavement-market chic.

I enquire how the course went after we last met. Naval's eyes glaze over a little as he thinks back to the evening classes. Then, a broad grin stretches elastically across his face. 'Very nice. The course, very nice and very glorious.'

He tells me some of the central lessons he took away from Mr Vyas's instruction. The five Ws, for instance: 'Where, What, Why . . .' A pause. '. . . and stuff like that.' He's learned of the importance of getting into character. With the glint-eyed passion of a mystic's pupil, he explains how to forget Naval, to forget self. 'Suppose that you could not forget self, this is not better for you. This is not true for character.' He regrets not taking the extra dance class. Singing might have been helpful too.

The glory came on the last day with the end-of-course performance. Each student was encouraged to act out a short skit. Drawing on his own experience, Naval chose to incorporate the persona of a street pedlar. The plot revolved around the relationship between Naval the aloo chard seller and his rich, handsome friend.

The memory appears to upset him. He sniffs. A purple sleeve reaches up to wipe his nose.

'I gave a very nice performance. Sidartha, my teacher of drama, he is also very nice.' Sniff. 'He suggest to me that don't fear. Your first-time performance drama, don't fear. Don't discourage. Mr Sidarth, very nice.'

He carried it off. Everyone clapped.

Naval takes a moment to compose himself. He is reliving that brief but luxuriant moment of triumph. It takes him a while to come back to the present.

'Auditions?' I venture. 'How are they going? Any luck?'

The question, unfairly perhaps, brings Naval back to earth with a bump. He mumbles something about callbacks and waiting. It seems he's been to four auditions. None has come to anything. For some, he's not right. For others, he's not eligible. 'No money, no honey, no funny,' he states plaintively. One casting director advised him to go back to his village, build his savings and then return to Mumbai. Naval dismissed the advice out of hand. 'You are winner. I am winner.' Instead, he's started doing the rounds of the local factories. Two thousand rupees a month. 'It's nothing. How to pay rent?'

His shoulders suddenly collapse in on him, his body visibly crumpling forwards as if an industrial air suction had been slapped onto his stomach.

He rights himself a fraction. As he does so, fat, warm tears begin to trickle down his cheek.

'I have two rupees. I am hungry. Last one week, I have no support. Not anythings. I've not any foods.'

I don't know what to say. His tears keep flowing, filling the silence between us.

He babbles an incoherent story – or is it a set of stories? I struggle to catch much of it. One minute, he's heading off to Gandinagar to meet a Member of Parliament. The next, he's hopping on a train to Bhopal to speak to a film director. None of it seems to make sense, to him or me.

Between his rib-shuddering chokes, I catch a strand or two: 'I am only water. Five days . . . Today, I go to church and pray to Jesus and ask for him to help me. I am feeling very, very sad . . .'

I wonder if I should offer him something. Some money? Food? Earlier, I'd suggested we chat in a cafe off the main road. He'd declined. I wonder how to console him.

'. . . Occasionally I feel like I'm going wrong way. What am I doing? But I feel God is saying, 'No, you are right. Take patience. My dear, my child, my son . . .'

Consolation. Is that really what he wants? Something – a sense, an intuition – holds back my full sympathies. His tears are real. Yet how quickly they begin to fall. And how dramatic the whole act.

I've no doubt he's hungry and broke. At one stage he pulls up his sleeve. 'Look how thin my arm is. Before, I was fat.' As he grabs at his taut skin, the truth of his pinched circumstances stares me in the face.

Yet could it just be that he's performing?

Naval's role-playing is, I am convinced, subconscious. Somehow, somewhere, he has developed an image of himself as a down-at-heel actor – yet a down-at-heel actor who, without doubt, will one day rise to become a star. Initially, I suspect him of aping Mr Kher's script. The thought proves mistaken. When I ask him if the struggles of the academy's director inspire him, he looks at me with genuine puzzlement. The high-visioner is oblivious to anything but his mentor's present. 'Anupam Kher is a very sentient person,' he assures me flatly. 'A very famous man.' If he has cast himself as the bench-sleeping Kher of yesteryear, he has done so by accident. Not that the rags-to-riches story is a unique one. It is there in every film Naval has ever watched, in every magazine he's ever read. It's part of the Bollywood myth. Part of the New India story. Little wonder he's imbibed the role as if it were his own.

All the while, Naval is still blubbering. He has to shift flat. Another shared room in the faceless blocks has become vacant. He will move in two days. The thought does not comfort him. His sobs increase. In Delhi, he also lived in 'very poor place'. Near to Dr Mukherjee Nagar police station. The trains would run right beside his room.

His thoughts begin to jump. He has fever. He once did a play in the slums of New Delhi about swine flu. His hunger is 'like crick in his bones'. He misses his mum.

I fear he's become so engrossed in his part that he might just turn hysterical. I try some practical, yes–no questions in the hope of calming him.

'Can the school not help find you a job?' No. 'Can Mr Shilabhadra not advise you about casting agencies?' Apparently not. 'Can I buy you lunch?' He's fine. 'Might you reconsider going home?' Never.

The last question has the opposite effect to that which I'd hoped. He puts both hands over his face and gives himself over to a fit of unashamed sobbing. For a full minute, he is lost in his own grief. Eventually, after what feels like an age, he draws breath and stumbles to his feet. On the sill of an air duct out into the corridor is a colour passport photograph. It shows a diffident-looking woman staring at the camera from beneath the hood of her sari.

Taking it between finger and thumb, he sits back down in front of me and addresses a short monologue to the stark portrait: 'My mother, I love her so much. I used to sleep in the same bed as her until I was thirteen years old. Every week, we speak on the phone. Each time she is asking me when I come. I say "soon", "one month", "two months". My sister, she has marriage recently. I couldn't go there. My sister says me, "when come, when come, when come." I tell her one month. I have two sisters and two brothers. I am the last.'

He rights himself and mournfully returns the photo to its original position, as if laying a private keepsake at the side of his mother's tomb. Beside the snapshot stands a school notebook. A picture of the monkey god Hanuman adorns the front, majestic with his golden mace and android features. Naval looks at the book, thinks to himself for a second and then removes it from the shelf.

'Would you like to hear my poem?' he asks, the suggestion of a smile brightening his tear-ravaged face.

'Very much,' I respond, anxious to pursue any avenue that might provide him some cheer.

He sits and opens the pages of the wide-lined children's notebook. The poem occupies the first page. Several lines are blackened out with scribbles. He coughs to clear his throat. I take out my Dictaphone. 'Would you mind?' Of course not, he replies. He takes the machine and, in a halting voice still stifled by tears, reads out the following verse:

I am hungry from many days but my dream is too much completeful.

I am shorrow but my dream is very pleaser ('happy, you know, pleaser').

I am slaver ('I am slaver, slaver, you know'), but my dream is free like bird.

I am gayle [jail] but my dream is flying in the sky.

I am live in hell, but my dream live in heaven.

I said to dream, what are doing?

Dream tell me, 'I am right and you are wrong.

'Don't fear my dear, you have God.

'Don't fear. You are good winner. You are good winner.'

I am good winner.

I take the Dictaphone from his clenched hand and press the 'stop' button. It seems a natural point for us to part. I wish him every success and promise to keep his poem on record. It will be worth something when he's famous, I assure him. He responds to the thought with a credulous grin.

Over the following months, I often find myself thinking what happened to Naval. Is he still in the Projects? Has he landed himself a job? Should I have done more to help him? When I least expect it – sitting on a bus in traffic, waiting for an elevator, watching the talented and talentless fight it out on Fame Gurukul – the last line of this poem comes back to me. 'I am good winner.' The words haunt me for reasons I cannot quite understand. Long after they've gone, I still feel an unease in my gut. It's akin to dread, as if I'm the sole insider to a disaster foretold.

Then one day in November (a Tuesday), a short message pops up in my inbox. It's from Naval. I don't know how he came to have my email address. I don't remember giving it to him. Google perhaps? Anyway, he has news to share.

HI nice and good journlist mr. oliver ji , namste . perhaps u forgetted me .but i cant . your work.i most like it.dear oliver i am working as assistent in new serial.a new chanel hom tv .i am workig free.than u

Working free. It's not much, but it's a start. Naval's script is unfolding. Who knows where it might lead? The Mizapur School of Acting stands an inch closer to reality. Thank God. And Ram, Jesus and Krishna too.

Indian cinema offers The Common Man an opportunity to be transported to another place, a place free of drudgery, a place full of life, love and song. The audience knows what they are watching is a fiction, yet that matters little. Aspirations require the boundaries of truth to be stretched occasionally. The fantastical is a gateway to the possible. Not so with cricket, though. At the crease, dreams are counted in wickets and boundaries. Physical realities, matters of life and death.

5

Sporting Chance

[sport]

'Yesterday was the first day of the Games. Today we are sorting everything out and from tomorrow we will have a free flow of everything.'

Suresh Kalmadi, Chairman of the Commonwealth Games Organising Committee

Mumbai

The elderly ice-cream seller reaches for the rail to steady himself as Brabourne Stadium erupts around him. Sanath Jayasuriya, the Master Blaster from Sri Lanka, has been given the ball for the seventeenth over. The crowd screams. Horns blast. Whistles shriek. Hands clap. Drums beat. The din is saturating, a cacophonous flood of noise crashing and raging like a storm at sea.

The authorised vendor is the only person with his back to the cricket pitch. Spectators bustle around him, inadvertently pushing and nudging him. He seems not to care. Trade is good. The evening is warm and the Mumbai Indian fans are feeling jubilant and flush. He pulls the Kwality Walls ice-box down from his head and rests it in the aisle of the raised stand.

The man beside me cups his hand and yells an order. 'Three Cornettos.' It's no good. We're sat mid-row. His request is lost, swallowed up by the clamour. Resolving that the ice cream is worth the fight, he leaves his seat and enters the scrum of spectators. I watch him struggle through. He treads on toes, trips on bags, blocks the view. No one scowls. The crowd is too elated. Life is too sweet. The Indian Premier League, the IPL, is back. The magic of cricket is upon us.

Jayasuriya is pacing back for his second ball, his first having been driven towards mid-off by the determined Paras Dogra for a single. The huge scoreboard to the right of the main pavilion reveals the runs required.

58 RUNS, 23 BALLS

Batting first, the home team of Mumbai Indians scored an aggressive total of 212. Jaipur-based Rajasthan Royals, who won the inaugural IPL tournament in 2008, are giving chase admirably. Time is against them, however. Of their twenty overs, fewer than four remain.

Jayasuriya begins another run-up towards the wicket. He bowls a full toss, which is top-edged towards a fielder at long-off. The batsmen run quickly between the wickets, collecting a single.

Rajasthan Royals desperately need boundaries. Fortunately for them, burly Yusuf Pathan is still at the crease. The big hitter from Gujarat is on song. Eighty-three runs off thirty-four deliveries so far. It's a slogfest for the broad-shouldered Test player; precisely the kind of combative, untamed performance for which the IPL was invented.

'Come on, Mumbai Indianssss!!!!'

The tannoy screeches into life. The snippet of a popular Hindi soundtrack booms across the field. Over the loudspeaker system, the game's over-excited compère begins a countdown.

'Five, four, three, two, one . . .'

The words are mirrored in numerical form on the big screen. Jutting exclamation marks accompany each number. The sound and shape of Zero sends twenty thousand sets of arms thrusting into the air. The crazed screech of 'In-di-anssss' courses across the city.

This is entertainment in the raw, exhilarating and unencumbered. I sit in my seat, ears ringing, enjoying the ride.

The batsman on strike drives the ball to mid-on. A fielder collects it cleanly. Another single for the Royals.

Outside, the crimson sun is sinking into the Arabian Sea. Beautiful, broad brushstrokes of mottled purple light up the wispy evening clouds, which swirl and sway like feathered petals in a field of lavender. Nature's visual evensong is wasted on us. Pressed close in the cavernous hold of the stadium oval embrace, all eyes are focused forward, not up. Never once do they waver from the rectangular stretch of buzz-cut grass, twenty-two yards in length and bathed in the stark white of the floodlights.

The bald head of Jayasuriya bobs towards the stumps. Pathan lifts his bat in anticipation. Another full toss. Dispatched back over the bowler's head. The ball scorches through the illuminated night sky, re-entering orbit well over the ropes.

SIX!! SIX!!

A band of musicians, elegantly attired in long-trained turbans and starch-white kurtas, jump to their feet and thrash out a tune from beside the boundary rope. The celebrations are universal. The IPL is too young to have built up strong fan allegiances. There are no grudge-ridden derby games as yet. Pathan is first and foremost an Indian hero. Rajasthanis and Mumbaikers join in applauding him.

Next ball. Pathan swipes. Edge. Scuttles off behind to the boundary for four. More uproar in the stands. The next. Full toss. No mercy from Pathan, The Beast, The Lethal Weapon, The Steeler. Up over long-on.

SIX RUNS!! SIX RUNS!!

The consecutive boundary brings his hundred up, the fastest century (off thirty-seven balls) in IPL history.

The entertainment machine shifts immediately into action. Music. Fog horns. 100!!!! in gigantic font, yelling from the screen. TV footage of Pathan close up, helmet off, bat aloft, saluting the crowd. He's a modern-day gladiator, clad in his armour of pads and encircled by a squadron of vanquished fielders.

A commotion follows, off to the left. Wolf whistles and clamouring. Balanced on a small stage, right in front of the cheap seats, three cheerleaders are launching into an energetic routine. Pompoms thrust. Hips wiggle. Legs kick. Men everywhere are screaming and stomping their feet.

At the scoring of every boundary, the fall of every wicket and the end of every over, the foreign girls flaunt and the Indian audience froths. It's a perverse rehearsal for an impossible tryst. Even so, introducing fair-skinned blondes in skimpy outfits to the game of cricket is marketing genius. It triggers all the right buttons for your average red-blooded, sofa-sitting Indian sports viewer.

Naturally, Old India took immediate umbrage. Calls quickly came for the gyrating cheerleaders to be banned. 'It goes against our culture.' 'It will corrupt our children.' As long as the ratings rocket, however, the girls will stay.

Sexing up cricket is what the IPL is all about. The organisers – a for-profit consortium headed by the Board of Control for Cricket in India – have employed every trick in the book to turn their six-week tournament into one of the most watched sporting events on the planet. Over twenty million households tuned in to watch the opening game of this series. Shopping malls register a twenty per cent drop in footfall on match days. Nor is the appeal just in India. IPL games play out to huge prime-time audiences in Bangladesh, Pakistan and Sri Lanka. Further afield, millions tune in via satellite. This year, Google is even streaming matches on YouTube.

At the core of the IPL's appeal is the game's revamped format. The new league strips the game down to its essentials and re-packages it for the mass-market. In a sport in which matches can last for days, the IPL squeezes everything into an evening's viewing. Keeping the games short means more action, faster runs and closer finishes – perfect TV fodder.

Viewers love it. So too do advertisers. The IPL can count nearly one hundred corporate sponsorships, most of which run into millions of dollars. As for the broadcasting rights, they were snapped up by Sony. The ten-year deal cost the Japanese firm a cool $1.93 billion.

The team owners themselves are not blind to the IPL's promotional potential. Film actors are first in line. B-Town celebrity Shah Rukh Khan never misses an opportunity to be photographed in the colours of the Kolkata Knight Riders, a team he part-owns. Likewise, C-list actress Shilpa Shetty – whose career rebounded after the *Big Brother* race row – uses her stake in the Rajasthan Royals to keep herself in the spotlight.

Back in the stadium, the ball disappears into the crowd over mid-off as Dogra belts right-armer Rajagopal Santish for six. It's a stinging riposte to the dismissal of Pathan, unluckily run out a few balls earlier.

The umpire, whose shirt and broad-brimmed hat are plastered with the injunction to 'Fly Kingfisher' (part of a $23 million tie-in with the airline), points two fingers to the darkening sky. The camera hones in on the batsman. He too is a walking billboard. The cement brand 'Ultratech' splays across his chest, while analgesic pain ointment (and Rajasthan Royals' 'Official Fitness Partner') Moov covers his top pocket. The rest of his outfit is similarly bedecked. Puma owns his trousers, HDFC his back and Kingfisher his arms.

19 RUNS, 12 BALLS

Rajasthan Royals are back in the game.

The diminutive figure of Sachin Tendulkar, India's undisputed King of Cricket, stands idly in the covers. Everyone loves Tendulkar. His name is stitched onto the back of every Mumbai Indians shirt. A teenage prodigy with the bat, Tendulkar's illustrious international career spans two decades. No one in the history of the game has scored more runs either in Test cricket or the sport's one-day format. He's a living legend, as close as any human can come to being an incarnate deity. 'Cricket is my religion', many Indian fans will even say, 'and Sachin is my God.'

The IPL has not let his fame go to waste. He is one of five players to be accredited with 'icon' status. In the inaugural auction, securing his services cost Mumbai Indians twenty-five per cent more than any other player. The thirty-six-year-old veteran would not let his employer down. In this, the IPL's third season, the home-grown Mumbaiker would go on to score 618 runs in fourteen innings – more than any other player before or since. He went on to win the season's award for Best Batsman and Best Captain.

For decades, it was the glory of the game that lit the desire in every young boy's heart to one day become a cricketer. Names like Azharuddin, Dravid, Gavaskar, Laxman, Hazare and Mankad draw a smile wherever you go in India. These are the men who, with bat or ball, stuck one in the eye of the English or smote the Pakistanis in Lahore. To mention them is to demonstrate good-will, to open a conversation, to cross a barrier.

In the public mind, India's cricket stars compare with the pin-up paladins of Bollywood. When the legendry Sourav Ganguly was dropped as the national captain, riots broke out in his home city of Kolkata. Politicians would have to reach deep into their pockets for such a show of popular support. Cricketers' motives are perceived as purer, their hearts more patriotic. 'A Proud In-dian' reads Tendulkar's strapline on Twitter. No political leader could write that and be taken seriously.

However, when youngsters look at their cricketing heroes today, they see something other than glory. They see money, bucketloads of it. The IPL has turned India's top-flight cricketers from quasi-amateurs into business professionals. In the inaugural auction, mouths dropped when Chennai Super Kings parted with one and a half million dollars for Indian captain Mahendra Singh Dhoni. On a pro rata basis, colossal salaries such as these make the IPL the most lucrative league in the world after America's National Basketball Association.

Little wonder then that foreign players have come sniffing. Eng-land's Kevin Pietersen, Australia's Adam Gilchrist and Graeme Smith of South Africa are among some of the world-class crick-eters whose bank balances have grown prodigiously thanks to the IPL. Even the incredible – though very much retired – West Indian batsman Brian Lara tried brushing down his pads to win a piece of the IPL pie.

'Say Malinga, Mummm-baiiiii!!' The compère's booming voice is back, zapping the audience with a verbal cattle prod.

We're down to the last over. Not a single spectator remains seated. Not a mouth stays closed. The two Royals batsmen confer in the middle of the pitch. Then they punch fists and walk nervously back to their respective ends. Sri Lankan Lasith Malinga, brushing back his dyed, curly lion's mane, rocks on his heels.

12 RUNS, 6 BALLS

Malinga the Slinga prepares to bowl. First ball. A classic yorker. The batsman, desperately digging it out from under his toes. The ball, squirting forward, not far enough. Dogra, sprinting from the other end. Malinga, out ahead. The bowler bending, scooping, diving, throwing. The bails, flying off. Dogra, lunging. Too late. Malinga, spread-eagled, thumbs pointing up. The umpire, finger raised.

OUT! RUN OUT!

Pandemonium ensues. Spectators dance and shout, jump and twist, scream and holler. Pounding music pumps, manna to the mayhem. Even the stand itself is celebrating, its metal struts reverberating to the thunder of a thousand thumping feet.

The new batsman walks out to the centre, whirling his bat like the sail of a windmill.

12 RUNS, 5 BALLS

Amit 'Mitu' Uniyal takes his mark, assesses the field, watches Malinga running in, raises his bat, prepares to strike and . . . OUT! The ball careers off his inside edge and clatters into the stumps. The middle stump catapults out of its moorings, pitching through the air in graceful, luckless cartwheels.

Australia's Shane Warne enters the throng. Hostile jeers rain down on the Royals' player-coach. He strides towards the wicket, acting impervious.

12 RUNS, 4 BALLS

He scrapes over Uniyal's freshly made mark with a gravedigger's detachment for the dead. Malinga steamrollers in, arm crooked, gold chain glinting. A blistering ball. Warne manages to get bat on ball. The fielder at square leg is on to it like a shot. The batsmen try returning for a second, but are forced to settle for a single.

'Ma-lin-ga! Ma-lin-ga! Ma-lin-ga!' The bowler's name resounds around the ground, a war cry in all but name.

11 RUNS, 3 BALLS

The ball is driven through mid-on. The batsmen scamper for two. The fielder throws. The bails come off. 'Howzat?!' The home team screams for a run-out. Over to the third umpire. A pause.

Suspense. The big screen flits to the cheerleaders, then to the dug-out, then to Shilpa Shetty, then to a Royals supporter yanking at her hair. The verdict flashes up.

NOT OUT

A reprieve.

9 RUNS, 2 BALLS

Malinga bowls. Down leg side it darts. A wide, bringing an ex-tra run. The crowd is chanting, champing, choking the game of its final fix. Malinga the Slinga bowls again. He's hit into the covers. The batsmen gallop down the pitch, adding a further one, then two, to the score.

The tannoy bursts into life. 'Six runs to win!' Any pretence of non-partisanship on the compère's part is long gone. 'Mumbai winning!!' A bugle fanfare sounds. From the terraces, 'Ma-lin-ga! Malinga!' The last play of the dice, the final volt in the charger. 'Ma-lin-ga! Malinga!' Again and again, the cry goes up – five, ten, twenty times. The stadium shudders and sparks, racing its way to-wards a final crescendo.

The scoreboard screams what we already know, the fact on which twenty thousand minds are solely focused.

6 RUNS, 1 BALL

Out on the pitch. Two men, bowler and batsman. A classic showdown, an all-or-nothing duel. Malinga, speeding in. The batsman, steeling his courage. The ball, launched down the wick-et. The bat, wielded wildly. Thunk. Leather against willow. But the timing, tragically, is off-centre. The ball does not sear into the stands as the fairy tale holds. It scurries along the ground, straight into the path of a sure-handed fielder. A single is secured, a mo-ment of crowning glory missed. Malinga celebrates, fist in the air. His team-mates pile in, football-style, one on top of the other. The heap of bodies collapses, victorious.

MUMBAI WINS

Fly Kingfisher. Fly Kingfisher.

The party continues outside. The crowd swells as the ticketless masses at the stadium gates join the swarm of departing spec-tators. Most are men, and most are ecstatic. Even the Royals supporters. They leave with most of what they came for: not a victory perhaps, but a forty-over feast of adrenalin-fuelled highs. What's more, the whole season lies ahead, nearly sixty games overall. The two will meet again.

Elbowing my way out of the thickest part of the scrum, I turn left and head down Marine Drive towards Nariman Point. The road is banked by the oil-blue sea, which languishes quietly and alone, a million miles away from the ceaseless, sleepless streets of the city.

On dry land, the air is damp and salty and rent with klaxon horns. The pavement remains thick with people. I continue on, bodies moving all around me. The mood is festive, but I have a growing desire to be away from it all. I love the constant jostling of India, yet it can gradually work me over. India is a nation of the masses, a nation that instinctively inverts the private into the public. Indoors becomes outdoors. My space becomes our space. Unused to living in a crowd, the presence of so many people leaves me craving quiet.

I duck off the road and into Geoffrey's pub. The British-era refit is located in a smoky corner of the Hotel Marine Plaza. I find a stool at the bar, and order a murgh malai kebab and a beer from the waistcoated barman.

An even mix of Indians and expats divides the room. The split is by age, not nationality. The younger crowd occupies one end, with their lagers and lounge seats, while the old-timers lay claim to the other end, nurturing their whiskeys and escaping their wives. My seat at the bar places me between the two camps. It's a neutral zone, with pots of peanuts to keep the peace.

A wide-screen television is tuned in to the sports channel, Max Live. The studio is kitschily decorated and painted in a bright bordello red. A child-faced presenter with a Brylcreemed quiff and a silver suit is rhapsodising about the 'cracker jacker' of a game just gone. Highlights of Pathan's innings are played back. The Sixes, Max Live's on-screen bulletin reveals, are Brought to You by Hero Honda. Ad breaks flow copiously. Lux Beauty Cream, Samsung Dual Sim Phones, 7 UP 'The Lemon Drink'. All are told in a polyglot hybrid of English and Hindi. A let-up comes with the IPL's Green Tip of the Day. Plant a tree, the nation's viewing public is encouraged.

The message is lost on the old guard. Their backs are turned. The success of the IPL may be galactic, but its appeal is not entirely universal. Cricket purists cannot abide it. A ratings-led barbarity, a desecration of the sacred game, they say. They bemoan the loss of strokeplay and deride its dumbed-down simplicity. The Mickey Mouse format is ruining young players, the critics allege. Their temperaments are too flighty. Their techniques too flashy.

For others, the rot runs deeper. The IPL stands for all that is ill in India. Everything, not just cricket, is becoming tainted by cash and greed. Life used to be all about 'being'. Now, it revolves around buying. People want their pleasures now, not later. Patience, respect, history – such values are disappearing job-lot in an India bamboozled by the novel and new. The IPL, like reality TV and fast food, speaks of a country that is losing its way. India is prioritising the present over the past, and endangering its future in the process.

As a metaphor, the IPL is a flexible construct. Just as it can be viewed as the road to ruin, it can also be portrayed as a harbinger of hope. Cricket in India is a majority pastime. Yet, for years, its top-flight players have come from a minority of the population. Sourav Ganguly, for example, belongs to one of Kolkata's richest families. His family house reputedly has twenty-two bedrooms. V. V. S. Laxman, captain of the Deccan Chargers (and later Kochi Tuskers), comes from a family of affluent doctors. Though of more modest means, Tendulkar's father was a Marathi novelist and teacher. All are Brahmins. Today, a new breed of stars is coming to light. Yusuf Pathan, the son of an impoverished muezzin, burst on to the scene from nowhere. Likewise, millionaire heart-throb Mahendra Dhoni, the son of a steel-factory worker, clawed his way up from the backwaters of Bihar to become captain of the national team. The IPL is giving ambitious young cricketers an unprecedented shot at fame and fortune. Talent is being noticed.

The gifted now have a chance. And India too – so the parallel runs – is becoming an equal-opportunity enterprise.

Drunken laughter breaks out from the far end of the pub. Behind me, ice chinks frostily in whiskey glasses. It's time I left. Outside, Marine Drive has grown quieter. I hail a cab and head down the crescent highway to the exclusive Oberoi Hotel.

The hotel's foyer is five-star chic and almost empty. At the indication of a liveried doorman, I take the lift down to the basement function room. The button pings. The door slides open. And into a different world I walk. The carpeted Regal Room is rammed. New India, dressed in its designer best, has come out to play. Air-kisses fly. Diamonds sparkle. Champagne flows. At an IPL Party Night, everyone has their part. The day's cricketers meet and greet. Mumbai's cool crowd shimmers and struts and smiles for the cameras. Leggy models saunter down a catwalk in seductive, semi-clad strides.

Around midnight, the same crowd ups and leaves for Bandra. I follow in pursuit. Shilpa Shetty is hosting the launch of her new nightclub, aptly named Royalty. A red carpet and bank of paparazzi line the route to the door. Inside, three blonde Eastern Europeans sway in the middle of the packed dance floor, half a foot taller than everyone else. The Indian cricketers have all gone, leaving the foreign players to monopolise the models. The silver-sequinned Shilpa presides over the VIP lounge, an entourage of actors and impresarios swooning at her feet.

At three a.m., the lights come up. Partied out, the IPL juggernaut retires for the night. The photos of the evening are already with the newspapers. The cricketers can sleep easy. On and off the pitch, they have given people what they want.

Delhi

'Sure, a pop-up – that makes sense. Let's run it throughout the afternoon. "Viv Richards, live at nine p.m." Rajesh. Can you get on to that please?'

All eyes are on Rahul Kanwal. A semicircle of senior editors sits poised around his desk, pens and notepads at the ready. Behind them, a back-up troop of reporters and sub-editors form a more scattered, outer ring.

We're twenty minutes into the morning editorial meeting at Headlines Today, an upstart English-language news channel beamed out of the Videocon Tower in Delhi. Its coverage is 'fresh' and 'alternative', according to Rahul, the precociously young chief editor. Three years into the job, he's still shy of his thirtieth birthday. His tabloid, newsflash style – borrowed from Aaj Tak, Headlines Today's longer-standing Hindi sister channel – is proving popular with today's viewers. Ratings are creeping up. Rahul's star is shining.

'That's good. Let's play this up in a biggy?'

Rahul's focus is turned to the bank of television screens fixed to the wall in front of his desk. On one, a block of flats is crashing to the ground. A minion runs off into the busy newsroom to relay the message.

The screens show Headlines Today's competitor channels too: CNN-IBN, Times Now, NDTV and Breaking News. All four combine to create a frenetic montage of bold graphics, shaky camera work and non-stop bulletins of 'Exclusive!' news.

Viv Richards' visit to the Headlines Today studios marks a veritable scoop. The former West Indies cricket captain is passing through the Indian capital for the Commonwealth Games, which kicked off three days ago.

'Saddath, get me a print out of the promos quickly.'

The cub reporter jumps from his chair and disappears.

Rahul is visibly excited. He taps his pen on the desk and runs a hand through his wavy side-parting. The charismatic editor is anxious to milk the Richards interview to the full. It'll run over the hour-long Centre Stage show, the prime-time evening slot hosted by Rahul himself. That much is decided. Now, how to market it?

'Let's think of a contest, right. You know, erm, "Which batsman has the most similar style to Sir Viv?" We'll get him to answer the question on air and give the winner . . .' Rahul pauses for thought. 'Everyone, what can we give the winner?'

'How about an autographed cricket bat?' suggests the goatee-bearded copy-editor.

'Good idea. We'll need someone to go and buy a bat. Imran, get onto that. And, Rajiv, put something up on the website right away. And prepare some tweets on it too.'

Richards is due to arrive just before three o'clock. A protracted discussion follows about who from the guest team should go down to meet him. It has to be someone who knows about cricket, one of the editors points out. And someone who can butter him up, says another. 'He's a moody guy. We need to try and pump him up a bit.' A junior assistant is mentioned and the name agreed.

Rahul is jotting furiously on a piece of paper. A waiter in a frayed black jacket approaches his table with a steaming cup of tea in a Headlines Today mug. 'Refreshingly Different', the caption reads.

The editor looks up, a glint in his eye.

'So I was thinking, let's lead on a history of his career. We'll call it, "King Richards' Life". Right? We'll need to dig out some footage of him at his prime. The Original Master Blaster. The Most Feared Batsman Ever. That sort of thing.'

The programme manager raises a hand. 'He's very particular about being referred to as Sir Vivian.'

'No, that won't work,' the head of investigations chips in. 'We've got to say, "Sir Viv".'

Another debate unfolds. The Delhi bureau chief goes off on a tangent about Richards being called Smokin' Joe, 'you know, like the black US boxer Smokin' Joe Frazier'.

Rahul cuts him off. 'Sir Viv' has his vote. He shifts to the question of graphics. Ideas are thrown in about what will work and what won't.

Meantime, Saddath comes back with the promos. Rahul scans them, his ear still tuned into the discussion around him. 'Too long. Cut it back. And make it punchier.' Saddath skulks off.

'Settled then?' Rahul looks to his colleagues, who nod hesitantly. 'So, not full frame. We want his picture on screen too. Remember, he's a big guy.'

Thirty minutes pass before any mention of the interview questions is made. Two story editors taking hurried notes at the end of Rahul's desk wait expectantly.

'We'll just talk about his glory days, and which players he sees coming up after him,' says Rahul.

His manner is offhand. No one adds anything. He'll be the one fronting the interview. The questions are his call.

'Then a bit about how the West Indies are declining and how India are in the ascendancy. Sound good?'

Again, no comments. Rahul himself voices what everyone else is thinking.

'So that'll take about twenty minutes. How can we string it out over an hour?'

Legs crossed, a biro wedged down the side of his shoe, the copy-editor lifts a hand. 'How about Kapil Dev?' Kapil and Richards were Test contemporaries. The two could banter about old times. The chief editor likes the idea. A phone call is put through to his PR. Kapil is in Kolkata. 'Talk to Avijit,' Rahul responds immediately. 'Check the outside-broadcast van is available this afternoon.' A follow-up call is patched through to the former cricket star himself. The receiver passes across to Rahul.

'A small request, sir. Can you give up twenty minutes for us this afternoon? . . . Of course, we'll send the van to wherever you are . . . Sure, the Taj Bengal . . . Three o'clock, great . . . Brilliant, sir. I really appreciate this.'

Rahul runs his hand through his hair again. He talks out loud to no one in particular about the logistics. Visuals would have to be ready an hour before. Someone would need to speak with the manager at the Taj Bengal hotel. The relevant team members take notes.

Time is running on. Packages for the evening's other shows have to be decided too. Attentions turn to Ground Zero, the channel's other prime-time slot. The older of the two story editors reads from a list of top stories: a Saudi prince beating up his male lover in a London hotel, a toxic leak in Hungary, racist comments by New Zealand television presenter.

Rahul takes notes, interjecting with questions all the while. 'What are the images like?' . . . 'We can run the blurb on the side.' . . . 'Get Sunita Narain from TERI for a two-way?' . . . 'Who's got the phone number of our local fixer there?' . . . 'Fantastic.' . . . 'So what do we all have?'

'Then there's the Commonwealth, of course,' the story editor continues, raising his eyebrows.

'Anything positive?' Rahul asks.

The story editor stifles a laugh.

For weeks, Headlines Today has joined every other Indian media channel in slamming the Games. The swathe of bad press began as a trickle. First came reports about 'eleventh-hour mayhem' and Delhi not being ready in time. Then charges of sleaze and missing millions began to filter out. Next, stories emerged about slums being flattened and beggars being deposited outside the capital. News of ill-paid workers, safety lapses and traffic gridlock followed.

'Global Scorn for CWG Fiasco.' So ran the headline for a *Headlines Today* exposé in the days just before the Games kicked off. The story played out against grainy photos from the multi-million-dollar Athletes' Village: paan-stained toilets, broken stairs, stray dogs on the beds, faeces in the corners. The programme then shifted to a collapsed pedestrian bridge and the caved-in ceiling of the weightlifting venue. 'Should CWG be called off?' the show's host asked provocatively. Viewers were invited to post their comments at twitter.com/rahulkanwal.

The Commonwealth Games were supposed to be the opportunity for 'Shining India' to dazzle the world. It wasn't turning out that way. A spectacular opening ceremony did little to allay the criticism. For the first two days, news-stands still flooded with reports of empty stadiums, ticketing problems and condom-blocked toilets in the athletes' village. Many Indians were embarrassed. Some were angry. On screen, Rahul was righteously indignant.

For all the emotional fervour, however, I sensed no one deep down was that surprised. After all, this was a sporting event, and India doesn't really do sport. Sport that's not cricket, that is.

By any measure, India's performances on the international stage are dire. The country has never had a world champion sprinter, gymnast or racing driver. Its national football team has never graced a World Cup. It took a century of the modern Olympic movement for India to lay claim to its first individual gold medal. The contrast with China, which wrapped up the last Olympics with fifty-one gold medals, is telling.

The lack of priority given to sport in India is lamentable, but understandable. In a developing country, precedence has traditionally been given to schools and hospitals, not leisure centres and athletics tracks. Even now, two million Indian children die every year from easily preventable diseases. Were the country's social needs magically done away with, Indians would still remain sceptical about investing in sport. To the public mind, there's a childish frivolity to men and women running laps and chasing balls. Indeed, the Hindi word for sport is 'khel', which also translates as 'play' or 'playful'.

In as much as Indians do engage in sport, it's generally from their lounge chairs. Formula One Grand Prix attracts almost twice as many television viewers in India as it does across all of Europe combined. By the same token, only one in every fifty pairs of Nike jogging shoes sold on the sub-continent is ever used for running.

All the same, enough is enough. Rahul feels a change of tack is needed. The public mood is switching, he says. The self-flagellation needs to end. He wants some success stories. 'So, really, any going?' He scans the faces of his deputies. No suggestions are forthcoming. 'What else have we all got?'

The second story editor pipes up. 'The political crisis in Karnataka?'

There's a note of scepticism in his voice. The Karnataka affair is an ongoing saga centring on a vote of no confidence in the state government.

Rahul is uninspired. 'Anything else?'

No answer.

He exhales slowly and picks up his pen. 'So, what will we call it then?'

A few days later, I head over to the Shyama Prasad Mukherjee Swimming Complex. I am in search of a good-news story of my own.

The whiff of wet paint still hangs over the newly built stadium. It smells as it should do, fresh and unused. India has never had a heated Olympic swimming pool with a roof before. On seats of polished plastic sit fans from across the Commonwealth, excitement written on every face.

In the pool, it is Australia's day. Their national anthem stays on perpetual loop as one broad-shouldered champion after another takes gold. The Indians in the crowd cheer as loudly as the rest, their buoyant mood strengthened by a large dose of low expectations. Swimming is not a sport in which India has much heritage or success. So when Prasanta Karmakar walks out for the start of the Para fifty metres freestyle, the home supporters greet him with enthusiastic applause.

Poised and professional, the lone Indian swimmer looks the part. A fraction shorter than his fellow competitors, his upper body is compact and his stomach muscles corrugated. A plastic racing cap covers his head. His trunks, which run down to his knee, are the latest in low-drag design. He raises his left hand to salute the crowd. His right arm, which ends abruptly above the wrist, stays at his side. He starts in Lane Six.

The athletes step onto the elevated starting blocks. Prasanta checks his cap and fixes his goggles in place. Knees bent, arms down, head up, he waits for the starting gun.

Collectively, we hold our breath.

Prasanta has travelled far to be there. Born into a poor family in Kolkata, he lost his hand in a bus accident aged seven. He couldn't swim until his mid-teens, learning in a lake close to his home. His parents encouraged him to join a club and he began clocking up first-place finishes shortly afterwards. Now aged twenty-nine, his first national record came almost a decade ago. He now holds four.

Away from the pool, life is distinctly less glamorous. He lives in a shared room in a student garret. He has no job, no money, no girlfriend and no commercial sponsor. He swims for four hours a day, with weight training on top.

We'd met several months previously. Nandan, a friend of a friend, had put us in touch. A lawyer by profession, Nandan runs a small charitable foundation that supports up-and-coming sportspeople. He has a dozen or so boxers, swimmers, hockey players and badminton hopefuls on his list. All are young, poor and glowing with talent. The Go Sports Foundation provides each with a monthly stipend. Not enough to live on, but sufficient to cover some basic essentials.

Mindful that the Commonwealth Games were coming up, I was interested in meeting a potential competitor, someone who had fought against all the odds to make it in their chosen field, someone who summed up the spirit of aspirational India. Nandan had given me Prasanta's number. 'If it's tough odds you want,' he'd said, 'he's your man.'

Prasanta was working out in the antiquated weights room at the K. C. Reddy Swim Centre when I arrived. Located in down-town Bengaluru, the outdoor pool is on temporary lease from the government. Three rusting lifeguards' chairs lined the pool's edge. All stood vacant. A dilapidated row of concrete terraced seating ran along one side. Along it sat a scattered gathering of vigilant mothers. Their faces wore tense and slightly pained ex-pressions, as though they were stuck standing out in the rain. In the shallow end of the pool, decked out in armbands and goggles hawked from the back of a van at the club's entrance, swam their little ones. A sign at the door advertised the three-week beginners' course. It was Week Two.

We sat on a bench in the municipal park beside the pool. The seat's central slats were missing. I'd asked Prasanta why he'd moved away from Kolkata. 'My trainer,' he'd replied. 'He's based here.' Nihar Ameen, India's national swimming coach, runs a training camp for the country's elite swimmers at the rudimentary K. C. Reddy Swim Centre. Prasanta is the only Para swimmer in his squad. His fellow training companions include Sandeep Sejwal and Virdhawal Ghade. Aged twenty-one and nineteen respectively, they are the fastest swimmers in Indian history. Both are more or less on the breadline too.

Prasanta is not one to mince his words. Our short conversation clarified just what India's swimmers are up against. At the time, India had only two heated pools of competitive size (the Commonwealth pool in Delhi was still not finished): one in distant Assam and one in Pune. Neither is well maintained. Australia, in contrast, has more than fifty. As for the Bengaluru centre, it's closed for half the year. The water is too cold to swim in.

Last winter, Sandeep and Virdhawal trained in Spain during the off-season. They hope to go again this year, but they need a government grant. Though promised, the money has yet to materialise. There is no similar training budget for Para swimmers. Nor does the reservation system, which earmarks jobs in publicly owned companies for top sportspeople, have a category for disabled athletes. Prasanta's applications to the national swimming federation and his provincial sports ministry have also come to naught. To keep him going, a business contact in Kolkata has loaned him some money. He has to pay him back with any future prize money that he may win.

Although swimming is particularly badly funded in India, competitors from almost every sporting discipline face financial hardship. The winner of the Mumbai marathon, for example, had to spend the night before the race on a hostel floor because he lacked the cash for a hotel. It is no coincidence that the country's top-performing athletes come from wealthy backgrounds. Olympic marksman Abhinav Bindra is a prime example. He trains at a private shooting range built by his millionaire father on the family's thirteen-acre estate. Tennis greats Vijay and Anand Amritraj, badminton champion Prakash Padukone, chess Grandmaster Viswanathan Anand and billiards ace Pankaj Advani all credit parental support for their success. In Prasanta's case, ill health has prevented his father from working for the last decade.

After the meeting, I'd called Nandan to thank him. He'd asked how I'd got on. I told him what I felt: how inspiring Prasanta's dedication was and yet how mystifying it was that anyone should choose such a course. Nandan had agreed. Excepting cricket, sport seems like a thankless option in India. That's why so many talented youngsters drop out. Those that stick it out generally fall into one of two camps, Nandan had explained: those rich enough to afford it, and those so poor they have little else to lose.

It was then that he told me about Sourav Shah. The fifteen-year-old swimmer is the latest addition to his Foundation's books. Like Prasanta, he too is from Kolkata and he too learned to swim in a lake. If I was ever in Kolkata, I should look him up, Nandan had advised.

Several months later, I find myself passing through the Bengali capital. Recalling Nandan's suggestion, I contacted him again and asked for Sourav's details. I called his father and set up a meeting for the next day.

The Shah family lives in a single, cramped room off B. T. Road in the north of the city. Nine feet square and shaded by a crumbling block of government flats, the room has space for a large bed, a steel wardrobe and little else. Sourav sleeps on the floor. He is an only child. That is fortunate. The floor area could not accommodate a sibling. His orange Vodafone swim shorts are hanging from a string attached to the room's only window. A framed photo of him rests on the sill. He's a good-looking kid, with a wide, even-toothed smile.

Pinaki, Sourav's father, was there to greet me. Thin as a bird, he walks with a severe limp. 'Polio,' he'd said good-humouredly, tapping his withered leg. With similar cheer, he'd apologised for the lack of space. Times are tough. He runs a tea stall on the footpath near Shyam Bazar. After rent and food, there's little left. He's sorry too: Sourav had to go out. He went to the hospital. No, no, he was fine. The swimming authorities required him to take some medical tests, that's all.

Pinaki was evidently proud of his son and talked animatedly about his prodigious talent as a swimmer. He told me about his punishing training schedule: up at four-thirty a.m. every day, an hour and a half by bus to the pool, two hours swimming, back home for breakfast, then the same in the afternoon. What of school and friends? He had little time for either, Pinaki admitted. It was regrettable. But what could he do? Sourav wanted to represent his country. What troubled his father more was his diet. 'He needs extra food.' Even with Pinaki and his wife going without, the tea stall didn't cover three square meals a day. They'd applied to the provincial government for a sports scholarship. A decision, they'd been told repeatedly, was 'pending'.

I looked around the spartan room. Thoughts of the hardship that lay ahead came to mind. Was it really worth it? Pinaki merely repeated his son's ambition. He believed the boy had the talent. He'd pointed to the tiny television in the corner. 'The London Olympics in 2012. I shall watch him on this.' It would require hard work, he'd acknowledged. And sacrifice. 'You may have ambition in mind, but without these you cannot get.' They were the price of success.

Pinaki gazed at the floor. A look of sadness crept over him. The tea vendor was under no illusions. For his son to become a champion swimmer, he knew he'd need more financial support. 'If this is not coming, it will be very difficult for him. I think he cannot continue.' He'd never tell Sourav that, of course. He spoke with a deep, almost guilty remorse, as though by expressing the truth he'd somehow betrayed his son's dreams.

I got up to go. Pinaki rose too. He seemed anxious, keen that I shouldn't leave on such a note. He wanted me to know that Sourav was an 'honest boy . . . a good boy, determined'. He opened the heavy wardrobe door and rummaged through a drawer at the bottom. He re-emerged holding a bulging plastic bag. 'Look at these.' He laid out the contents on the bed: newspaper reports, race certificates, winners' medals.

I leafed through the pile of memorabilia. For a moment, neither of us spoke.

Then Pinaki broke the silence. The evidence of his son's potential, splayed across the patchy bedspread, had given him a new resolve. 'Sourav's first chance is to be a good swimmer. We don't have any means, so if he can succeed then he might be able to build himself a future. His opportunity to enter business or government service is very little. Sport is such a thing that it can bring a man to the top. Only this.' He hesitated, before repeating himself again. 'Only this.'

Instinctively, Pinaki knew the truth of Nandan's observation. His boy had nothing to lose. The son of a lame tea wallah, Sourav must have known it too. Why else did he rise before dawn? What other reason did he have to sacrifice his schooling, his friends, his youth? Of course, swimming is not cricket. Wealth and fame do not necessarily wait at the top. Prasanta is proof of that. Still, the outlook at the top beats the view from the pavement. Of that, both father and son were in no doubt.

Back in the pool, the starting whistle goes. Prasanta is a fraction late out of the blocks. Kicking his legs in tandem, his head is the last to emerge from under the water. Two across from him, in the middle lane, is world-record holder Matthew Cowdrey. He's one of three Australians in the race. His bobbing yellow hat begins to pull out in front of the chasing pack. By halfway, he has a lead of more than a yard. Powering along beside him, his legs kicking fiercely, speeds Simon Miller. The two of them inch further out ahead. With ten metres remaining, first and second place look set.

The real race is on for third. There are three in the running. Each is enveloped in a churning swell of their own creation, three white foam shapes streaking through the water. In lanes two and three charge the other Australians, blasting into the home straight neck and neck. On their shoulder, clawing at the water with every ounce of energy, comes Prasanta.

The crowd is on its feet. I'm up there with them. Screams of support resound through the stadium. 'Come on, come on.' 'Go, go, go . . . gooooo.'

Austin edges ahead, then Cochrane, then Austin. Prasanta hangs in there, striving, battling, contending. The trio enters the last five metres. The final wall nears. The Kolkata-born swimmer kicks madly. A final spurt. An arm outstretched. A desperate lunge for the finish.

And then it's all over. Thud, thud, thud: three healthy hands collide in unison against the pool's end wall. Who pipped who? It's impossible to judge. Eight panting swimmers emerge from under goggles and hats. Arms rest on the plastic lane dividers. Cowdrey and Miller have bagged gold and silver. But who took bronze? Every head in the pool swivels round to the digitalised scoreboard at the starting end. The crowd's gaze follows. Five or six tense seconds pass. Then individual names and stop-clock times begin appearing, flashing up one after the other on the computerised screen like flight numbers on a rebooted departure chart.

MEN 50M FREESTYLE S9 EVENT 120

TISSOT RESULTS

1 COWDREY MATTHEW AUS 25.33

The yellow-capped Australian punches the air ecstatically. Whoops from the crowd. The winning time is followed by the two letters, 'WR'. World Record. Cowdrey has just reinforced his status as the fastest one-handed swimmer on the planet.

2 MILLER SIMON ENG 26.70

The camera hones in on the runner-up. He's turning to congratulate the record holder. The St George flag on the back of his white cap temporarily fills the screen.

3 KARMAKAR PRASANTA IND 27.48

The home spectators explode in joyful celebration. Prasanta's clenched fist shoots defiantly out of the water. One twentieth of a second separates him from Austin, two tenths from Cochrane. The son of an unemployed Bengali taxi driver has secured third place. The bronze medal is his. India has its first ever top-three finish in a Commonwealth Games swimming event. Prasanta has entered the history books.

A few minutes later, at the other end of the pool, a troop of Punjabi soldiers marches in goosestep towards the flag posts. They look glorious in their elaborate headgear and waxed,

handlebar moustaches. The three medallists step towards the podium. The bleached white gloves of the soldiers pull at the guy
ropes. Above them, unfurling in the windless stadium, the Indian
ensign appears to view. It's crisp and new and greeted with a surge
of ecstatic cheering. Back at the podium, a former air marshall of
the Indian Air Force slips a ribbon over Prasanta's bending neck.
He waves his good hand and then joins the applause for his fellow medal winners. Music strikes up. We rise from our seats. The
anthem may be Australian, but the joy in the terraces is quintes-
sentially Indian.

India has a new hero. Sourav has a role model. And Rahul, at
last, has a good-news story from the Games.

Seven years previously, Indian delegates had travelled to a swanky
resort in Jamaica to persuade the Commonwealth Games presiding committee to permit them to host the Games. They showed
slides of gleaming malls, futuristic airports and five-star hotels. India was on the up, they argued. Its rise was unstoppable. Its time
was now.

In the end, the Games proved the lie. The much-maligned prep-
arations revealed a side of India that the country's administrators
would rather keep hidden. The nation's upbeat public branding hides a less flattering reality. Short cuts still vie with central
planning, chaos still undermines systems and graft still challenges
honesty.

The truth of this was not lost on everyday Indians. It wasn't just
Rahul and his editorial peers that damned the authorities as 'in-
efficient', 'callous' and 'corrupt'. Their barbed criticisms echoed
the feeling on the street. India's leaders had let the country down,
disgraced them on the world stage. 'Incompetence Raj', joked the
Wall Street Journal. 'Shoddy', mocked *Time* magazine.

The day after Prasanta's victory, I took the new metro line out
to the site of the Games Village to meet with him again. We talked
about the race and his plans for the future. His sights are set on
the next Olympics. After that, he's not sure. If he can, he'd like to

set up a dedicated training academy for disabled swimmers. Before I left, I took a picture of him holding his bronze medal.

Several months later, I return to the photograph. In the background, a concrete pedestrian bridge rises in the air. Its concourse is crowded with people coming and going from the newly inaugurated metro station. Below the bridge runs a dual carriageway into Noida, Delhi's business-oriented satellite town. Construction tape and bollards line the road's edge. Cars are passing. There's also a rickshaw and a bicycle. In the middle distance, a hotch-potch of roofs jars against smog-smeared sky. The overcast tones merge with the yellowing grass, short and brittle, which spreads across the foreground. In the centre of the frame sits Prasanta, his expression proud and hopeful, his medal sparkling.

The image brings clarity to the opposing visions of India. Order alongside disorder. Hope against helplessness. New beside Old. And positioned in the middle, people such as Prasanta, aspiring for something better.

Arduous training and self-sacrifice are the price Prasanta paid for his piece of the New India dream. Millions of others are heading to the mall for a taste of the same.

6

Chasing Lakshmi

[consumerism]

'Earth provides enough to satisfy every man's need, but not every
man's greed.'
  Mahatma Gandhi

Kochi

Rahul Ravindran chomps methodically on his popcorn. He is a
young man of precise habits. One sweet. One masala. One sweet.
One masala. He slurps on his Sprite.

Meanwhile, in the celestial realm, a bearded Zeus (alias Liam
Neeson) is debating with his evil brother Hades (Ralph Fiennes)
about the fate of Ancient Greece. The arrogant earthlings have
turned their backs on the Gods. They must pay. Argos is given
ten days to serve up the sensuous Princess Andromeda in propiti-
ation. That, or the monstrous Kraken would be unleashed on the
city state. Annihilation pends.

Rahul takes another slurp.

The citizens of Argos are in luck. A demi-god is lurking in their
midst, the muscle-bound Perseus (Sam Worthington). So off our
hero heads on an explosive journey of slaughter and special effects
to save his people.

Just as Worthington finishes off a pair of gigantic pincer-snap-
ping scorpions, the lights come up. The packed cinema hall collectively stretches and gets to its feet. The sudden curtailment
of the film marks an old-fashioned interval. The harmonised
shopping-aisle chords of a popular Hindi film track play out over
the digital Dolby Stereo sound system. A sizeable proportion of
the audience shuffles to the door in search of refreshments.

The film's subject-matter has got Rahul thinking. He turns to me in his seat. 'I am an atheist, you know.' Even in contemporary India, this remains a startling confession. The Hindu computer programmer stopped believing when he was seventeen. His family are devotees of Sai Baba. The way he sees it, though, life doesn't offer much in the way of a higher purpose. Each man must become master of his own fate. As for immortality, genomics represents our best chance in his opinion. Have I been following developments in bioprogramming and artificial intelligence? I should. It's very exciting. And had I seen *Matrix*? Personally, he found it very inspiring. In fact, it's fair to say that it is his favourite film of all time.

A trailer for the latest Shah Rukh Khan movie flashes up. The Bollywood superstar is cast as a US émigré who defies all odds to reunite himself with the Latino love of his life. Rahul is rapt. The clip finishes to the sound of latecomers retaking their seats, laden under Cinemax's veg snack 'n' drink combo. Soon it's back to Greece and our hero Perseus slaying more mythical creatures, each uglier and fiercer than the last.

The cinema idea had been mine. Oberon Mall in downtown Kochi had just inaugurated a brand new multiplex. Demand is high. The newfangled four-screen cinema is the first of its kind in the entire state of Kerala. We plump for the Sunday matinée. Rahul had booked the tickets online. With our printouts in hand, we had neatly circumvented the lengthy queues at the box office. The air-conditioned hall smells of new car interiors. It is a far cry from the cinema experiences I recall from my first visit to India as a teenager. The high-density foam seats are brightly buffed and devoid of rat nibbles. Sticky stains of indeterminate origin have yet to mark the carpeted floor. In short, we are enjoying the classic mall experience: clean, sanitised and free of riffraff.

Argos is, predictably, saved and we are free to go. Red neon strips zigzag along the floor. We trail the largely male audience to the 'exit' sign. Outside, the queue for the next showing of *Clash of the Titans* has already begun. The artificial light in the atrium is momentarily blinding. We stand on the edge of the crowd a while, allowing our eyes to adjust and the images of high-pixel violence to dissipate.

'Wanna grab something to eat?' Rahul suggests, his accent muddied between the India of his birth and the America of his dreams.

'Sure,' I agree, 'but can we first take a quick look around the shops?'

I am keen to check out the mall and was hoping Rahul might act as my guide. We had met a month or so before at an entrepreneurs' networking event. He'd come to tout for business. From the office in his bedroom, the young programmer had developed a complex software package for the real-estate market. His invention would help property developers save a fortune off their advertising costs, he'd told me. He just needed a backer.

Rahul's black shiny polyester shirt and matching trousers had made him stand out among the crisply dressed businessmen. He had done up his top button in place of a tie. On his feet he wore a pair of scuffed Nike trainers. His top lip was etched with an uneven, sprouting moustache. Acne blemishes clustered on the upper ridge of his cheekbones. To the unkind eye, Rahul looked like a man who worked from his bedroom.

We had chatted briefly after the presentation. Rahul turned out to be amiable, entertaining and, most interestingly for me, at odds with himself. The self-trained programmer had just dropped out of college. At twenty-one, he saw his future clearly. It didn't involve staying in Kochi. He'd go to the US, obtain a Green Card, earn his millions, marry an American (preferably blonde and buxom) and live happily ever after. He was pursuing his dream with a vehement single-mindedness. He speaks almost exclusively in English, dropping into the vernacular only as a concession to his mother. The usual pursuits of a young Indian his age hold no interest for him: he claims to loathe cricket, he 'never ever' watches Bollywood films and he abhors Hindi music. As for food, his preferred diet is Chinese or American. All he seems to retain of his Indian roots is his vegetarianism.

When it comes to his social life, it is predominantly an online

affair. His friends fall into one of two categories: fellow programmers from technical chatrooms, or fellow gamers from multi-play-
er sites like World of Warcraft and Guild Wars. Most live abroad.
He talks with them via Skype. His contact list currently stands
at seven hundred and fifty-seven. His best friend is a techie from
Alabama who supplements his computer habit by dealing low-
level narcotics. The two used to hack together. They have never
actually met.

We leave the fourth and uppermost floor where the cinema is
located and head down to the level below. The rectangular box-
shaped building is structured around a central oval atrium. Railed
balconies encircle each successive floor above, creating the effect
of an open chimney flue running up to the ceiling. Escalators zigzag like an untidy chain of window-cleaners' ladders from top to
bottom. Security staff stand around idly. A troop of female jani-
tors in uniform red saris with white polka-dots mops the floors
with robotic disinterest. Only the man welcoming shoppers at the
entrance seems to be approaching his job with any gusto. He is
dressed as Mickey Mouse.

The layout of the mall is prominently displayed on a colour-
coded notice board by the escalator. The plan indicates a total
of sixty-five branded stores over a three-hundred-and-fifty-thou-
sand square-foot floor space. International brands such as Nike,
Lee, Sony and Puma drum for custom alongside less well-known
domestic competitors. My attention is drawn to the latter. Most
are new to me: Infocomm computer accessories, Zapp! kidswear,
Smart Opticals 'eye fashion'.

What is immediately striking is the desire of the local retailers
to sound – well – not very local. The more international (and non-
Indian) their branding, the logic appears to run, the more alluring
their products. Depressingly, repeated consumer surveys endorse
such thinking. If it's foreign, it's 'cool'. If it's 'made in India', it
ain't. So the Oberon houses clothing stores with names like Bits
Indiana and Planet Fashion, a childrenswear shop called 'Gini and
Jony' and a make-up store evocatively entitled 'Cosmetic Island'.

From Rahul's sloping shoulders and resigned gait, it is evident he is not an over-eager shopper. Neither am I. To his relief, I suggest we keep the tour short.

We embark on Level Three. 'The Man who Sold the World' by David Bowie is playing faintly over the mall speaker system. It seems a fitting choice as we pass Frizbee, a toy store stocked with enlarged teddy bears and a child-sized Lamborghini. The identikit outfits in Mantra, Lamoda and Anarkali keep us moving on. Rahul tarries a while outside HP World. Though a Dell man himself ('I know the district manager'), he likes to keep abreast of what the competition is up to. 'A laptop is NOT enough,' a poster advert in the window informs us. This surprises me. Laptops remain a luxury item in India. But take HP at its word and if it hasn't got a built-in scanner and printer, it's simply 'not worth the Rs 39,990 you paid for it'.

For the integrity of our research, I feel the need to cross the threshold of at least one store. We opt for a high-street clothing outlet on Level One. It belongs to Reliance, the giant Indian conglomerate. The company's consumer arm covers everything from supermarkets and mobile phones to bathroom fittings and footwear. Most are on show in Oberon.

I head to the area for men's fashion. Neutral colours, humdrum lines and an inordinate amount of beige chino trousers dominate. Mid-range labels like John Player, Terrain, Pan American and Dockers are each given a corner to tout their lookalike wares. I move through into the teenagers' section. The same theme is repeated there, only in two sizes smaller. Racks of T-shirts are organised under brand logos like TeamSpirit, Naomi, Lilliput and Forever 17. A pubescent mannequin is wearing a white round-neck from the newest of Reliance Trend's collections. The words 'I have a boyfriend on sale. He's cheap,' are emblazoned across her pert, plastic chest.

As we navigate our way back up the escalator, a teenage boy of around fifteen or sixteen years old passes us. He's going down as we're going up. Rahul's head turns a fraction. I wonder why. The boy looks to me like your archetypal mall rat: branded T-shirt, baseball shoes, three-quarter-length shorts and hair painstakingly gelled to look scruffy. I turn to watch as he descends, puzzling over what caught Rahul's eye.

'You can tell he's lived abroad,' Rahul says.

'How?'

'The way he dresses, his hair, the way he walks. He's definitely lived overseas. Gulf mostly likely. Loads of people in Kerala go to the Middle East to work. Isn't it obvious?'

It both is and isn't. Most of the teenagers in the mall are dressed in Western clothes. Plenty also gel their hair. But closer inspection reveals some clues. Every other teenager in the mall is wearing trousers, not shorts. Their haircuts are short at the neck and carefully combed, not loose and scraggy.

Rahul spells out other differences too: the way he is talking loudly, the swagger in his step, the belt round his hips not his waist, and the fact he's with two girls.

Aha, so that was what had grabbed Rahul's attention. The opposite sex was a considerable preoccupation of my programmer friend. Girls – at least, available girls – are thin on the ground in Kochi.

'Look around. How many girls do you see? Hardly any, right? And those you can see. Who are they with? Their parents, right?' says Rahul, motioning to the packed walkways of the mall.

It is true. A typical mall on a Sunday afternoon in Europe or the US would be heaving with young people, boys and girls – and few, if any, with their parents. In Oberon, the foreign boy and his cohort is the only example to be seen.

'You'll hardly ever find girls just hanging out in a mall,' Rahul complains. 'Their parents won't let them. If they do, they have to go with friends and have to go home at a set time. To bring a girl to a mall is still a big thing in Kerala. And anyhow, ninety-five per cent of these guys' – he waves his hand towards the scores of young men lounging over the railings at every level of the mall – 'wouldn't have a girl to bring anyway. If you see a couple together, they'll either be married or from North India. And it's just not the done thing to go up to a girl in a mall in Kerala. When her family is there, it's a big no-no. And if she's with friends, well, that's intimidating. And, anyway, it'd just be weird. Of course, in the US, it's different. There you can just walk up to a girl and ask for her phone number.'

Rahul's obsession with America colours his perspective. Nothing in India could ever be quite as good as the promised land across the Atlantic. I fear disappointment might be lurking for him should he ever make it to Nirvana.

We reach the 'Full Circle' food court. Rahul heads straight for the Krispy Chicken counter. In case the name was in anyway ambiguous, a placard by the till spells out 'No pork. No beef'. Faithful Muslims and Hindus can gorge without guilt.

Rahul orders a veggie burger with french fries. The waiter hands him a plastic contraption designed to look like a small detonator. 'It'll light up when your order is ready,' he advises him. I pass down the line of fast-food counters. All palates are catered for. Dosa Express and Rasoi Indian Cuisine cover local fare and attract an older clientele. Noodle King and Arabian Treat meet the growing appetite among younger diners for Chinese and Middle Eastern food. Papa Milano wraps up the gastronomic world tour. As a house special, the Italian pizzeria offers a 'MacCheese': a bowl of macaroni with real American cheddar-cheese sauce. A long queue of hungry adolescents dissuades me from waiting to try it. I double back up the line and order a tikka sandwich from Krispy Chicken. I am duly issued my own detonator.

The food court's four hundred and twenty places are almost entirely occupied. We find an empty half table next to two university-aged men. Standing beside the adjacent table is a middle-aged man dressed in a cotton shirt and mundu, the Keralan equivalent of the lungi or dhoti. The long sarong is made from a single piece of plain woven cloth. It ties around the waist and, when not folded up to the knee, is left to fall down to the floor.

The gentleman is casually holding up one of the garment's corners with his left hand. The action produces a flap, as if a sudden gust of wind had darted under the hem and caused the cloth to billow. A double-turn of the mundu ensures his lower half remains covered and his modesty intact. In the man's right hand, he carries a mobile phone. He is speaking Malayalam in bossy, insistent tones. He is not the only man dressed in a mundu. I saw several others on my tour of Oberon, including a couple of younger men. But their numbers are few enough to be noticeable.

I ask Rahul, who is dressed in an airtex Adidas running shirt and jeans, why it is that a small minority comes to the mall in traditional dress.

He looks over and sizes up the man. 'You know, it's strange. If you walk outside, you'll see plenty of people wearing mundus. They'll be taxi drivers or labourers – ill-educated people. But a mundu in the mall? Then you can be pretty sure they're wealthy. It's an issue of pride, really. Most are old businessmen who've already made their fortunes or who work in traditional Keralan industries like coir or spices. They always wear the traditional clothes. It makes people look at them differently. See, just like you are now.'

I immediately drop my gaze. Rahul smiles. 'They like that. They are used to getting respect. But in a mall everybody dresses the same so nobody would know them. Which is why they wear the mundu. It makes people recognise their social standing.'

I rather liked the idea of people flouting the advertisers' pressure to take up Western dress. Malls spell homogenisation. Everyone shopping under the same roof. Everyone bombarded with the same merchandising. Everyone buying the same brands. For all their Western trappings, it pleased me that Kochi's mall-goers had hung on to their culture. Try as he might, the zealous Mickey Mouse had not divested them entirely of their identities at Oberon's revolving entrance door.

The food hall gives me particular reason for hope. Despite the array of burgers and pizza slices that fill people's trays, a large contingent is still eating biryani and appam. In the main, diners still eschew cutlery for fingers. A special row of extra sinks caters for their hand-washing needs. And, by and large, people eat in families. Parents, grandparents and children sit together – not adults on one side and youfs on the other, and certainly not alone.

Full Circle is heartening for another reason: it is crammed to capacity. The retail area of Oberon is busy with people too. But most are not strictly 'consumers'. They come to window-shop, mill around and generally pass the time. Malls are still new enough in India to be enjoyed for their novelty value. They act as recreation. Families used to travel across the bay to Fort Kochi to visit the Chinese fishing nets or take a boat ride in search of dolphins. Now they go to Oberon, the air-conditioned consumers' play park. The shops themselves, however, remain more or less empty. Which is where the food court comes in. In a second-tier town such as Kochi, 501 jeans or Air Jordan shoes remain beyond most middle-class budgets. A Brownie *à la mode* at Baskin Robbins or a family-sized box of nuggets, on the other hand, fit perfectly.

Our detonators explode simultaneously.

Rahul enters the fray and collects our meals. When he returns, I try and steer the conversation towards the impact that malls are having on Indian society. Are they ushering in a new materialistic mentality? Might their Western mores, as some argue, represent a threat to Indian culture?

He toys with a sachet of ketchup. Eventually he prises it open with his long fingernails and squeezes a dollop on the side of his plate. He dips in a chip and sucks off the sweetened tomato sauce.

'How can I put this in a nutshell?' he muses, half to himself and half to me. His Nokia N95 phone sits on the table beside his fries. He picks it up and clicks on the camera function. 'Check out this photo,' he says, pointing the screen towards me. The image is slightly blurred but the two decorated elephants and accompanying village backdrop are clearly decipherable.

'I took it last weekend. It's from Irinjalakuda, the place I grew up. We went on a family visit: me, my little sister and my parents. My cousins and everyone still live there. The local temple was having a festival. That's why the elephants are there. Last year, one of the elephants killed somebody, can you believe it?' he says, showing me the photo once more before resetting his phone.

'The village hasn't changed at all. I swear. In the five years since I was last there, I can see no difference at all. There's one mall in the whole region – thirty kilometres away, in Thrissur. They've hardly ever been. Malls might influence a certain class in the cities. Richer, better-educated people, basically. But these people, my relatives . . .'

His teeth crunch down on the chip between his fingers. '. . . malls aren't going to change their lives any time soon.'

As I travel around the country in the succeeding months, I visit a wide variety of other malls. They differ in size and shape. The balance between international products and domestic lines varies between big cities and small. Some malls have cinemas, others don't. As with Oberon, few classify as strictly 'out-of-town'. India's sprawling urban centres make the very notion increasingly implausible. In general, the essential dynamics are the same: a rich elite buying, an aspirational middle-class browsing and the low-income Other serving their meals or guarding their cars in the parking lot.

As for Rahul's views about the progress of Western consumption habits, I find a more mixed bag. Some agree that malls cater to a privileged few and that their broader impact is minimal. Others see them as a kind of Trojan horse within which Western retail culture will sneak into the country without anyone really noticing, until it's too late.

Gautam Singhania takes a more pragmatic view. I go to speak to him at his multi-storey apartment block on Altamount Road, an exclusive enclave of south Mumbai. He is renting the luxury premises while his own personal skyscraper is being built down the road in Breach Candy. To get to his second-floor private office requires entering through the lobby car park. Under tarpaulin sit a handful of Mr Singhania's favourite toys: a red Ferrari, a yellow Lamborghini and a blue Lotus Elise.

The son of a flamboyant retail millionaire with a penchant for hot-air-ballooning, Mr Singhania has inherited his father's business empire and his high-octane daredevilry. He served his apprenticeship in the company's latex condom division. Prophylactics are now in the past. Since his father's retirement, he's trimmed down and spruced up the family firm, turning the Raymond Group into a profitable consortium of popular high-street brands. The company's premium line sells the most expensive worsted cloth in the world.

Mr Singhania's own playboy life is a parody ('personification', his PR team would prefer) of the company image. He is the kind of businessman who appears in the Indian edition of *Hello!* magazine at the helm of his huge teak yacht, who sets speed records and who talks liberally about his globetrotting and perfect marriage ('the woman that tamed him'). Raymond's strapline is the 'Complete Man', an image of Indian masculinity that the company's chief executive projects both of himself and onto others. Few have a better handle on Indian consumer patterns.

Sitting at the head of his large mahogany boardroom table, his feet sunk into the shag-pile carpet and his eyes fixed on a brimming trophy cabinet, the retail mogul spells out how he sees India's consuming public.

'If you took a typical middle-aged guy ten years ago in this country, he'd say, "When I get to fifty-five or sixty-five, I'll have saved enough money to buy myself a house and then I'll retire in it." There was no credit available back then. Today a twenty-five-year-old kid, as soon as he gets a job, he wants a mobile phone, he wants a car, he wants a house. And to buy them, he gets a loan. The mindset today is completely different. People are spending. They just want to be told how to spend. So now it's all about marketing, helping consumers make a choice.'

I ask which kind of twenty-five-year-olds he has in mind. Is it the minority elite who I saw shopping on their credit cards in Oberon? Or does the net of eager consumers stretch further?

He leans forward. Today, people can be in the smallest of villages and see his advertisement on a television that they didn't own a decade ago, he says, repeating the revelation that Captain Gopi obtained on his helicopter ride. 'They can sit in their house with a modem and a mobile phone, and be virtually connected to the world.' The power of that is 'phenomenal'. Indian consumers know the latest trends. And not just those at the high end of the spending spectrum. 'Aspirations in Class Three, Class Four, Class Five, down the list, are much higher.' Prahalad's Pyramid, in other words.

The idea of potentially more than a billion people buying his worsted fabrics understandably excites Mr Singhania. If he is only partially right, the garage of his new mansion had better be equipped for a good deal more sports cars.

'But what of Gandhian notions of austerity? Aren't they central to Indian culture?' I venture with a degree of hesitation.

One of the images of India that first drew me to the country was its reputation for other-worldliness. India – at least the India projected for decades to the outside world and the India I grew up reading about – was supposed to cherish simplicity as a spiritual virtue. Greed, consumption, the accumulation of possessions – these belonged to the ego, to venal desires that tie us to this world and blind us to the next.

'You can't change it,' he fires back, clearly uninterested in worn-out notions from another century that may or may not once have held true. 'Aspiration levels are now too high.'

I blanch at his directness. The Complete Man is sensitive to his public image. He doesn't want to be construed as a vulgar capitalist.

He offers another, more rational argument. 'Materialist things are rewards for performance. If you want the country to perform, you have to reward people for it.'

Gandhi would have argued the exact opposite. The gift for performance – for the hard work of austerity, of self-denial, of godliness – is inner peace and communal harmony, not mountains of branded goods to call your own.

The retail impresario and one-time condom manufacturer hunches his shoulders. 'After all,' he says, in a tone that suggests conciliation but invites no debate, 'everyone has their desires.'

It's one of the few points on which Singhania and Gandhi, the Retailer and the Renouncer, are in accord.

A month or so later, back in Kochi, Rahul's desires continue to be US-bound. His dream has inched considerably closer since we met to watch the adventures of Perseus & Co. He's accepted a job. I am looking at Global Infonet's new Chief Software Architect, responsible for 'troubleshooting and tricky coding'. Rahul makes the job at the software company sound glamorous, the programmers' equivalent of slaying Kraken. Global Infonet is based in Jacksonville, 'in Florida, the US!' His new software bosses are proposing to relocate him, conditional on a probation period and visa requirements.

'It's between New York and Florida at the moment. They've not decided. Man, I could earn upwards of sixty-five dollars per hour there. That's a one-hundred-thousand-dollar salary.'

Rahul is, to put it mildly, excited.

We are sitting in Barista coffee store in Bay Pride Mall, a down-at-heel precursor to Oberon. The new entrant to India's coffee-shop market offers an illustrated timeline on the wall. It starts with the year 1600, when coffee enters Europe, and finishes a few years ago with the first Barista store in Delhi. The chain's burgeoning network now stands at two hundred and thirty outlets. In Bay Pride, its customers stretch to six: a young married couple sitting mutely over two voluminous Iced Caffe Mochas, two young men dressed in rugby shirts and smelling of Davidoff aftershave, and a pair of Chinese businessmen humming along to an Elton John soundtrack. Are they a picture of how India is evolving, the next entry on the historical chart? I would like to ask Rahul what he thinks, but his mind is on other things.

'. . . so for the full H1V work visa, I need a degree. And for a L1V visa, I need at least one year's work experience. So the current plan is to go initially on a V1 visa, and then change to . . .'

Mentally, if not physically, Rahul has already moved on. The tech fairs and electronic gadgets ('I'm going to buy a Windows Phone 7 as soon as I get there') in the US are calling him. Has India moved on too?

I look out of the window. It's early evening. The wide promenade overlooking the bay is bustling with families enjoying a weekend stroll. A crowded ferry chugs out of the harbour terminal. From the industrial shipyard across the water, the foghorn of a tanker bellows. Sugar-hungry children jump around the re-frigerated cart of a street hawker, pestering their parents for a twenty-rupee ice cream. With their backs to the railings, a line of men sit on their haunches eating masala-coated peanuts out of old newspaper cones.

The scene inside the overpriced coffee store speaks of a different world from outside. One has moved, the other is moving. Whether the two will ever meet and, if so, how long such a coalition would take, remains unknown. For Rahul, the transition is too slow. Young and ambitious, he hasn't the patience to wait. He wants his New India now, and if he has to leave India to get it, he will.

That the two worlds should be inching together, however, seems inescapable. Just a few kilometres down the road, construction workers are putting the finishing touches to Lulu Mall. Pitched as India's largest shopping centre, its developers are banking on the strolling masses of today becoming the brand-hungry shoppers of tomorrow.

With no crystal ball, it's impossible to say where India's new-found consumer culture will take it. An extreme version of the future is waiting in the capital. I travel to Delhi and buy a ticket for the city's biannual Fashion Week.

Delhi

Ashdeen's knickers are in a twist. The opening show is running late. Nina will be beside herself.

He pulls a tissue from his handbag and dabs his perspiring forehead. A dribble of sweat escapes, edging down his shorn sideburn. It is heading towards the folds of his neck and the collar of his navy satin shirt. He double-dabs. The sweat bubble is caught.

'I mean, it's just all just sooooo amateur, don't you think.'

The pronouncement floats across the chattering table. The words are directed at no one in particular and they die away on the current of fashionista blabber.

'Dyed. Yes, definitely dyed. What was she thinking?' a thin-hipped fashion editor at the far end of the table snipes.

'Well, it's better than those,' her plain-faced colleague replies, gasping in mock horror at a middle-aged brunette a couple of tables away. 'I mean, if you're going to get extensions, yaar, at least make sure they match.'

In their early twenties, both women are equipped with upper-class St Xavier accents and posh salon haircuts. Their summer dresses – both floral, both crimped at the waist and both ever so slightly flounced at the shoulder – shout style. Throw in a discreet gold necklace, a silver butterfly clip in the hair, designer heels. They are cool. They are *Elle*.

Ashdeen hovers on the edge of the group. He is wearing crisp white boating shorts and a newish pair of steel-grey Converse.

The twenty-nine-year-old Parsee embroiderer crosses his legs nervously. He twitches his head from side to side, uncharacteristically tense. The fingers of his right hand begin drumming on his kneecap, like a trumpeter going through his practice scales.

'Rumour is they've closed the gates. I mean, it's a complete dii-saaa-sterrr.' He is speaking into thin air. Flapping his hand, he reaches for a Diet Coke.

He takes a small sip and places the glass back on the table. He fears a full bladder as it'll mean having to use the venue's public toilets.

We are sitting in Olive beside a knee-high wicker gate. Within minutes of Delhi Fashion Week opening, the high-end eatery has been designated as the place to be. Ensconced on its white iron-framed seats are rows of bottoms wrapped in gorgeous silks and printed satins. Bony fingers reach greedily for tomato bruschettas topped with shavings of imported Italian Parmesan. Chilled Californian Chardonnay washes against expensive dental work. Circular, oversized dark glasses bob at one another in visual monotone.

We've ordered drinks, and now refuse to move. Like soldiers in our bolthole, we have staked our claim and will defend our territory tooth and varnished nail.

'Fashion is like war,' opines Julian, a colourful Brit dressed in tartan trousers and a voluminous bow tie. 'There's lots of sitting and waiting around for the action.'

The opening midday show is already half an hour late. Where better for a fashionable delay than a fashion event? Yet Ashdeen's predictions seem to suggest something more serious is afoot. The evidence begins to mount. Ant-like assistants carrying walkie-talkies are pacing frantically up and down the venue hall. A sycophantic huddle forms around a harried Sunil Sethi, the white-bearded doyen of Indian fashion and the event's chief organiser. Three police officers follow in his wake. A mêlée of television cameras attach themselves to the khaki-clad sergeants. An impromptu press conference is held at the far end of the venue. Still we do not budge. Word will come to us. Quickly enough it does.

'Apparently, the place hasn't been cleared by the fire department. All hell's broken loose. The police say everything's off until the proper papers are signed,' an excited press photographer passes on, evidently best pleased by the chaos.

The news is met with equanimity by the group, and a grimace from Ashdeen. Julian breaks the tension. Leaning across the table, the fluffy teddy bear in his top jacket pocket lurching forward, he raises his glass and proposes a toast. 'No one stops a fashion queen getting to their fashion, darlings.' Everyone laughs.

The chatter gradually renews itself. Talk moves from general idle bitching to specific criticism about the delay. Some suggest the fire department is looking for publicity. Others hint at corruption, the popular catch-all for India's woes. 'When the backhanders got given out, someone forgot the fire inspector,' jokes a manicured stylist. The majority opinion places fault with the event organisers.

'This whole place is like a big . . . urghhh, what's the word – a big tent,' exclaims Nonita, the petite, barely-out-of-college editor of *Elle India*.

She waves her hand at the huge marquee, pitched in the inelegant conference complex of the National Small Industries Corporation. India's haute couture brigade is a pampered lot. Fashion shows happen in five-star hotels. Not on industrial estates in the deepest, darkest recesses of South Delhi. Nonita is disgusted. 'It's so . . . well . . . tacky,' she exhales, as though the organisers' taste and the delay were directly linked.

India's designer fashion industry may only be a decade or so old, but it lacks nothing in self-importance. The launch of *Vogue India* and similar foreign fashion titles over the last few years has given it heightened confidence.

Underlying everything is the knowledge that the wealthy in India are getting wealthier. Dollar billionaires now beat the fifty mark, up from a dozen five years ago. Nor are the New Rich slow to spend. Sales of luxury sports cars, private jets and exclusive yachts are all rocketing. The waiting list for the top-of-the-range Rolls-Royce Phantom runs to several years. Luxury real estate is booming too. Industrialist Mukesh Ambani is just putting the finishing touches to his twenty-seven-storey 'Skyscraper mansion'. The first six floors of the multi-million-dollar home serve as a car park. Six hundred staff will be on hand to service the modern-day maharaja, who intends to occupy the towering Mumbai apartment block with his wife and three children.

The fashion industry is taking off too. India's luxury-brand market is reckoned to be worth around half a billion dollars, up from almost nothing a decade ago.

Atsu Sekhose, a rising star in the burgeoning fashion business, sidles up. 'He's very trendy, very bang-on,' whispers Ashdeen under his breath. 'Showcased in Miiii-lan.' The suave, besuited designer from Nagaland greets everyone with an elaborate air-kiss. The table mwaa-mwaas him back. 'Oh, delicious dress,' he exclaims to a flattered Nonita. He sits and orders a Diet Coke. Behind his smooth exterior, his nerves are jangling. His afternoon show, he fears, might be cancelled. Beckoning back the waiter, he changes his order. 'Make it a regular Coke.'

My eye drifts to a group of models on the neighbouring table. Ashdeen follows my gaze. 'Diva,' he says. That much is evident. Sitting with her back to the wall, chatting to her friends, is a long-haired siren. Blessed with luscious lips, dreamy hazel eyes and a divinely sculpted nose, she's the whole package. She's an Indian Andromeda, the advertiser's dream, a billboard knock-out.

'Diva Dhawan,' Ashdeen elaborates. 'New face of Garnier. Sikh, hence the long hair. From New York. Brainy as well. Studies long-distance.'

The gay embroiderer counts off the rest of her table. 'Nethra. What can I say? She's a massive hit right now. Just won this TV show, *Khatron Ke Khiladi* [*Who Dares Wins*]. Then that's Tamara next to her, on the right. Getting on a bit, but, again, massive. And the girl next to her, the one smoking with the short spiky hair. That's Tinu. Seriously cool. DJs and stuff.'

'And the short lady?' I ask, indicating a dowdy woman eating her Difiore pasta with considerable nonchalance and evident good appetite.

'Dunno. Must be a modelling agent or something,' Ashdeen answers.

The four models are all tall and waif-thin. Their hair is uniformly lustrous, like the shampoo models on TV. But then they are the shampoo models on TV. I watch them from a distance, out of strict professional curiosity of course. Each picks at her salad as she chitchats. Tamara sips at a glass of water. Tinu checks her Blackberry for incoming mails.

Then it dawns on me: this is about as close as it gets to an Indian version of a *Sex in the City* all-girl lunch date. We have the overpriced food, the hip venue, the low-cholesterol, everything. Only the tone of the conversation is different. Less lewd, I imagine. Twenty-year-old Diva still travels everywhere with her mother as chaperone. But their poise, their effortless sense of style, the carefree way they giggle, the confidence with which they scan the room, the sheer sultry femininity with which they hold themselves – all of this encapsulates the women idealised by Nonita and her colleagues.

Are these the women Indian girls are growing up longing to be? Do the picture-perfect creatures across the room epitomise the shape and style of tomorrow's India? I watch the other women in Olive stealing glances at them. I wonder if they are craving to be like them. Or do they see them for what they are, as the mannequins of fashion designers, as projections of an abstract ideal?

The answer strikes me as important. Women the world over want to be more beautiful. The issue rests on *who* defines the parameters of such beauty. Women themselves, or a bevy of ad execs and fashion editors in Lower Manhattan? There's a larger question here too, a question that lies beyond hem lengths and seasonal colour tones. It's about direction. If India is on the move, where is it heading? Is it aping the West, a copycat case of cultural transition, or is it drawing on internal reference points and charting an Indian course all of its own?

'. . . did you hear Sonam's deal with Ray-Ban fell through . . . ?'

The talk around the table draws me back. The *Elle* girls are judging designers by the pretension of their after-show 'thank yous'. One of the sub-editors is mimicking Ashmia Leana, drawing her hands together in a prayer-like 'namaste'. 'I mean, how ridiculous. She looked like some rustic behenji.' The imitation brings a cackle of unpleasant laughter.

Just as I think there will be no escape, the *Hi Blitz* photographer creeps into view. Julian spots him first. He is no fan. 'Run for cover,' he squeals, pulling his spotted top hat down over his eyes. *Hi Blitz* is the paparazzi-based in-flight magazine for Kingfisher, part of the Vijay Mallya empire.

'They don't airbrush,' he gasps theatrically. 'I swear, it's positively criminal. That guy could make a supermodel look ugly.'

Ashdeen suggests we leave the exclusive enclave of Olive and visit the designers' zone in the next-door building. We skip by the photographer and head through the twee wicker exit gate.

Delhi's top designers line up their collections in three neat rows. Each is assigned a boxed room in the enclosed conference block. These they endeavour to deck out in the style of their Hauz Khas Village boutiques, with tinted lights, eclectic window displays and clothes racks lolling under the weight of their latest creations.

Ashdeen runs his finger over the floor plan by the entrance. 'J. J. Valaya, Rohit Bal, Tarun Tahiliani . . .' He coos as he numbers off the industry's big players. The most prestigious designers are given the spots closest to the main door. Occupying the building's far recesses are the new kids on the block.

We set off in a clockwise direction. A few designers are busy with private clients and retail buyers. Most are not. It's early days. As an institution, Fashion Week is yet young. To keep from looking underemployed or, worse still, overlooked, they tap away at miniature laptops or fervently study their catalogues.

Four sewing machines encrusted in gold and brown beads occupy the storefront of Stall No. 33. I stop to look at them. As I do so, an Arab gentleman and his wife step out. She is veiled from head to foot in black. Two wide walnut eyes stare out from the visor of her burkha. She carries a shopping bag in either hand.

I wander in after her.

Rahul Khanna greets me warmly. A congratulatory smile is writ large across his face. The Arab customers had paid handsomely. Rahul is all helpfulness and charm. Dressed in a white open-necked shirt and tapered black jeans, he could pass as Italian.

'I'm just in from Paris,' he says, laying out his international credentials upfront.

Rich Indians love to boast about their foreign holidays: a sojourn in Switzerland, a fortnight in Florida, a fleeting shopping trip to London. They are the signs of having 'arrived'. Arriving is very important for India's affluent. It's as if they're endlessly popping out and feel the need to announce their successful return.

I am not an habitué of boutique design shops and begin rustling through the minimalist clothes racks with a brutishness that clearly concerns Rahul. He joins me at my elbow. As I move my way through his collection, he realigns each of the dresses back to their original position.

Rahul's current collection is inspired by shadows, he tells me. A play on themes of light and shade. He is obviously itching to say more about his creative process, so I pull out my notebook and gesture for him to continue.

'Well, as you'll see, there's a strong vintage influence. A touch of military too. Lots of drapery, lots of pleats, lots of folds.' He strokes the dresses lovingly as he talks about them. 'The colours

are all very metallic. Lots of layering. You'll see there's an emphasis on the shoulders. The Eighties are a big influence on my show
this year.' The fabrics? 'Yes, the fabrics . . . a lot of chiffon, treated
sand-washes, embossed silks, lightweight wools, hand-made se-
quins.' He pulls out a low-cropped evening gown with a jagged
hemline. 'Laser cutting. You see? All very new. No scissors, no
nothing. It gives it this fraying, flaring effect. Gorgeous, don't you
think?'

I agree, although my real interests lie elsewhere, back on the
question I'd left hanging in Olive. Where did he look for inspira-
tion, to home or abroad?

As a roundabout way of asking, I enquire where he sells his
designs. It's a mix, he tells me. He owns stores in Delhi, Mumbai
and Bengaluru, but exhibits overseas. He has shows coming up in
Singapore, the Middle East and Europe. 'In Paris, they love all the
glitter, glamour and gold,' he insists. 'I'm very appreciated there
for my cuts and fabrics.'

I try refining the question, more interested in knowing how he
perceives himself than in how others perceive him. As a designer, would you describe yourself as Indian or international? His
response, like his designs, refuses to commit to either. The very
premise of unitary categories, of exclusive either/or definitions,
runs counter to his creative philosophy. 'I use Indian techniques,
but the style is very Western, very contemporary.' Others see him
not as an Indian or Asian designer, he adds, bound by his profession to reference the opinion of industry insiders. 'In fact, people
are surprised to hear that I'm from India.' I have a hunch he likes
it that way.

The idea of being Indian and international, of entering one
world without leaving the other, is an attractive one in theory. It
suggests an inner confidence, a willingness to engage as equals.
How feasible it is in practice is another question. Can cultural time
zones be merged? Is there a universal date line out there that remains true to itself as well as to an amorphous, universal Other?

Rahul the Programmer had chosen not to try welding the two,
shedding his origins as a snake might its skin. Rahul the Design-

er, in contrast, had given his best shot at striking a balance. Yet the indistinct origin of his work left me unconvinced. His style sounded less like a fusion of identifiable parts and more like an experiment in global ambiguity, the fashion equivalent of a planetary no man's land. I'm sure it made his designs very edgy and in vogue, but it didn't make them very Indian.

Unless New India is actually Post-India, a country loosed of its cultural moorings, floating free in an indeterminate sea. Even for the fashion world, however, that sounded like a step too far. As an analogy for India, it most certainly did. The idea of future visitors spending a week in Delhi, Kolkata or Hyderabad and being 'surprised' to learn they were in India is impossible to conceive. Change as India may, it could never become a Transit Lounge nation, devoid of distinctive markers.

I leave Rahul's stand impressed by his efforts to globalise, but sensing ultimately that the Indian had lost out to the International. His cultural weathervane pointed more to Dolce & Gabbana than Delhi or Haryana.

Ashdeen, in his own way, agrees. 'You need to understand that the fashion industry is still very young in India,' he says, talking as we walk. 'A new, more experimental generation is just emerging. But it's difficult to pick out any particular style, like say, an Alexander McQueen or Giorgio Armani.'

We continue our way around the stalls. The embroiderer has a critic's ability to pass swift judgement in a few, well-chosen words. So Ashi Maleena, I learn, is 'a big hit with the rich, older crowd, but so aunty-ish'. Prashant Verma, on the other hand, is 'very young, very grunge'. Abraham and Thankere, 'older lines, classic style'. Rabani and Rakha, 'super-dressy, satiny, red-carpet stuff'.

The last remark sparks a tangential thought. He stops at the window, eyeing a chiffon gown with intricate crystal work around the plunging bodice. 'It's all very confusing for Indian women today,' he muses. 'Formal used to mean your best sari. Now with all these cocktail dresses and international designs, no one is quite sure what to wear.' He's thinking of the men too. Do they wear a Western suit or a kurta? To help avoid the dilemma, most party invitations these days say 'black tie' or 'Indian formal'. 'That way, everyone is happy.'

We turn a bend and come to Nida Mahmood's show-cubicle. She is sitting on a stool behind a circular metallic table, one hand on her brow, looking forlorn. Nida and Ashdeen are friends. It is her show that has been delayed because of the dispute with the fire department. It is mid-afternoon and it looks likely that she'll miss her slot. The organisers have assured her that they will re-schedule, but she'll have missed her debut place. Months of work and no little expense, down the drain. Ashdeen enters first. A tête-à-tête ensues. She breathes deep and rallies herself. Her delicate shoulders stiffen with resolve. 'Please, come on in.'

Nida features on the hip list of young Indian designers. A little over five feet tall, her minuscule waist and swan-like neck imbue her with a porcelain fragility. We talk of the fashion world in general, anxious to keep off the subject of today's debacle. She credits the likes of *Vogue* and *Marie Claire* for bringing India into the international arena. In her opinion, events such as Fashion Week debunk the common perception that the industry is 'just a frivol-ous world'.

This desire to be taken seriously crops up repeatedly among India's design community. 'Adolescent' is the word Ashdeen had used earlier to describe how some people viewed him and his colleagues. He blames the offspring of the rich and famous who dabble in fashion as 'a hobby'. These 'socialite designers', as he dismissively calls them, only keep afloat by selling to their rich, heiress friends. The comments sound spiteful, yet they make sense in a nascent industry desperately vying for credibility.

I look over Nida's array of garments. Bold patterns and bright colours dominate. The influence of international trends is more moderated in her designs, compared with Rahul's. She works with 'Indian clothes', she tells me with deliberate emphasis. Above all, the sari. 'I try and reinvent it each time.' She's launching a sil-houette of a sari, she says excitedly, temporarily forgetting the postponement of her show. 'It's extremely funky, extremely cool. It has a front drape in a pleated fabric, like this.' She imitates the look by clasping both hands around her doll-like midriff. 'It's scrunched in a very unique way. The whole thing is held together by a brooch. The way it falls with a very trendy belt is something else. And it's draped over jeans, so it has a very different feel.'

I am surprised to learn that the sari – this unstitched strip of coloured cloth, so graceful, so timeless – needs a makeover. No item of clothing could be considered more archetypally Indian. One of the strongest images I have from my previous travels, in fact, is gazing out of train windows and seeing the countryside sparkle with paint-pot flecks of brilliance as sari-clad farmhands went about their labours.

According to Nida, however, the sari is becoming a less frequent sight. Women in the country's cities, especially in the north, are opting for the more practical shalwah kameez or, in the case of younger generations, Western attire.

The urban consumer is Nida's market and therefore the focus of her creative preoccupations.

'Everybody likes to see something these days. Everyone is becoming very Westernised, very cosmopolitan. People want to make a statement. They want their clothes to say something about them. So I'm trying to balance the Indian and Western together. That's my take on fashion. That's my niche.'

An SMS announces its arrival with a ping. The urbane designer checks the screen. Her face takes on some of the despair of before. Will we excuse her? The reinventor of the sari slips out into the corridor. She is dressed in a cashmere V-neck and black trousers.

With her departure, Ashdeen calls it a day. The official line from the fretful public-relations woman is that the show will kick off in thirty minutes. But Ashdeen is sceptical. He is right to be so. The opening day ends up being suspended entirely. Nida is shunted to a graveyard slot late on Monday, the day after the closing party bash.

I reflect on Nida and her collection as I make my way back towards the main hall. As philosophies go, her desire to assimilate what's Indian and what's not echoes that of Rahul. Only their starting points are different: hers beginning from within her own culture; his, predominantly, originating from outside. Eclectic as Nida's saris may be, they are recognisable for what they are: a new take on an old idea. They are tethered to something with a discernible history, a natural continuum of ideas and cultural associations.

I spy Eddie, the fashion editor at *Vogue India*, outside Olive. Ashdeen had pointed him out earlier. He's easy to spot: a reverse quiff, three-quarter-length trousers, pointy leather shoes with no socks, oversized dark glasses, an oriental tattoo on his neck and a tight denim jacket with the sleeves rolled up to his armpits. Delhi's *homme de mode* agrees to a quick chat and we take a seat by the Wills Lifestyle enclosure.

We talk shop to begin with. Birkin Hermes is the new 'it' bag, apparently. Jodhpur pants and one-piece tunics, also 'very in'. 'We're all over dresses as well.' We are? Eddie deals primarily in superlatives. The arrival in India of high street brands Zara and Top Shop is, in his opinion, 'just fabulous news'. The opposite is true for dressing in a hot climate. Layering, forget it. 'It's quite impossible.'

He pauses. I exploit the break to ask about the impact of Western fashion on Indian design. Rahul seemed to claim the differences between the two were disappearing. Nida believed otherwise, claiming a lasting uniqueness about Indian dress. Ashdeen thought people were confused. Where does Eddie stand?

'How do I answer that? There's a feeling – how do I say? – a feeling about the need to be cool. In that sense, we're more and more exposed to what Western culture is telling us. On the other hand, we're very traditional still. You cannot not wear a sari to a wedding. We're globalising, yes, but we're also sticking to what we have. India is one of the very few countries where you can't just adopt Western culture. Look at MTV. It started out playing international music, but now it's mostly Hindi. That's what the consumer wants. In terms of fashion, people are still trying to set the boundaries between Western and Indian wear.'

I'm conscious the fashion fraternity operates in a bubble of its own creation. That's as true for Delhi as anywhere else. Few Indians, even those that can afford to shop in the malls such as Oberon and Lulu, know their Givenchy from their Gaultier. That makes analogies to broader trends a dangerous game. Yet Eddie's analysis rings true. Not about the Jodhpur pants and tunics. Those will come and go, the fads of fashion. What resonates are the inherent cultural tensions associated with globalisation, the fact of the world arriving on your doorstep. Like a good host, do you throw open the door and ask it in? Or do you reach for the padlock and key? It's a trend that Indians are facing in all walks of life, not just in Delhi's design studios. And it's a trend that won't go away. How the country answers will define the shape and form of New India.

I return to the NSIC complex a couple of days later. A fire truck is now parked ostentatiously outside the entrance gate. Ashdeen has tickets for the Pankaj and Nidhi show at three p.m. I spot him sitting beside his butch boyfriend halfway down the banked seating. The room is packed. I pass an empty seat with a *Vogue* reservation sticker on it. No sign of Eddie.

Ashdeen is all a-quiver. Clutching a new handbag, he points out members of the industry's A-list in the front row. None of the names I recognise. I'm reminded again of how divorced the world of the catwalk is from normal life.

But what's 'normal'? Definitions are changing. Inside the fashion show, all is new to me. That makes it exciting. It also makes it disorientating. Do everyday Indians feel the same about the changes unfolding around them? As the ground beneath their feet begins to shift, as their aspirations begin to be realised, as New India inches ever closer, what's their response?

The lights come up. A trip-hop beat kicks in. Sinuous models begin sauntering down the ramp. They stop, pose, turn on their heels. An artillery fire of flash bulbs tracks every step. Ashdeen gushes. The crowd erupts. Pankaj and Nidhi, a husband-and-wife team, appear from out of the wings to a chorus of clapping. They smile in thanks and, with the most modest of waves, return again backstage.

Fashionistas occupy the furthest end of the trend spectrum.

They are provocateurs by nature, pushing the boundaries of style, testing the limits of acceptability. The extremes of Delhi Fashion Week are not indicative of what's unfolding on the street. Many iterations await the creations of Atsu, Rahul, Nida, Pankaj and Nidhi before they filter down to the nation's malls.

Change is coming, all the same. Indians know it. Rahul, Ashdeen, the man in the mundu – they are all responding in their own way. Some are expectant, some fearful, some belligerent. But respond they must. New India leaves them no choice.

Part III

Change

7

Dear Agony Auntiji

[relationships]

'Her hand touched his, owing to a jolt, and one of the thrills so frequent in the animal kingdom passed between them, and announced that their difficulties were only a lovers' quarrel.'
E. M. Forster, *A Passage to India*

Kolkata

An untidy file of typists sits in a line outside Kolkata's family court. Each occupies a rickety wooden desk with his back to the perimeter wall. The collars of their shirts are frayed and their cuffs dark with ink stains and accumulated grime.

They make for a down-at-heel bunch, like office workers reduced to the pavement after successive demotions. With each rung down the ladder, a little of their dignity has disappeared. Yet never their trusty typewriters. These they have clung to come what may. Soot-black Remington Portables dominate each of their open-air workstations, sitting square in front of them as proof of their literacy and collateral against further demotion.

Bony fingers press down a finger at a time on the knuckle-bent keys. Click-clack, click-clack. The metallic sound of typed legalese fills the overcrowded courtyard.

One scribe, with pallid skin and half-moon spectacles, is feeding carbon paper into his antiquated machine. A client is perched on a low bench beside him, reading out his claim in a tired, nasal voice. '. . . the petition decree holder has repeatedly requested that the counterparty . . .' He stops. A discussion breaks out. Is 'counterparty' the right term? Or should it be 'contraparty'?

I butt in before they come to a final decision. Do they know where the divorce hearings take place? The typist nods and extends a lazy hand to point out a flight of stairs across the courtyard. 'Up there,' he mumbles.

I thank him and press on into the busy courtyard. To my right stretches a bank of restaurants, little more than trumped-up food stalls with plastic awnings and a few long tables. They offer the usual fare: rice, dhal, steamed vegetables and Bengali favourites like alu posto and begun bhaja. It is too early for lunch, but the smell of milky tea and pakoras has drawn a couple of punters. They sit on the eateries' benches in morose silence.

A line of rough-hewn tables fills the middle part of the court-yard, each accompanied by a squat bench. On these sit a second breed of court worker. They appear marginally less slovenly than the typists, but just as lacklustre. Their trousers are stained with age and greasy fingers, the remnants of long-dead suits. Each has with him a scratched briefcase from whose innards legal papers spill.

With resigned expressions, they occupy themselves reading case notes and making annotations. A few are sat with petitioners, pen in hand, asking questions and then transcribing the answers. Several are asleep. I take them to be notaries.

The lawyers proper, on the other hand, are easier to make out. They wear the barrister's uniform of white shirt and kipper-tail tie. They also have the plum seats, on the shaded side of the courtyard. In front of their desks runs a passageway linking the courtrooms to a separate administrative block at the back. This second building has a holding cell, but no prisoners. I feel slightly cheated. I would like to see an incarcerated suspect or a fully fledged criminal. The clink of handcuffs would bring a sense of gravity to the scene; would confirm it as a place where wrongs were righted before the law. As it is, the family court feels like a mix between a refugee camp and a dilapidated classroom.

The barristers' location affords a direct view on to the court traffic. This comprises a steady flow of brow-creased litigants, supportive family members and expert witnesses. Their number also includes a small assortment of lost souls. Slumped on the floor or wandering in slow circles, these are the unfortunate few for whom the twists and turns of the justice system have become too much. Fate has consigned them to India's legal labyrinth, leaving them to pursue fruitless claims and counterclaims until they gradually become mad. Perhaps the court has its prisoners after all.

I head up the wide, exterior staircase to the first floor. The final step gives way to a broad corridor, which, with a low wall running along one side and a view back down to the courtyard, feels like a veranda of sorts. The air is muggy and heavy as a stone. Not a breath of wind passes. Along the corridor, people are milling around in small groups. There are no seats, so everyone is standing. Some are smoking. Others are in conference, heads pressed together, discussing their case in whispers. The atmosphere is listless. Everyone is waiting. I lean on the wall and wait too, watching the typists and notaries go about their business below.

I've come to the Kolkata court to learn about divorce. As with a good watch, a spouse is traditionally regarded in India as something you keep for life. In many circles, the prospect of breaking the marriage covenant remains taboo. New India is challenging that, with legalised separations doubling over the last decade. That doesn't mean the country is overrun with divorcees. Far from it. Unsuccessful marriages remain barely above one per cent – roughly forty times lower than in the United States. Yet the trend is upwards and I'm interested to know why.

Kolkata, I'd chosen on a whim. The one-time capital of the British Raj is New India's ailing aunt. Though still admired for her intellect and pristine manners, the years have not been kind to her. Long back now lies her golden youth, when the world's trading ships would rush to her quaysides and music would fill her streets. No wars are fought for control of her heart any more. Her dogged citizens have enough battles just staying afloat.

In New India, most cities run. The smaller ones might walk. Only a few hobble. Kolkata is a hobbler. Of course, she's very proper about it. Her walking stick has a handle of herringbone and is crafted from a shaft of finest Indian willow. But the creaks in her knees and her shuffling step are unmistakable. She's struggling to keep up. Of all New India's metropolises, it is here in poet Rabindranath Tagore's birthplace that tradition is best loved. In Kolkata, more than elsewhere, marriage remains an institution, a bulwark against the tide of modern mores.

The sound of high-pitched shouting startles me. A young woman storms out of the room in the middle of the corridor. She slams the door behind her. Gesticulating wildly and spitting out oaths in Bengali, she wakes the court from its mid-morning slumbers. In a torrent of noise, she disappears down the stairs. Scurrying after her is an older lady, who, from her facial similarity and evident concern, I take to be the shouting woman's mother. I walk across to the room where the outburst occurred. 'Court Counsellor' says a small sign on the wall. Not a successful session then.

The commotion seems to jolt people into action. A ripple of activity spreads through the corridor. Lawyers stub out their cigarettes and give a tug to their jacket cuffs. Bystanders shuffle up and down. A handful of litigants go to recheck the court timetable. The order of events is hanging against the wall by a hook and a string, carefully typed onto seventeen sheaves of thin printing paper.

I approach to take a look myself. The faded pages speak of the interminable nature of the legal process. There are expert hearings, hearing applications and hearings of miscellaneous cases. The list goes on: submission of new documents, requests for payment, applications for guardianship, cross-examination of witnesses, security reports. The shortest, and most honest, simply reads 'argument'.

Shortly after the woman's outburst, a group of plaintiffs and their lawyers emerge from Court No. 1. (There are two courts in total, one at each end of the corridor. The other carries the predictable name of Court No. 2.) The heads of thirty onlookers swing in their direction. The defendant, a well-built man of around thirty, is in animated conversation with his lawyer. They stop close to me. The lawyer lights up a cigarette.

I approach and explain that I'm investigating divorce in India.

Both men raise their eyebrows. Do they have time to answer a few questions? To my surprise, they readily agree. The defendant, who is dressed in jeans and wears an expensive watch, explains that the judge has ordered him and his wife to meet with the court counsellor. If mediation fails, a divorce will be granted. He appears happy at the prospect. I pry as to why. She's a lesbian, he responds flatly. His lawyer is evidently entertained at the look of surprise on my face. She wanted a triangular relationship, the bespectacled advocate adds, a hint of perverted derision in his voice. His client, naturally, declined. The two head off, smirking.

Stationed a little further up the corridor stands his estranged wife. She is also talking with her lawyer. Her mood is less jovial. Separated for the last two years, her husband pays nothing towards the upkeep of their four-year-old daughter. Indian law allows a wife one fifth of her husband's income. She merely wants what is owed to her, she tells me. Her estranged spouse swore before the judge that he works as a street pedlar. The idea is risible, she says, citing his various business interests. I mention the allegations he had made about her sexuality.

Her lawyer interjects. 'False,' he insists, 'totally false.' She left because he used to beat her, he adds. In my brief conversation with her husband, he'd mentioned her owning a mobile-phone shop. There is no shop, the lawyer states. She has zero income. 'What can I say? Men are beasts.'

The lawyer turns back to his client and shares a few words about the next step in their case. I sense myself excused. I retire to my spot by the balcony and watch him wave the woman off. He then walks up to Court No. 2, checks his watch and enters. I follow. He has taken a seat in the front row talking to a stocky man in late middle age. The man looks like a client and indeed the two soon approach the low wooden dais before the judge.

Sitting high above the proceedings behind a monolithic desk, the wiry judge commands his courtroom. It is not a taxing task. Other than the aggrieved couple and their legal representatives, his domain is almost empty. A grey-haired stenographer sits huddled below the judge's seat. Head down, he winces as he types, as if tiny electrodes were implanted into the keys. Twenty or so chairs fill the remainder of the room. They are lined up in two rows against the mouldy back wall. Fewer than half are occupied. Above the heads of the court spectators, a thick film of patterned cobweb hangs. A single fan whirrs noisily beside it. The machine makes no difference to the soporific humidity of the room. What little breeze it creates is for the benefit of the spiders only.

I follow the proceedings from the doorway. Both sides are pleading vigorously with the judge, speaking over one another in their attempt to be heard. Tempers fray. The two lawyers turn on one another. A serve-and-volley sequence of cruel invective unfolds. 'It's just greed,' the barrister from Court No. 1 shouts mid-rally. 'Behave like a lawyer,' his opponent replies with a clinical backhander. Eventually the judge calls order and, after a few summary comments, adjourns the hearing. The whole proceedings last no more than ten minutes. That is about standard length. So is the outcome. Most hearings end in an adjournment. Occasionally, a case is dismissed. Final judgments are rare.

The jobbing barrister whom I'd followed from the other court rushes off. He's sorry, but he doesn't have time to talk right now. He has another case to prepare. India's rising divorce rate is at least keeping a small quarter of the legal fraternity busy. His adversary dawdles a while at the door. I ask if I might be able to speak with her client briefly, indicating the younger lady at her side. 'You mean me,' she responds abruptly. 'I'm the client.' I apologise, aware all of a sudden that both women are in fact barristers. The mix-up embarrasses the younger of the two, who, despite presumably being paid to represent the defendant, has hardly said a word.

'Asha Gutgutia,' the middle-aged barrister says, proffering a hand and a firm shake. She looks me in the eye and asks my business. Her questions reveal a professional directness that is both refreshing and slightly scary.

At her invitation, I join her on her walk back to her chambers a couple of blocks away. The route takes us down a lane cluttered with stationery shops and booksellers, tea stalls and typesetters. A group of men are washing by a fire hydrant, naked but for their thin dhotis and body-suits of soapsuds. We reach a corner beside the High Court, a grandiose red-brick building of arched colonnades and Gothic church windows. The gates are locked. The court workers' union has called a wild-cat strike. West Bengal, Mrs Gutgutia explains, is run by Communists. It is not a figure of speech.

The junior barrister says farewell and peels off into the crowd. Mrs Gutgutia turns right and ducks into an open doorway beneath a neon Xerox sign. Inside, the air is pungent with mildew. It's dark as well, almost black. My guide doesn't hesitate, plunging into the cavernous office building and striding up a rickety flight of wooden stairs. Groping for the handrail, I do my best to keep up. On reaching the first floor, I'm surprised to see her approach a second set of stairs, no wider than a stepladder, and then disappear through a hole in the roof.

Curious, I clamber up behind her. I expect some kind of attic. Instead, I find myself stumbling into a cramped mezzanine office. It comprises two windowless cubbyholes. The first room is wall-papered floor to ceiling with legal documents. Tightly pressed, each caseload is bound with a red ribbon. A black gown hangs from the metal shelving. The cut denotes Mrs Gutgutia as an attested barrister for the Supreme Court. A small shrine to Ganesha and Laxshmi surveys the room from atop a filing cabinet.

She leads me into the adjoining room and invites me to sit behind her glass-topped desk. A bookshelf of legal titles stretches across one wall. I examine it as she busies herself with her computer. A hardback block of Supreme Court adjudications fills a full four rows. The remaining books concern themselves with her specialist areas of constitutional, corporate and private law. About halfway up, wedged between a bulky tome on joint-property rules and another on Hindu law, sits a second-edition copy of *Marriage, Separation and Divorce*. The paper cover is torn. It looks well read.

We talk in general about her workload. She is seeing many more maintenance and non-compatibility cases these days. She puts the trend down to the empowerment of women and the in-crease in female education and literacy. There's another, related issue too. Put simply, Indian women are becoming less patient. Levels of 'mutual understanding' between men and women are de-creasing.

I ask her what she means exactly. She spreads out her hands in front of her and explains: 'Today, women are increasingly allowed to work. But their husbands still want them to be the usual house-wives. It's impossible to have the two extremes. My generation – those women aged from thirty to forty-five, say – find themselves in a transition period. They are not able to live in the old systems or values, yet they can't obtain their new demands either.'

'And is that your own experience?' I ask hesitantly, conscious that my question crosses the fine line between the professional and the personal.

She looks at me with a considered gaze. Her professional in-stinct, I sense, is telling her to terminate the conversation here. She doesn't. At least, not explicitly. Instead, she turns back to her computer. She has an affidavit that needs finishing. I interpret this as an adjournment rather than a dismissal, and decide to wait.

'My case is one of many cases,' she says, pressing 'send' and swinging her chair back to face me. 'I am separated. He deserted me.'

I had been warned before arriving in Kolkata that I would be lucky to find anyone willing to discuss their own divorce. As a conversation topic, it's up there with herpes or bankruptcy: not something to be broached in public, especially between strangers.

Evidently a rare exception, Mrs Gutgutia spends the next thirty minutes describing the breakdown of her marriage in great detail. It hadn't been her idea to get married in the first place, she states upfront. She was content building a career and a reputation for herself as a trial lawyer. Her parents pressured her into it. They said it was a good thing to marry, so she thought she should ex-perience it. Tensions soon arose though. Her husband didn't like the fact she continued working. He wanted control over her life, she says. 'In his mind, I'm not equal to him.' It's all bound up in his ego, she thinks. That makes him jealous. Her theory is that deep down he resents the fact that she is more successful than him.

Then there's the small matter of S.E.X. She spells out the word letter by letter in preference to verbalising it. She hints at an incompatibility. He is more indirect. He's accusing her of having an 'illicit relationship'. It's a lie, she says. An attempt to bolster his case in court.

The comment brings her on to the legal wrangling between the two of them. Clause 13B of the Hindu Marriage Act is the easiest way to obtain an annulment in India. Divorce through mutual consent. She'd prefer it that way. As a lawyer, she knows how nasty and time-consuming litigation can be. He objects. His reasons, she says, are irrational. From her perspective, it comes down to his ego again. He'd rather carry on fighting than give the appearance of having lost. She calls him a 'frustrated personality'. He won't let her live in peace. Nor will he accept the judge's suggestion for counselling. She tried that route before. They had three sessions with the court-appointed counsellor. Her estranged husband didn't turn up to any. All of which leaves her marital status in legal limbo.

The focus of their legal battle is now over maintenance. That brings Mrs Gutgutia round to talking about her four-year-old daughter. Her voice contains a mixture of tenderness and steely determination. Her husband is trying to turn the little girl's mind against her, accusing her of being a bad mother. And then she checks herself. She has gone further than she intended. She lets the matter trail off.

The conversation drifts back to the realm of the impersonal. I ask about other cases she has dealt with. She tells about the husband who tricked his illiterate wife to unknowingly thumbprint her own divorce papers. Another man forced his wife into kinky sex against her wishes. Not all her clients have been women. She once represented a man whose wife had eloped with her lover, taking all the papers for their house and investments with her.

A number of the stories are coloured by domestic violence. Wife-beating is not uncommon in modern India. A third of adult women under fifty have experienced spousal abuse, according to official figures. In Bihar, the figure climbs to three-fifths. Not that such violence automatically translates into divorce proceedings. Most incidents are never reported. More than half of women believe men are justified in beating the missus from time to time, the same government survey finds.

In cases where domestic violence is cited as the cause for divorce, it is not always possible to determine if the factor comprises the whole truth. To obtain a divorce in India, the woman (or man) needs to prove 'torture'. The term is used in its broadest sense, encompassing not just physical abuse but social, religious, mental and emotional harm as well. So, as in Mrs Gutgutia's case, being told last-minute that thirty people are coming for dinner and could she 'quickly rustle something' up could be considered torture. Modest though the requirements are, the tendency to juice matters up for the court must be tempting.

I return to the court after lunch and the following day. In no special hurry, I stroll the courtyard and fall into conversation with some of the idling barristers. One of the kipper-tie club, a young lawyer with a wispy beard and a gravy stain along his lapel, offers me an animated briefing on the differences between English and Indian divorce law. Another also finds it incumbent on him to deliver me a second short lecture, this time on the specifics of 'rule nisi'. ('Special Marriage Act, 1954, Article 28, Section 13. Look it up.')

A third is more relaxed. He sits stroking his belly, a post-lunch coffee sitting on the shaded bench beside him. High child maintenance, that's what it boils down to, he ruminates. He has evidently given the matter considerable thought. Not out of a sense of social justice, it should be said. His own interests are at stake. Many married Indian women are not financially independent. They depend on their husbands for money. Given that they can't be expected to go to their spouse and request cash for divorce proceedings, covering their legal fees presents a difficulty. In such instances, the barristers often settle on a no-win-no-fee deal.

Lose and they come out empty-handed. Win, and they get a cut of whatever child allowance they have eked out of the judge.

Back in the first-floor courts, I sit in on a succession of hearings. The proceedings are doused in drowsiness. The court's somnolent eyelids collectively droop in the mid-afternoon heat. Even the spiders look comatose. The judge is forever calling recesses. During one of these, I find the door to the court counsellor's room open. Inside, an elderly lady sits behind one of three large desks transcribing notes into a ledger. Against the wall beside her stands a tall filing deposit made from rusted bars. It is three quarters full, piled high with a jumble of discarded case folders. I leave at the close of the afternoon sessions, the pages of my notebook gloomy with the ink of litigants' complaints: overbearing in-laws, alcoholism, financial stress, dowry harassment, sterility, miserliness and just plain unhappiness.

By the end of the second day, my enthusiasm as a court reporter is beginning to wear thin. The family court is not a happy place to be. It's as if the acrimony of countless couples has seeped into the brickwork, filling the building's very pores with hate and ill feeling. The atmosphere of bitterness and ennui, more pressing by far than the waterlogged air, is beginning to darken my mood. I move on before it squashes me completely.

I am reluctant to leave Kolkata before confirming one nagging question. Marriages fall apart for all sorts of reasons. Violent husbands or querulous mother-in-laws are not new to India. Such factors alone cannot explain the leap in divorce rates. Of all the reasons I'd heard, only one had the ring of a genuinely new phenomenon: namely, the rise in career women. The emergence of professional women leads to inevitable tensions in traditional family roles. Yet female high-flyers such as Mrs Gutgutia remain the minority in contemporary India, as they did in the corridors of the family court. It was women from everyday walks of life who I'd come across there: homemakers and hairdressers, full-time mothers and part-time teachers. No, there must be some other driver at play.

Mrs Gutgutia had hinted at something else. Back in her office, she had talked of a change in attitude among younger women. 'Less patience,' was how she'd put it. Before, women trapped in an unhappy marriage would suffer in silence. Now a brave few are saying 'enough'. They want out.

It certainly sounds feasible. I wonder if it could be true.

To corroborate, I decide to ask some marriage counsellors. If anyone knows what is driving women to divorce, it should be those in whom they confide. There's only one problem. Other than the court-appointed mediator, there aren't any. Well, that's not strictly true. An afternoon spent hitting the Internet and phone directories turns up a dozen or so names. Once I take out the clinicians in psychiatric units, I'm down to four. Not many for a city of over sixteen million people. One permanently engaged phone line and one email bounce-back reduces my shortlist further. The following day, I set out to the southern suburbs of Kolkata to meet the remaining two.

The Association for Social Health in India is a well-meaning NGO located down a winding back street in the Bansdroni district of town. It operates out of a large, tumbledown house with a scruffy yard. A caretaker opens the gate to me and ushers me towards an office area at the front of the house. There I find a kindly gaggle of elderly women seated around a table. They offer me tea and biscuits and explain the goals of the Association. These focus mostly on providing assistance to women and girls in difficulty. I'm handed a promotional leaflet. It enumerates a host of services, ranging from the offer of temporary shelter to the promise of 'family enrichment'. Marriage counselling falls into the latter bracket.

The director takes me through to the back of the Association building to meet with the counsellor. On the way, we pop our heads into a tailoring workshop. Fifteen teenage girls in matching white saris scramble to their feet. 'Good morning, ma'am,' they chant in unison. The director smiles and tells them to get back to what they were doing, which consists of some basic needlework. The Association runs a home for distressed girls, she explains. These are their current crop of residents. Some are the victims of sexual abuse. Some orphans. Some too poor to marry. Some the subjects of prostitution. The marriage prospects for all are dim. Hence, the sewing lessons. Tailoring is a means of future upkeep.

The director pushes open the door to the counsellor's room, introduces me to Mrs Mukherjee and promptly leaves.

Mrs Mukherjee is a motherly lady in an orange sari and colour-coordinated fringe. She is busy with clients, a married couple with worry lines etched around exhausted eyes. They sit in two straight-backed chairs looking fraught. The woman seems to be on the verge of tears. The object of all the tension is lying with his feet in the air under the counsellor's chair. Then he's up on the desk pulling at her stationery. Then he's back again on the floor, doing circuits of the room on his knees. Seven-year-old Antarish cannot sit still. Nor will he stop shouting 'Baba, Baba'. A slogan on his yellow T-shirt reads 'Stand Out'. He is at least accurately attired.

The beleaguered couple leaves with the name of a specialist for attention-deficit disorders and advice regarding various foreign-sounding medications.

Mrs Mukherjee turns and invites me to take one of the recently unoccupied seats in front of her. She was informed of my visit and is ready with her answers.

'We deal with all types of people. Anyone with marital adjustment problems,' she explains, anticipating my first question before I've even voiced it. 'Most are referred to us from the courts, but the police, protection officers and other local authorities send cases too. Some couples come of their own accord, but not many.'

The chief difficulty, she reveals, is persuading the couples to talk. Men are especially reluctant to open up. Often the women come alone. While their husbands won't speak because of pride or privacy, their wives' reluctance stems from fear. Marital problems are supposed to be resolved within the family (which, it strikes me, explains the shortage of independent counsellors). Women worry that by voicing their dilemmas to others, their future shelter and economic security will be put in jeopardy. Many ask for their comments not to be documented. The request guarantees privacy, but effectively rules out legal action too.

Not all are so reticent. A number of female clients ask for legal support to pursue a divorce. For the Association, it's a last resort. Mrs Mukherjee repeats the line about marriage being an institution and reiterates the Association's desire to help couples patch things up.

'Many just don't have the patience nowadays,' she concedes, her shoulders hunching in a way that suggests it is a battle that she is resigned to losing.

'Why have things changed, do you think?'

She shrugs. And then she sighs, a long and tired sigh of resigned acquiescence.

'Formerly there was an attitude of making adjustments. Couples would take more time to work things through. Today, attitudes are shifting. There's no time to think about these issues. If something is nagging at a couple, rather than fix it they just say, "Okay, better to separate." Like that.'

As a good counsellor, Mrs Mukherjee tries to see it from her clients' perspective. She may be pro-marriage, but can appreciate why some women are not. Family life requires compromise, she admits. Yet there must be room for individuality too. I nod. The right of the individual seems commonsensical to me. In India, however, the notion remains up for grabs. Family trumps everything, even – or, perhaps, especially – the personal interests of its members.

'Yet why now?' I press. 'What's happened to make opinions change?'

She shrugs again. It's a convoluted story, she says, suddenly looking dog-tired. With another heavy sigh, the experienced counsellor talks of how globalisation and 'computers and all' are leading to a greater exposure to the wider world. She mentions the education of women. She speaks of the confidence that comes from self-reliance. All are causes for celebration, she insists. 'But . . .' Her explanation trails off.

Mrs Mukherjee is an intelligent woman. She sees where the

trend is heading and realises she can do little to stop it. The more
women are empowered, the more her caseload will increase. She
wishes things weren't that way. Family and freedom need not be
incompatible. Young couples are more attuned to the shift in roles
these new demands require. They are working 'hand to hand'. As
long as India remains male-dominated, however, women will suffer. And marriage will bear the brunt.

She points to a poster on the wall. It depicts a chain necklace
with seven circular amulets. Each is amateurishly yet colourfully
illustrated with a scene of domestic harmony. In one, the husband
is building a wall for the family home, while his wife hands him
the bricks. In another, the man is doing the ironing. A third shows
them seated in conversation. The sequence ends with a family
photo: the happy couple, in-laws and offspring, all smiling. The
necklace encircles a caption in Hindi. 'A happy family is the responsibility of all the family.'

The slogan travels with me on the train to Rashbehari Avenue.
I walk the gauntlet of the pavement, assailed by shopkeepers on
one side and market vendors on the other. Eventually I find escape down a narrow passageway that leads to the ground-floor
offices of Kanash Lifestyle Management Centre. Located beside a
'multi-sex' clothing outlet called X&Y Chromosome, the private
counselling service shares the building with a drug and alcohol abuse charity. There's no signage outside. Kanash is not the sort of
place you would stumble on by accident.

I'm met at the door by Shilpi Mondal, a warm-hearted lady
in her late thirties with a rounded face and eyes as dark and
liquescent as a West Country mire. The hallway opens into a sizeable room with orange curtains, yellow walls and purple wooden
chairs. A vase of plastic flowers adds to the well-intentioned efforts at cheeriness. The head of a nameless Indian woman, dark
as soot, surveys the room from a pedestal. She is dressed with a
lopping bridal nose ring and wears the Indian national flag as a
headscarf.

'Doctor? Mrs?' I enquire, as I take a seat beside her desk.

'Miss,' she says emphatically.

Miss Mondal teaches at a prestigious primary school during the day and offers one-to-one counselling sessions during the evening at the Kanash Lifestyle Management Centre. Counselling is her passion. It's also the source of a steady second income. She is separated and has two children to maintain. Her husband is a Bengali from Kolkata. He is also an only son and therefore doted on by his mother, a traditionally domineering character in Bengali culture.

'Oh god,' her friends used to say to her when her and her husband first met. 'You've got something not so pleasant to look forward to.'

As it turned out, they were right. Early on in their marriage, her husband took a job as the manager of a tea plantation up in the hills of West Bengal. With the loneliness of the place and boredom of the job, he gradually turned to drink. Coming from a conservative family, Miss Mondal had no experience of alcohol. They returned to Kolkata, but his drinking continued. She tried to get him to go to rehab. He refused. Eventually, after seven years, she left. She's not officially divorced as yet. He won't turn up to the hearings. He's sought no contact with his children for the last three years.

Miss Mondal says sorry. It's usually her asking the questions. She hadn't intended to reveal so much of herself. What is it I wanted to know again?

That's quite all right, I assure her, privately glad to have stumbled upon my second talkative divorcee. For a while, the conversation steers back on to less personal ground.

She talks quickly, like an excited teenage girl gabbing to her friends about a boy she likes. Much of what she says tallies with the accounts I've already heard from Mrs Gutgutia and Mrs Mukherjee. She too identifies how fast attitudes are changing among young, educated women. They want their own independence, she says. They want to earn well. They want to lead a life of their own. So why marry? They see their mothers running from pillar to post trying to hold down a job, manage the home, keep the in-laws happy. 'Young women think "I don't need that."'

The new generation is not naive either, Miss Mondal asserts. They know what marriage will entail. It'll require adjusting their lifestyles. It'll mean 'bowing down' to someone else. They have a lot of pride in themselves. So many are therefore putting off marriage until they are older. Some get wed because they want kids. Others don't want to grow lonely when they are old. Either way, for once it's about what women want. Not what their families want for them.

Whom they marry is a case in point. Most would prefer to find someone themselves. Not that they'll rule out an arranged marriage. 'It's a helpful back-up option.' Interestingly, many parents are going along with it, the teacher-counsellor maintains. 'Their daughters have good salaries and they realise there is not much they can do about it.'

The same could be said increasingly for divorce. It's a question of attitude, according to Miss Mondal. Today, once one party has decided that the marriage is over, 'like it or lump it, it's over'. Parents are slowly coming round to the idea too. Before, daughters were perceived as someone else's property almost from birth. That's changing. 'Daughters are seen as an equal part of the family.' If a marriage breaks down, the parents are now more likely to help her out. Especially in cases of 'love marriages', where the contractual bond with the boy's family is not so strong.

Miss Mondal suddenly hesitates. Just so I'm clear, I should know it's the upper classes she is talking about. For the middle classes and everyone below that, there's very little flexibility. Social change in India can be a piecemeal, protracted affair.

As she talks, I struggle to ascertain exactly where she personally stands on the issue. With Mrs Gutgutia, I sensed there was an element of zealotry in her divorce proceedings. Her stance was unabashed and unrepentant. It wouldn't surprise me if she secretly hoped Mr Gutgutia vs Mrs Gutgutia might one day make it into the series of Supreme Court adjudications lining her bookshelf. Mrs Mukherjee, in contrast, was torn. Her belief in family stood challenged by her recognition of women's rights. For her, divorce was a last resort, to be avoided if at all possible. But what of Miss Mondal? How did she feel?

I ask her outright and am surprised by the calm measure of her response. She married for love, she explains. That love died. She feels no particular animosity towards her estranged husband. Unlike her sisters, who want to beat him black and blue, she has emotionally detached herself from the situation. She told him when they separated that he had to choose between the bottle and his family. It took her two years to realise he had made up his mind.

So with admirable pragmatism, she set about rebuilding her life without him. She realises it will be difficult for her to remarry. Few men would take on a divorcee with children. Yet she is in no rush to do so. Not that she's anti-marriage. Her parents and siblings are all happily married. For her, for now, she is happy where she's at.

Time has run on. It's close to seven o'clock. Just as our conversation is winding up, her phone rings. It's her nine-year-old daughter. She is with the ayah. She's calling to say goodnight.

For the first time, a look akin to sorrow passes over Miss Mondal's face. She would like to be at home putting her daughter to bed. But such is life, she says, biting her lip and looking around for a distraction.

Her eye settles on a semicircle of chairs at the opposite end of the room. She points to them. They remind her of something that brings a smile to her face, expelling her momentary sadness. She runs a group counselling session every Saturday morning, she explains. 'Personal growth classes', the lifestyle-management folk at Kanash brand it.

'It's designed to help people get in touch with themselves. You know: Who are you? What makes you tick? What do you want out of life?'

Manipal and Mangalore

Sunny's father strides into his room with a hammer. The teenager braces himself, an arm flung over his head. His father, lips blue with fury, sweeps past towards the room's only window. Wrenching four nails angrily from his pocket, he hammers the shutters closed. The window is never to be re-opened. Natural sunlight is banned. From now on, Sunny will have to study by the light of a desk lamp.

Five years on and now a third-year journalism student, Sunny recalls the incident over a bottle of fizzy orange in his university canteen. A good-humoured smile flashes across his cheeky face. His grin is semi-permanent, as though it came with his name.

Sunny is dressed in rolled-up, retro jeans and a branded red T-shirt. He is the campus funny guy.

The violent incident stemmed from a girl, he tells me. 'Opposite my window, on the other side of the road, was a flat with a balcony where a girl used always to come. I used to keep looking at that girl. And she'd look at me. It went on for almost a week. On the day I was talking about, my father was cooking in the kitchen next door and he saw the girl standing there. That's when he came rushing in and locked the window. Afterwards he asked me if I was looking at her. Of course, I said "no, no, no". Can you believe it? It's a crazy thing. I know it is. But in my village, everyone has that kind of mentality.'

The window episode occurred in Patna, Bihar, Sunny's home state. His father was working in the city as a teacher. Although he himself was only a high-school graduate, he was adamant that his son would go to the Indian Institute of Technology. And so Sunny spent his late teens cramming at his artificially illuminated desk. His father banned anything that might distract him. Especially girls.

'He used to consider even looking at girls a sin,' Sunny says with a rueful smile. 'If I looked at a girl, he used to ask me, "Why are you looking at her?"'

Sunny, as it turned out, had no aptitude for science or engineering. Girls, not numeric equations, were what filled his post-pubescent brain. The more his attentions drifted from theorems to hemlines, the more repressive his father became.

Prevented from so much as speaking to a girl, Sunny became

'desperate', as he puts it. He began masturbating. Only his dad caught him at that too. He looks at me straight in the eye, appalled, for a moment forgetting his mask as the resident course comic.

'Do you know how much fear he sent into my heart about masturbating? He said I'd become weak, that I'd not become tall, that I'd lose my memory power. And I was so frightened that though I had all the urges I used to be so scared of all that. You know, it was only when I came here to university and researched thoroughly on this matter, that I realised that masturbation was not injurious to health.'

The Indian Institute of Technology never worked out. He struck on journalism instead. The wide-eyed boy from Bihar entered the campus gates as fixated as he was naive about sex and relationships. Until then, the opportunity to actually 'go out' with a girl had been inconceivable. Not that dating in the Western sense is really an option. Most Indian teenagers are left to lust from afar. Or from the couch.

Sunny somehow succeeded in keeping his pornography habit silent. At sixteen, he came late to the porn scene. For many Indian youngsters, blue movies provide an alternative to the blanket classroom silence on the subject of sex. Earlier it was all on pirated DVDs, watched secretly round at friends' houses. The arrival of the Internet has made accessing pornography easier, according to Sunny. At first, he didn't care what he watched. Over time, he's become something of a connoisseur. He'll always opt for an imported film over local content. 'In Indian porn, the woman is not very participative. Just the sex and it's over. That's the difference.' All his friends agree.

'Would you like a drink?' he asks.

'Sure, thanks. Whatever you're having.'

He returns from the canteen checkout with two more orangeades. I ask how he's adapted to university life, 'with the girls and everything'. Sunny makes a show of looking abashed. He's not. Not any more, at least. In the beginning, it was different. As with all the boys from rural or conservative backgrounds, he was struck dumb by shyness.

'When you come from the villages or any other part of India to a place like Manipal, the society over here is very open,' he says, referring to the suburb of the small coastal town of Udupi in Western Karnataka where the journalism college is based.

'Open in what sense?'

'Here people talk about anything, anything, I tell you. Take this girl in my class. One day, she sits beside me and she starts drawing body parts, male and female. She asked me to name them. I named her ears, mouth, nose and everything. Then she drew a penis, huh. I didn't know what to say. Then she said "penis". I thought, oh my goodness, what is this?'

In such an environment, Sunny's tongue-tie problem soon passed. After that, his reticence swung to the other extreme. He used to go round 'proposing everyone', university slang for asking a girl out. When that failed, he tried the 'rakhi sister' ploy.

The scheme derives from ancient Indian custom. Tradition has it that, on nearing adulthood, a girl ties a holy thread (or rakhi) to her brother's wrist and her sibling then commits to protect her for life. It is all rather gallant. 'Brother' and 'sister' need not always be linked by blood. Close family ties sometimes suffice. The students have adapted this loophole to their own ends. To gain a rakhi sister is not to gain a girlfriend, as such, but it does offer access into her friendship circle, which, by Sunny's previous standards, marks a promising first base.

A pretty girl from his broadcasting class approaches. She is wearing a pair of tight-fitting denim jeans. The cut of the trousers accentuates the thinness of her legs. Her one-size-too-small T-shirt has a similarly pronouncing effect on her modest bust.

Her arrival marks a break in our conversation. The two begin discussing a pending assignment. They are clearly on familiar terms. Sunny starts ribbing her – or, as he puts it, 'taking the liberty' – about a fellow classmate whom he alleges she fancies. He calls her 'Mal', which in Hindi literally means 'item'. Colloquially, it translates closer to 'hooker'.

Not all Sunny's classmates conform to the 'open culture' that he has so readily embraced. A number remain 'conservative', a term he uses frequently and only ever as a pejorative. Girls dominate the category. Most come from rural backgrounds such as his. They prefer studying to socialising, he says. And they blush at his graphic jokes. These 'behan jis' ('sisters') stand out as prudes in Manipal only because of the university town's reputation as a cosmopolitan hub. Much more representative of middle India is Mangalore, an hour down the coast and a world apart. There the prudes reign.

A provincial port town, important in the export of coffee and cashew nuts, Mangalore has a homespun and mildly forlorn feel to it. The main road is being resurfaced when I arrive. It is part of a drive to spruce up the place. A flattened road surface to go with the town's first all-shining, half-empty shopping mall.

One of hundreds of third- or fourth-tier towns, Mangalore has no more than a walk-on part on the national stage. In that sense, recent years represent something of an aberration. Not once, but twice, the port town has hit the headlines. The second incident occurred a week before my arrival, when an Air India plane overshot the runway and killed almost everyone on board. Before that, there was the 'Pink Chaddi affair'.

The hullabaloo began in Amnesia, one of a handful of bars popular with Mangalore's young crowd. During the day, students from nearby colleges – St Aloysius, Madhyama Kendra, SDM, Besant – would come to hang out, play pool and drink beer. At weekends, a DJ would play and a bigger crowd might gather. The scene was never as raucous as in Manipal. Most students originate from Mangalore itself and are subject to parental curfews. Closing time at Amnesia used to be eleven o'clock.

One February afternoon, a group of around forty or so slogan-chanting young men gathered outside the pub. Their saffron-coloured headbands and scarves identified them as militant Hindus, part of a radicalised group called Sri Ram Sena (literally, 'Lord Ram's Army'). Reports of what happened next are sketchy. What seems certain is that the mob broke in, grabbed a number of young women from inside and partially stripped them. Then, in broad daylight, they dragged them outside and beat them up. The police were called but arrived long after the thugs had disappeared. No arrests were made.

The case was then taken up by a group of women's rights activists in Bengaluru, the state capital. In very contemporary India fashion, they coordinated their protest through the social-networking site Facebook. The group opted for a suitably provocative name: 'The Consortium of Pub-going, Loose and Forward Women'. Their Facebook page attracted fifty thousand members in the first week. In addition to much emailing and wall-posting, supporters were encouraged to take direct action. The call went out to send the chief minister a pair of pink chaddis (or underwear) for St Valentine's Day.

Voices within the Hindu right have long inveighed against Valentine's Day as 'un-Indian'. Its religious-minded opponents deride it as a celebration of all that's rotten and impure about the promiscuous West. In the run-up to the Amnesia attack, Sri Ram Sena, the self-appointed custodians of India's cultural traditions, issued a warning. Any unmarried couples found together on 14 February would be marched to the nearest temple and forced to tie the knot. Sending their underwear was the Consortium's literal way of saying 'Eat my Shorts!'. Women responded in droves.

What good the campaign did is difficult to tell. The media concerned itself as much with the underwear's cleanliness (were they used or not?) as with the cause they were designed to symbolise. Certainly, the chief minister did not appear overly put out. Despite official promises, he declined to enact the strong-arm Goonda Act against the attack's perpetrators. Nor have the police advanced any further with their inquiries. As for the women attacked, they have gone into hiding.

I spend a couple of days traipsing around Mangalore trying to find out more. Through a local journalist, I track down the number of Pawan Shetty. The twenty-six-year-old shot to fame after intervening in the brawl outside Amnesia. He was the only bystander to do so. The television footage shows the rickshaw driver's son throwing himself into the throng and disappearing under a hail of punches. His intervention distracted the thugs for long enough to allow a few of the girls to escape.

I put in a call to him and fifteen minutes later he pulls up at my hotel on a noisy Yamaha motorbike with a flatulent exhaust. He indicates for me to jump on the back and we roar off into the traffic.

We head to Liquid Lounge, a busy bar just in front of Amnesia. The latter stands empty. After the attack, government inspectors slapped it with a temporary closure order. Copious red tape and legal wrangling have resulted in the measure becoming permanent. Rumour has it that the owner of Liquid Lounge was in cahoots with the Sri Ram Sena mob, Pawan says. True or not, the removal of the nearest competition is certainly working in its favour. The bar is packed with early-evening drinkers. Meatloaf is playing at full volume. We sit outside.

Pawan orders a jug of beer and we kill time waiting for it to arrive. A one-time bodybuilder, he evidently enjoys his new-found fame. Anywhere I want to go, anyone I want to speak with, he can sort me out, he assures me. Good-looking and a sharp dresser, Pawan is a born hustler. He works the university scene mostly. He's short on specifics. On other subjects, however, he's positively verbose: the girlfriend who wants to be an air hostess, the brother who works as a valet at the mall, the father who has fallen on hard times. He's a talker. He reminds me of Sunny.

The beer arrives and I pour us both a glass. 'So, the incident outside Amnesia, can you tell me a bit more about it?'

He falls strangely quiet. There's not much to tell really, he mumbles in an offhand way. He picks up a pack of cigarettes from the table and starts turning it between his fingers. 'I was just drinking tea in the Woodside hotel next door when I heard some shouts from the road.' He saw the mob arrive and watched them break into the pub through the back door. Next thing, he caught sight of about ten men dragging out a girl by the hair. 'They were slapping her around, calling her a prostitute and other such insults.' He approached to try and reason with them. Someone pushed him. So he pushed them back and, 'Well, that's about all of it.'

He takes a slug of his drink. I try pushing him for details. How many girls were there? Did he recognise any of the faces in the mob? He answers evasively.

'I was boozed,' the Shining Knight of Mangalore eventually admits, a little sheepishly.

The vagueness of his memory leaves me a little disappointed. It must show on my face because Pawan senses it. He tries to make amends. 'Do you do marijuana?' he wants to know. I don't. 'Coke?' I pay for the beer and he drives me back to the hotel. We shake hands. 'Remember, anyone you want to speak to in Mangalore. Just let me know. I can sort you out.' He disappears down the road and into the night.

The next morning, I decide to head to one of Mangalore's universities. I opt for the Jesuit college of St Aloysius perched on top of Light House Hill. Its chapel is reputed to be one of the few examples of baroque architecture in the whole of India. Struggling up the hill, I stop at a wayside juice bar. It is nothing fancy: plastic chairs and tables, a man behind the counter chopping and liquidising fruit, a Hindi pop song playing over the radio. I order a banana shake, which arrives spilling over with froth and tasting sweet and sugary. Three of the tables are occupied, all with young folk in their teens or twenties. They lounge on the seats and fill the room with excitable chatter.

A few weeks earlier, I had picked up a report by a Bengaluru-based civil liberties group about 'cultural policing' in the Mangalore region. It is sitting in my bag, unread. Deciding to put off the hill and the heat a little longer, I take out the report and begin reading. It is comparatively short. It is also terribly earnest. Talk of constitutional protection, 'egregious' human rights abuses and 'social apartheid' fill its pages. The content itself, however, is illuminating.

The first section provides a review of local newspaper stories. The Amnesia attack, it would seem, was just one of many such vigilante incidents. Accounts abound of private parties being raided or couples being yanked from buses and beaten up. One irate article even describes Sri Ram Sena activists threatening the 'skimpy-dressed' participants of a beauty contest. The heated stand-off only calmed after the photographer consented to delete all the 'vulgar' images from his camera. The attackers' actions pass without comment. The article instead highlights the 'tragedy' of parents that allow their daughters to take part in such shameless events.

I flick though to the concluding analysis. Lying at the root of the violence, the authors argue, is the widely held belief among Hindu traditionalists that India's majority culture is being diluted. Comments from regional Sri Ram Sena chief Pramod Muthalik certainly give weight to the interpretation. 'Pub culture is not our culture,' the right-wing Hindutva leader is on record as saying. I'd heard the same in Kolkata about divorce. Muthalik also objected to 'taking drugs and dancing naked'. (According to the girls' testimony, they consumed only fruit juice and they were most certainly clothed.) The political leader did issue a muted apology, although only after television footage of the pub beating began circulating on national news. His backtracking came with a qualification. 'It is our right', the Sri Ram Sena frontman told the cameras, 'to save our mothers and daughters.'

I look around the juice bar. A boy has his arm stretched out across the top of the girl's chair next to him. His fingers touch her shoulder. His head rests against his upper arm, not far from her neck. His body position is designed to look casual. It is anything but. He's hugging her without hugging her. Is that grounds for an attack? What if they were to kiss? They don't. But what if they were to? Would that push things beyond the pale for the moral police?

Needless to say, Muthalik's comments riled the likes of the Consortium of Pub-going, Loose and Forward Women. Sri Ram Sena are 'fascists', they say. Renuka Chowdhary, a senior female government minister at the time, even accused the militant group of 'Talibanising' India.

The Karnataka-based group is by no means isolated, though.

Their anti-Valentine's stance was borrowed directly from the Shiv Sena, a powerful Hindutva group concentrated in Mumbai. This is the same outfit that said Pakistani cricketers should not be selected for the Indian Premier League. They also called for Rohinton Mistry's book *Such a Long Journey* to be removed from Mumbai University's syllabus because of allegedly derogatory comments about Maharashtrans.

Both sides have over-simplified the issue in Mangalore. A perceived threat to the town's sexual morals certainly stands at the forefront of the debate. Behind it, however, lurk other local tensions. Invariably the attacks involve couples of mixed religion, for example. The notion of Hindu girls fraternising with Muslim or Christian boys strikes Sri Ram Sena as particularly worrisome. They even have a name for it: 'love jihad'. According to this slippery-slope logic, a trip to the cinema today will become a religious conversion tomorrow.

Exclusion also forms part of the picture. Many of Sri Ram Sena's foot-soldiers in Mangalore herald from lower castes, particularly the Billavas and Moghaveeras. Some of their antagonisms are locally specific. The Moghaveeras work as fishermen, for instance. That puts them into regular conflict with Beary Muslims, who dominate the fish trade.

Wider trends are also in play. For all its down-at-heel appearance, Mangalore is actually coming up in the world. Banks, IT companies, private hospitals and commodity exporters have all set up shop here in recent times. Most of the new jobs that this has created have been snapped up by the better-educated Christians, as well as high-caste Hindus. Such 'inequitable development', the report ends, explains some of the 'tremendous alienation' and 'disgruntlement' felt by the upwardly mobile elements of the town's lower castes.

Churches feature among the more popular targets of the cultural police. Official records cite dozens of recent complaints by Christian groups of vandalism and intimidation. So it is a relief, when I eventually arrive at the St Aloysius chapel, sweating and out-of-breath, to find its fabulous wall-to-wall frescos in perfect order.

Outside, sitting in the college courtyard in the shade of an arching Indian cork tree, I spot four students. They are talking among themselves, shooting the breeze. I wander over. As I draw close, I observe that the tree's Latin name (*Millingtonia hortensis*) is printed on a small wooden sign fixed to the bark. The plaque reveals its originator as well: a Dr Smitha Hedge, of the laboratory of applied biology. The tree's test-tube birth contrasts markedly with the chapel's biblical motifs. The disparity strikes me as interesting, but not odd. New India is beginning to accustom me to the close proximity of polar opposites.

The students – Pravisha, Prajwal, Gautham and Noel – stop talking as I approach. I ask if they're happy to chat and they readily acquiesce, inviting me to sit with them on the low brick wall surrounding the tree. In their early twenties, they are all final-year students. They are identically dressed, in jeans and short-sleeved shirts. Pravisha and Prajwal even have the same style and brand of trainers. Their breath smells of alcohol. It's not quite noon.

I explain that I'm interested in understanding more about the dating scene in college. They giggle and bury their heads in their hands. Noel, a good-looking Goan with curly long hair and a sculpted goatee, is the first to speak. The religious authorities of St Aloysius do not prevent relationships between students, but nor do they overtly condone them. Campus closes each day in the mid-afternoon. So, while they would no doubt like the student body to remain modest and virtuous, the college's religious-minded authorities remain realistic.

After class, the four classmates sometimes head to all-day drinking spots such as Night Flight and Pegasus. 'We drink whiskey sodas generally,' Noel clarifies. 'Beer is for old people.' Sometimes they'll bunk off school and head to the mall or travel out-of-town to the Manasa amusement park. Noel prefers the nearby Summer Sands beach. He goes 'roaming' with his girlfriend there. 'When her parents are in,' he adds. 'Otherwise, we go to her house.'

Pravisha interjects. He is keen I get a balanced view. Unlike Noel, who comes from a Protestant family in Goa, Pravisha and the others hail from Mangalore itself. All three live at home with their parents. Their Hindu households are run on traditional lines: home by eight o'clock, no womanising, and no 'boozing or fagging'.

'We never get caught,' Pravisha assures me. 'If we go home stinking of alcohol or cigarettes, we brush our teeth or chew gum to hide it.'

It is Noel's picture of girls that his course companion primarily wishes to clarify. Many of the female students may be 'loose', Pravisha admits. Yet, from his perspective, there under the cork tree, such behaviour is neither commonplace nor appropriate. Mangalore girls, he insists, are 'good girls'. They obey their parents and cede to their wishes. Most of the girls Noel is talking about – those who go out drinking or 'go with guys' – are from out of town. 'Their parents are in other states or countries even. They stay in hostels and their parents don't know what they get up to.'

I suggest to him that Mangalore has to have some girls that fit Noel's description. If there are, Pravisha says, it's because of money. 'It corrupts them.' He knows a number of poor and middle-class girls from university who have chosen a boyfriend just because he can buy them clothes or because he owns a car. As Babu would say, it's a status thing.

On a roll, Pravisha reveals a number of other things that he doesn't think are appropriate. One is dress sense. 'Girls should be decent,' he says. He approves, for example, of the campus ban on skirts and bare shoulders for girls.

'Why?' I ask.

'When girls wear miniskirts, it tempts boys. They feel like having sex with them. That leads to rape and all.'

I begin to get an inkling of the ingrained prejudices against which the Consortium of Pub-going, Loose and Forward Women are fighting.

Pravisha's views on gender equality are similarly regressive.

'Girls', he says, 'should not have the freedoms of boys.' Not in the workplace, he clarifies. At home. 'Women in India are there for caring for the family and for motherhood.' If they are going out to bars and having boyfriends, the lines will become blurred. For Pravisha, the outcome promises not to be pretty: 'What boys do, girls will do also.'

The hypocrisy riles me. 'Sorry, help me out here. If it's okay for the guys to mess around but not the girls, who exactly are the boys messing around with?'

The question elicits no direct response. Prajwal, Gautham and Noel merely look at me, blank-faced. I can't tell if it's hostility they feel or bafflement. Pravisha, on the other hand, knows exactly what lies behind my question.

'We don't like Western attitudes,' he responds, deflecting my questions with an undisguised counter-attack.

Sensing that he might have been too abrupt or that his argument sounds bigoted (by my standards, not his), he pauses. Then, the alcohol in his bloodstream kicks back in and he repeats his opening salvo with a second round of fire.

'We've not been to these countries. We only see it on television and in the newspapers. But practices like eating beef and wearing bikinis, we don't approve of these.'

The conversation is taking a nasty turn. I raise my eyebrows, doing so in a way that I hope indicates continued interest on my part, not judgement.

Not all that 'they' say is correct, Pravisha continues in a more concessionary tone. The arrival of this mysterious third person into the conversation occurs quite naturally. I had not mentioned the Amnesia Bar incident nor Sri Ram Sena's cultural-policing activities. Yet the presence of both has hung over the discussion since we started talking. My questions – indeed, my very being in Mangalore as a foreigner – speaks of them.

I persist with the game, comfortable that there is no doubt of what and about whom we are speaking. 'Such as . . .?'

'Their opposition to Valentines, for instance. They say that more condoms are sold on Valentine's Day. On that day, they say men don't propose love, they propose sex. They are wrong about that. It's not a sex day.'

Given the growing tension in the air, I fight to stifle a laugh. But the urge to chuckle passes almost immediately. What initially struck me as absurd suddenly seems sad. Pravisha is trying to prove himself magnanimous, perhaps even enlightened, in identifying Sri Ram Sena's claims as exaggerated.

The idea of Pravisha giving the statement enough weight to consider them worthy of rebuttal is what kills my humour. It implies others might consider them serious too.

I thank them for their time and get up to go. As I do, Prajwal pipes up. He has yet to speak. Unlike Pravisha, his voice has a softer, more tentative edge to it. His classmate speaks for all of them – for all young men like them in Mangalore – he says. I must understand that they are all resigned to their parents' wishes. 'We will all have arranged marriages with girls from our own caste.' He is neither apologetic nor confrontational, just matter-of-fact. 'These things are organised. For us, love comes second.'

Love comes second. What a sorry thought. On reflection, though, we tell ourselves in the West that we marry for love. But how many folk are urged down the aisle by something other than Cupid's arrows? Money, status, fear, desperation, loneliness, children (born or unborn) – all are motivations that can lead to an exchange of rings. Perhaps Pravisha and his friends have a point? Maybe these young men from middle India are just more honest about how relationships work? So the element of choice falls predominantly with their parents. So courtship is a thing to be organised rather than left to chance. Are such things so bad?

Instinctively, I tell myself 'yes'. Young people should have the right to choose. They should have the right to fall in love and marry their childhood sweethearts. Despite a diet of Bollywood romances and television soaps reinforcing such an opinion, millions of adolescent Indians continue to think otherwise.

Back on campus in Manipal, meanwhile, Sunny's giddy with excitement. He has a girlfriend.

The two have been dating for a little under a year. She's from

Bengaluru, where she is living with her parents and studying for a post-doctoral degree. They connected via Orkut, the social-networking site.

The site hosts a chatroom for pupils at one of his former schools. Alumni would post notes and comments, while Sunny would write amusing ditties that he hoped would make him stand out from the crowd. Their online community also hosts a gaming function. The boys would take on the girls. His girlfriend acted as the Orkut equivalent of a house prefect, seeing to it that the girls won. Sunny would do his best to ensure that they didn't. Their online rivalry resulted in a 'friend request', which opened the door to lots of late-night 'chatting'. After a month or so, Sunny formally 'proposed' by email. It took six months for her to accept his online invitation to become his girlfriend.

Sunny's romance might be predominantly virtual, but it lacks none of the usual trials and tribulations of young love. Why did she make him wait so long? She had told him that she loved him. Or, at least, she had typed as much. But, in those early months, she'd worried it might be infatuation. So she'd told him to wait. Even now, she 'comes and goes' on him. Every other day, she cuts off mid-chat. Sunny's heart skips a beat every time her rosy little 'online' icon disappears. Is it something he said? Has she gone for good? Or is it her mum again, interrupting her at her computer. She's always doing that. Or so his girlfriend says.

The relationship is 'serious'. They know each other's passwords: Facebook, Gmail, Google Talk, Orkut, everything. In the world of modern relationships, there exist few greater testaments of true love. Sharing confidential data is what opening a joint bank account used to be: the surrender of singleness, a declaration of an entwined future.

That doesn't stop her testing him, though. Sometimes she says she's set up a new account, only to tell him later it was a lie. Their biggest crisis yet was sparked by a secret GTalk chat she had with an old crush. Sunny found out. He felt betrayed. She said it meant nothing. She'd have told him, but she didn't want him to become jealous. Like he was being now. Sunny had sulked for a while.

Eventually they had talked it out. Sunny has come round to the conclusion that real trust depends on 'having a heart that is totally clean'. That, for him, is the 'most modern thing' when it comes to relationships. Love, indeed, is changing him.

Again, Sunny is breaking the norm. While access to the Net is rapidly growing, bridges across the digital dating divide are yet to be built. Not that the Web isn't bringing lonely hearts together. Quite the opposite. Cyberspace is full of single Indians on the prowl.

Most of those searching for a soulmate have, at one time or another, passed through the virtual portals of Shaadi.com ('Shaadi' meaning 'marriage' in Hindi). The site's owners are explicit about their intentions, and dating is not among them. 'Redefining the way people meet for marriage' is what it's all about.

Here is how it works: India's single netizens log on, fill in a questionnaire and load up their profile. Applicants can choose any one of twenty-nine languages. Most post a photo of themselves too. Don't and people will automatically write you off as unattractive. It's a risk even ugly people can't take. Enter PhotoShop.

Shaadi.com even provides physical customer-service centres to assist those unfamiliar with the ways of the World Wide Web. Around one hundred are dotted up and down the country. There's even one in Toronto. The marriage-minded dot.com also has a tie-up with national cable operator Dish TV. Via Shaadi Active, singletons' profiles are piped directly into households across India. Pressing the red button gets you further details. Inevitably, there is now a game-show version too. Star Vivaah, 'India's biggest matrimonial show', gives the floor to young men and women to flaunt their wares and snare a spouse.

Behind the frills, Shaadi.com essentially serves as an online brokerage service. It and other websites like it mark an e-extension of the matrimonial ads that fill the weekend newspapers. Both formats are themselves replacements for the traditional village matchmaker. What used to be worked out on the hearth of the pandit's house is now resolved with the click of a mouse and the whirr of a search engine. The company's database carries millions of profiles. Thirty per cent belong to Indians living overseas. Payment only starts if you like what you see. Two thousand three hundred rupees will buy you the contact details for thirty people over a three-month period. A little extra will get you their blood type and astrological chart too.

Most suitors begin by getting to know each other online. Shaadi.com has its own chatroom. After a month or so, couples typically take things 'off line', as the site's owners put it. Bolder couples might meet alone in a coffee shop. The majority prefer to invite their parents along with them. In India, finding love is a family affair. In almost one in three cases, it's close relatives – not the suitor – who provide the original profile and sift through the potential candidates.

Online romance, as practiced by Sunny and as packaged by Shaadi.com, heralds a new dawn for the love-torn. Log on and luck out. When it comes to marriage itself, however, medium and mindset remain miles apart. It may be New India's hands at the keyboard, but it's Old India's finger hovering over the 'send' and 'delete' buttons.

Shaadi.com's profiling process proves the point. Should the applicant desire, they can include information about hobbies, pre-ferred foods, likes and dislikes, musical tastes and favourite films. These are designed to give a sense of the person behind the name.

Most don't bother. When it comes to online matchmaking, personality is mere window-dressing. It is ruthless out there in singleton cyberspace. Those in search of a life companion want to know about your age (above thirty-five sets alarm bells ringing), previous marital status (divorcees need not apply), education (postgraduate, double tick), profession (doctors and engineers win out), employer (all hail the magical 'MNC') and background (op-tions being 'upper-middle', 'affluent', 'middle-class'). There are more important criteria still. Income bracket, for one. Applicants are invited to place their earnings in one of a range of rupee band-widths, the highest running into a dizzying number of zeros.

Impressive salary stats wilt before the two dominating factors on every applicant's list: religion and 'community' (the euphemism for 'caste'). Even multimillionaires will be screened out if their faith or family doesn't match up. Brahmins can narrow their search down to sixty-three different sub-categories. Sindhis have ten from which to choose.

For Sunny, the future looks complicated. Storm clouds are brewing. He and his lady-love are talking of marriage. For that to happen, both parents must be on board. Elopement is technically a possibility. They wouldn't be the first couple to run away together. But neither wants to be ostracised from their families.

The first hurdle they face is caste, the indelible black mark of birth. You marry among your own, Sunny's Bihari father insists. The young couple are both from Brahmin homes, although from different sub-castes: Bhumihar in Sunny's case, 'slightly lower' in hers. 'Do you know what they say about marrying a lower-caste girl?' I didn't. 'They say if you die or if you can't satisfy her sexually, a girl from your caste isn't going to go to another man. In a lower caste, a girl hops from man to man.' I ask him if he believes that to be true. He's seen it, he tells me. 'It's a fact that exists.'

At least they are not from the same the same 'gotra' or clan. The most traditional corners of the Hindu-dominated 'Cow Belt' of the north still keeps strict rules against such marriages. In the old days, it made sense. Families were large and villages small. Marry too close to home and the chances of consanguinity were high. Over time, the prohibition became more muted. People moved on and others moved in. Populations grew. The term 'clan' became increasingly amorphous. The village roster gradually read more like a jumbled telephone book and less like a family tree.

Today it is improbable that the girl-next-door will turn out to be your second cousin. Yet recent years have seen a return to the medieval kinship norms. The reasons are unclear. One compelling theory is that the knap panchayats – the village-based caste councils who once dominated local affairs and who were responsible for enforcing the ban – are feeling marginalised by the pace of social change. Reinforcing the ban is a way of reasserting their power and influence, it's said.

Whatever the reasons, young couples from the same 'clan' face increasing hostility, shared DNA or not. At best, their marriage might be terminated. At worst, their lives could be. So-called 'honour killings' have become a regular feature of the daily news. Only a few days after meeting Sunny, I read in the *Indian Express* about the brutal murder of a young couple from Karora in Haryana. The village is located less than a day's bus journey from the national capital.

The article carries a low-resolution photo of Manoj and Bibli. A chain of orange marigolds has been thrown quickly around their necks. Expressions of stoic determination are etched on their young faces. The background reveals nothing, a plain blue wall. I imagine a busy civil servant at the registry office snapping it on a borrowed camera.

A few weeks later, two gunnysacks carrying their battered, putrefying corpses turned up in a canal. The burn of a rope mark was still visible around Manoj's neck. Bibli's internal organs, meanwhile, were found to be awash with agricultural pesticide. The newsworthiness of the twin murder (there are over one hundred honour killings a year in Haryana alone) rests on the perpetrators – Babli's own uncle and brothers – having been brought to book. It is India's first such conviction for an honour killing. It took fifty hearings and forty-one witnesses to secure the verdict.

The landmark decision is unlikely to bring about an overnight change. Opposition to same-gotra marriages is culturally entrenched and its standard-bearers seemingly indifferent to the wiles of reason or regulation. The Khap Maha Panchayat, an umbrella group for caste councils, is digging in its heels. Far from backing down, they are calling on the government to enforce a statutory ban on intra-clan marriages. 'This is a sickness, to marry in the same gotra. There is scientific proof to back this,' Dr Om Prakash Dhankhar, an educated voice in the panchayat echelons, tells the newspaper's reporter. 'Look at the English Royal Family.'

The second hurdle Sunny faces centres around how much his future bride is willing to pay. The payment of dowries was officially banned in India in 1986. Yet the law is porous. What was once called a 'dowry' is now described as a 'voluntary gift' – a practice permissible under the amended Hindu Marriage Act. His brother, a cadet in the merchant navy, is already receiving offers from prospective parents. One anxious father is promising forty-six lakh rupees, with a Mahindra Scorpio 4×4 jeep thrown in.

Sunny laughs to himself, as if it would be a travesty to pay even half the suggested sum for his brother's hand. 'Normally among our people, the most you'll get is a Bolero.' He seems unfazed by the treatment of marriage as a tradable commodity. He has lived in its shadow all his life. For that reason, he's under no illusions about his own value as a journalist. Not much.

Sunny's situation awakens my sympathies. As with millions of young people his age, he finds himself crushed between two worlds, squashed between orbits that are spinning in opposite directions. It must be disorientating, like returning to work after summer vacation to find your office full of strangers.

Beneath his feet, the landscape is constantly shifting and the signposts that guide his path are ever more dimly lit. The gap between the India of Old and New is widening. Will he one day have to choose? Or can a bridge be built between the two diverging banks?

For the moment, Sunny hopes to straddle the divide. He and his girlfriend have resolved to hold off marriage for a couple of years, until both of them are earning. Then they'll present their mutual desire to marry to their respective sets of parents. Not as a love marriage, he insists. They know that won't wash. 'What we'll do is talk to both our parents and have it appear like the marriage is something they have arranged themselves.'

A love marriage in arranged clothing. It is certainly a clever compromise. Perhaps Sunny won't have to decide after all? Maybe he can reverse the revolving orbits and have them turn together in concert? I don't know. Nor, I suspect, does he.

I wish him and his love affair well, and leave Manipal on the afternoon bus.

Change can cut like a scythe. For Mrs Gutgutia and Sunny, it's their personal lives that are feeling the force of its cleaving blade. For India's ancient tribes, the wound runs deeper. Change is slashing and cutting at every aspect of their lives, threatening to sever their moorings and cast them loose.

8

Outsiders

[exclusion]

'There is a whiff of fragility and under-confidence in the air, as if at any moment the entire facade of India as a rising power might simply blink out like a bad idea.'
Dr Harsh V. Pant

Gadchiroli District, Maharashtra

Jeevan scratches his head. I remain a puzzle to him. Sitting under the black tarpaulin roof of the village temple, he eyes me with a mixture of suspicion and curiosity.

His reaction is only natural. The village of Chavela receives few visitors and we have arrived unannounced. My sole point of contact is a young Communist Party delegate called Amol. Tall and lanky, with a downy growth of hair on his top lip, Amol has visited the backwoods settlement once before. Regrettably, no one seems to recognise him.

I turn for help to Nandeep, Amol's friend. An amiable maths graduate with an angular face and two-day stubble, he's been persuaded to join us on the bumpy motorbike ride out to Chavela. Nandeep speaks 'pretty good' Gondi, according to Amol.

'Journalist,' Nandeep says, jabbing a finger at me. 'From England.' Amol smiles. Jeevan continues scratching.

The Gonds, to whom the ancient Dravidian language of Gondi belongs, are one of the largest of India's tribal groups. Renowned for their historic warrior ways, they number around four million in total. Most are clustered in the remote corners of the country's central states. About half still speak their mother tongue. The Gonds, together with India's other adivasi or indigenous communities, feature among the country's most ancient people groups. They are also among its most neglected.

'Can you tell me something about yourself? How old you are? What you do?' I ask, entreaty in my voice. I look to Nandeep, who does his best to translate the request. Jeevan stops scratching and stares.

There are two others in our party. More of Amol's pals. Both grin continually, but remain conscientiously silent. I sense their Gondi is no better than mine.

Jeevan had been standing alone by the hand pump of Chavela's central well when we arrived. It had been just after noon. The mud streets of the village were otherwise empty, except for a few stray chickens and a morose cow tied to a bamboo post. The tethered beast lowed sadly and swished its tail at the flies.

Most of the villagers were inside, resting their limbs from a long morning in the paddy fields and awaiting lunch. The hum of our motorbikes had announced our arrival. It wasn't long before a cluster of men gathered around us. They approached drowsily, their limbs heavy with sleep and heat-induced fatigue. Still in that somewhere space between rest and wakefulness, they had walked over and now sit with us on the flattened earth outside the mud-brick temple.

All are dark-skinned, bare-footed and dressed in threadbare shirts and colourless cotton lungis. They too are inquisitive, their tone curious rather than aggressive. 'Who are we?' 'What do we want?' Nandeep does his best to explain.

Jeevan gradually relaxes. He utters something to Nandeep. His voice is soft and low, like the plod of footsteps in heavy snow.

'He's twenty-four,' Nandeep translates.

I would have put Jeevan at a few years younger. In his teens, even. His face is smooth and childlike, set by a geometrical jaw and topped with an unruly clump of jet-black hair. His clothes are those of a youngster too. His shirt has thick green stripes running downwards and a 'Due South' tab sewn onto the front pocket. It differs from those of the other villagers in being dual-coloured, multi-fibred and mass-produced. His trousers, meanwhile, are rolled up to the calf. The whole ensemble is several sizes too small for him, as if he'd had a growth spurt during the night. Only his eyes suggest his years. Two rounded lumps of charcoal, difficult to read; eyes that seem to have seen much and travelled far.

He mumbles something else. Nandeep passes it on, evidently more at ease working from Gondi into English rather than the reverse. 'He works in the fields with his father and brothers.'

I ask how an average day pans out in the village. It starts early, 'Up for the sun.' The able-bodied adults leave for the fields shortly afterwards and work the whole morning. Breakfast is a mug of tea. Lunch, rice and vegetable puri. Sometimes chapattis. After-noons are spent collecting water or firewood. In the evenings, the older men might drink. Alternatively, they watch television. There are two TV sets in Chavela, one of which Jeevan's family owns. It tunes into only one setting, the government-run Doordarshan channel. The electricity often cuts out.

The noise of young children playing in a nearby hut interrupts us. 'The primary school,' Jeevan explains. The teacher is absent, which, technically speaking, is one up on Jeevan's childhood, when there was no teacher at all. In terms of other basic ameni-ties, Chavela has no health centre of its own, relying instead on a weekly visit by two nurses from Marda, a larger village some dis-tance away. 'They help with coughs, colds . . . typhoid, malaria.' He seems not to differentiate between the relative seriousness of the conditions. Malnutrition is commonplace too, he says. 'Water is so much less now.' As the rains have dwindled, so too has the forest's bounty. For most of their vegetables, they must travel to the market in the local town. To worsen matters, the Forest Act restricts their ability to hunt for game, a traditional source of sustenance for India's forest-dwelling 'tribals' (as the *adivasi* are commonly referred to in India).

It took us an hour and a half to travel the thirty-five kilometres from Armori. A non-descript, pit-stop kind of place along the main highway to Nagpur, it's the closest Jeevan and his fellow villagers have to a town. No one in Chavela has motorised trans-port. People rely on bullock carts and bicycles. To get to town, they hitch. The village of Delanwadi is closer. A larger version of Chavela, it has an asphalt road. Jeevan bought his watch there, he tells me, turning his wrist to show me the fake gold timepiece.

Armori marks the limits of Jeevan's first-hand experience of India. His lack of knowledge about his homeland goes beyond the mere geographic. I ask him if he can name the Prime Minister. He can't. The state's chief minister – arguably a much more immediate force on Chavela's fortunes – also eludes him. As for the wider world, he has never spoken to a foreigner before. Never seen one, in fact. He has heard of Britain, though. 'It once ruled India, right?' He's heard of a place called Germany too. He cannot find either on a map. But then Chavela has no atlases. In fact, books of any kind are hard to find in this predominantly illiterate village.

New India, with its bright lights and global aspirations, might as well occupy another planet.

Jeevan points the finger of blame for Chavela's problems at the Indian government. The national Constitution identifies almost six hundred and fifty indigenous groups. These it categorises as 'Scheduled Tribes'. The 'tribals' number around eighty-five million in total. Politicians have tried to build careers out of defending their rights. Rafts of official affirmative-action measures and development programmes have been rolled out. Most, as the conditions in Chavela show, have rolled away just as fast.

Not all see the wretched state of India's tribal groups as the government's fault. Some blame the country's indigenous groups themselves for their 'backwardness', as if poverty and exclusion were products of their own volition. India's tribes prefer primitivism to modernity, the argument runs. They'd rather see their culture conserved than their communities developed.

India is changing fast. Are the citizens of Chavela happy to be bystanders, to watch the country speed forward as they stand still? I wonder what Jeevan thinks.

As a way of gauging his opinion, I ask about his views on Armori. His answers do not suggest a mindset closed to the prospect of advancement. In fact, city life positively appeals to him. He likes the way people dress, he says. And the festivals. And the girls. The last comment elicits a ripple of laughter from the group of villagers. Would he prefer to live there? He would. Only, there's no employment. No one in the history of Chavela, according to Jeevan, has ever obtained a job in Armori.

Lack of education is partly the reason for such dismal success in the job market. So too is lack of cash. The Constitution requires the government to earmark a quota of public-sector posts specifically for Scheduled Tribes. These, however, don't come free. Appointments are made via officials, and officials want bribes, Jeevan says. According to his reckoning, fifteen lakh rupees will secure you a teaching post. Three lakh for a clerical position. 'I've not got enough money to get a job in government service.' He doesn't seem overly put out. That's just how it is. How it's always been.

Something Jeevan says appears to upset one of the older men present. He scrunches up his pinched face and launches into a short, angry speech from beneath a bushy greying beard. The remonstration is directed towards me.

'In the village, they are used to going to the toilet in a free place. In the city, there is no space for going for toilet . . .'

Nandeep loses the thread of his argument and asks him to start again. The garrulous villager spells out his opinion in deliberate tones.

'In the city, life is always a struggle. Here, they have the peaceful life. From childhood, he has lived in a village. That is why he prefers it to the town.'

I turn back to Jeevan, who looks chastened by the older man's intervention. In an attempt at conciliation, I return to his earlier criticism of the government. 'Does it anger you, the government's lack of help?'

He nods vigorously, contented to be back on a theme with which there is broad consensus in the village. Government agents never come, he says. As for politicians, they only appear before elections. Nor do official funds arrive as they should. What they want most of all is paid employment. Under the National Rural

Employment Guarantee Scheme, the government promises one hundred days' work a year. In return for a minimal wage, the programme pays the poor to help build roads and generally lend their muscle to civil works. In Chavela, each adult is lucky to get fifteen days at most.

The same is true for house-building. The government promises one lakh rupees to build a hut. It's not enough, Jeevan maintains. He points towards a crumbling adobe house along one of the four tributary paths leading off from the temple. One of the building's external walls has collapsed entirely. The remaining three are sagging like dampened cardboard and look set to follow shortly. 'Even if it was enough, we don't receive all the money anyway.'

The Gram Panchayat, or coordinating village council, admits as much. We'd stop at their office in Delanwadi on the return to Armori. The main meeting room contained a large blackboard with close to two hundred names, all carefully chalked in five straight columns. Each entry corresponded to a construction order. The Gram Panchayat hoped to complete the list within five years, the duty official told us. He couldn't be certain, though. They were being short-changed as well, he'd claim. The bureaucrats above, they were simply skimming off too much for themselves.

I imagine the same line repeated by every official in turn, from the National Treasury downward. The result: more bureaucrats with bulging pockets, and a wall with little hope of ever getting rebuilt.

Jeevan, I suspect, could continue at length on the theme of government neglect. I try to shift the conversation on to a more forward-looking path. If a politician were to come here, what would you ask for? A lake tops his list. The village has three wells, all built more than three decades ago. It also has a pond. The latter is located behind the temple, its stagnant water insulated beneath a cap of green, luminescent algae.

He'd like a road as well. This second request brings me up short. A health centre, a properly staffed school, a mobile-phone mast: these would have made sense. But a road? Everything I've ever heard from indigenous-rights groups suggests that roads only bring trouble. It's a downhill spiral as far as they are concerned. Roads attract outsiders, who introduce external influences, which upsets the social fabric, which ultimately leads to a dilution of tribal culture.

'The village needs to travel to the market,' says Jeevan, his expression deadpan.

'But aren't you worried a road will bring more people to the village?'

Jeevan looks at me quizzically. 'We want people to come.'

The wizened old man responsible for the previous outburst shuffles noisily. Jeevan moves quickly to mollify him. 'Being adivasi means tradition to us,' the younger man qualifies. What traditions specifically, I ask. Worshipping the gods, he responds. Conscious that we're sat on sanctified ground, I push the point no further.

'Are you happy?' I ask instead. I meant the question collectively, rather than just Jeevan himself.

He smiles a forced smile. The older man is still listening. When Jeevan speaks again, his words are more measured and his posture more guarded. 'Yes,' he says, but with little conviction. 'This is a problem-less village.'

Amol is keen to be off. Rising from the floor, he taps his watch and motions that our visit is over. I thank Jeevan and climb back aboard Amol's motorbike. I turn to wave goodbye. Jeevan is standing alone again, back by the well, scratching his head.

'Hold tight, comrade,' Amol warns. The motorbike's wheels jar violently against the seared grooves of bullock carts as we navigate back through the woods. Created in the squelch of monsoon, the muddy rivulets have dried crisp in the sun. 'The path is not good,' he adds. The fact is self-evident. As is Jeevan's suggestion for a proper road.

Once we hit the tarmac, the journey back transforms itself into a magical ride. The sun sits high in the sky and a warm breeze rustles the crops. Wheat fields spread out towards the horizon in blankets of buttery gold. Beside them stretch acres of lush green paddy and groves of stubby mango trees with fruit so ripe their drooping branches nearly touch the floor. The bicycles of farm-hands lie in abandoned clusters by the roadside. The two-wheelers rest in the shade, their frames perched on the rubbery elbows of a handlebar like picnickers in the park.

Yet all is far from idyllic. Close to the border with Chhattis-garh, this remote district of eastern Maharashtra plays home to the most significant blot on the 'India Shining' story: the Nax-als or Naxalites. A disparate group of armed rebels, they first emerged in the late 1960s. Their fortunes have ebbed and flowed ever since.

Their ideology is vague (Maoism, they say; violent nihilism, their opponents), their public support is limited and their true strength is difficult to ascertain. All the same, they remain im-possible to ignore. Originating in West Bengal, the Naxals now extend across at least ten states, mostly in eastern and central In-dia. The area is dubbed the 'Red Corridor'.

Guerrilla attacks on police and army outposts are the Naxals' traditional speciality. They don't stop there. Their ambitions, like their firepower, have shown a recent shift in scale. In April 2010, a Naxal battalion killed seventy-six members of the Cent-ral Reserve Police Force less than one hundred kilometres away from here. Most of their intended victims wear uniform, al-though not all. Shortly after the blood-soaked ambush, they detonated an explosive on a bus in the same vicinity, killing forty people, including a good number of civilians. In the same month, the Naxals bombed the railway line as the Jnaneswari Express chugged its way from Kolkata to Mumbai. Over one hundred and forty passengers died.

In the wake of this glut of murderous blood-letting, Prime Minister Manmohan Singh described the rebel movement as the country's 'gravest internal security challenge'. He's since author-ised a massive military crackdown – codenamed Operation Green Hunt – to rid the country of the 'ultra' scourge.

Amol had warned me that Naxals operate in the region around Chavela. Only when we arrive back in Armori does he let on that the guerrillas had paid a visit to the village just two days beforehand. Suddenly the presence of our unspeaking pair of bodyguards makes sense. As does Jeevan's anxiety. Chavela, it seems, is anything but 'problem-less'.

We pull up outside the half-built house of Dr Manesh Kopulwar. Amol shows me up an open flight of concrete stairs to the first-floor apartment. We edge past a pile of bricks and cement, the building blocks of a future upward extension.

Dr Kopulwar, a moustached, middle-aged man of evident education and ill-concealed confidence, invites me to sit on the mottled armchair of his floral three-piece suite. Amol, Nandeep and the two silent minders squeeze onto the sofa beside me. Dressed in his home attire of shorts and shirt, the doctor sits cross-legged on the last remaining piece of furniture, a low-lying bed. He runs his own Ayurvedic practice. He is also district secretary for the Communist Party.

We make small talk about life in Armori and the local political scene as his wife prepares tea and biscuits. The noise of trucks passing along the Nagpur trunk road below competes with the hubbub from the market opposite. Conversation is difficult, although helped by our huddled seating arrangement.

Dr Kopulwar's wife arrives from the adjoining kitchen pushing a white plastic drinks trolley. Her appearance provides the opportunity for a switch in subject. I'm interested to know if the Naxals enjoy local support and, if so, why. Amol had been reluctant to be drawn on the question when I'd asked him earlier. He was a Marxist, he'd insisted. Naxals are Maoists. 'As the Communist Party of India (Marxist), we have no dealings with the Maoists.' He'd declined to elaborate. Dr Kopulwar strikes me as a straight talker and I try the same question on him.

All of a sudden, I'm grateful for the clatter outside. It allows the Communist leader to speak plainly, without fear of prying ears. Men need food, water, shelter, clothes, education and health, he tells me. These are the basic necessities. 'The tribals want these things. Because they are tribals, though, the government says development isn't necessary. Sometimes the government plans something for their development, but nothing happens.'

These communities are 'totally illiterate', he continues. 'Without education, how can they develop?' Of course, the government blames the Maoists. The Maoists don't want development, they say. 'Because of that, these communities are not developing. But that's not a fact. The government says this, but it's not a fact.'

He pauses a second or two, not in anticipation of an answer but to allow time for his point to sink in. The pregnant pause is one of several rhetorical habits picked up by Dr Kopulwar. Another is the ability to cast himself in his audience's shoes. Years of soap-box speech-making in Armori have infused the doctor's Marxist beliefs with a healthy dose of day-to-day reality.

'So what will these communities do? Their lack of education and their illiteracy means they cannot work. So they join the Nax-al movement because they have no employment. They say, "At least with the Naxals, we get some salary."'

He raises a hand of caution. The local Communist Party leader is anxious I don't assume that his knowledge on the subject is first-hand. The salary is something 'people tell me about', he insists. He can't verify the information. He's a Marxist, after all. Not a Maoist. Even so, he's adamant that most young people don't join the Naxals for ideological reasons. 'Most don't even know what the Maoists stand for. They just want to help their families and escape poverty.'

As with Jeevan, he talks at length about government interventions that promise much yet produce little. His list culminates with the Recognition of Forest Rights Act. The law exists to provide tribal communities with legal tenure to their ancestral lands. According to Dr Kopulwar, who has a politician's knack for churning out statistics with absolute authority, only twenty thousand two hundred and twenty-four applicants in Maharashtra have so far met with success. I ask the total number of applicants. 'Fifty-eight thousand,' he assures me, with equal confidence but marginally less precision. More than a third, then. Given India's reputation for red tape, the ratio doesn't sound too bad to me. 'But the government has so far actually given over very few lands,' he adds, as if guessing my train of thought and curtailing it.

If his party were to come to power, he'd follow Marxist principles and pursue social equality through land distribution. Electricity, fertilisers, water – whatever is needed to make agricultural land more productive – would be provided at a concessionary rate. That's what happened in West Bengal, he affirms. 'And the Communist Party of India (Marxist) has stayed in power for almost four decades.'

I had experienced Indian-style Communism during my stint in Kerala. In practice, the state seems to run much the same as any other: the same inefficiencies, the same complaints of corruption, the same volume of political infighting. Only in Kerala, there are more strikes than in any other state. With the exception of Communist-run West Bengal, perhaps. I say nothing.

'The tribals are trying for development, but whatever they need they are not getting,' Dr Kopulwar reasserts by way of conclusion.

'Exactly how are they trying?'

Unfairly, I feel, he takes the question as a slight. An awkward silence prevails. Amol begins work on the grime beneath his fingernails. Nandeep straightens and unstraightens his legs as if to relieve sudden muscle ache. Only the bodyguards remain unperturbed, smiling away. I wonder what it is that I've said.

Eventually, Dr Kopulwar points to the shorter of Amol's grinning companions. 'Without education, they cannot develop or think for themselves. They need to understand each and everything. Then they can do the development. Otherwise, they continue doing what they've been doing for generations.'

From Armori, I catch a bus to Gadchiroli, the next large town down the road and the district's capital. The same picturesque countryside unfolds outside the window. It ends abruptly as we enter the city limits.

Dust-covered houses and a down-at-heel pavement market replace the open fields and colour-soaked landscape. The market stalls are piled high with flip-flops, dark glasses, kitchen equipment, eggs, vegetables, CDs and bicycle tyres, all looking slightly sorry for themselves, like strays in a dog pound. Scraps of frayed festival bunting hang from a lamppost. Beneath it, a barber is giving his client an arm massage.

Gadchiroli's main roundabout is clogged with school kids on bikes, women riding pillion on motorbikes, rickshaws, goods carriers and the occasional rattling car. A yellow bus with 'Carmel School' plastered on the side trundles straight over the junction, oblivious to the traffic. A short avenue of oil-stained mechanics' shacks squashes along the roadside. The last has a billboard erected above it. Two young men are looking happy in front of a laptop screen. 'ME Mobile Excitement for You', reads the slogan. A cow arches its head in the direction of the advertisement and then, apparently resigning itself to a non-digitalised future, continues its plodding walk along the central reservation.

The town's two hotels are fully booked so I beg a room at the government guest house. Unlocking the door, I startle the occupying guest – a tiny brown mouse – and send him scuttling down the open latrine.

Evening is beginning to settle in by the time I arrive at the Deputy Collector's office. A journalist in Delhi had passed on his name to me as a helpful local source. In my experience, government officers know much and say little. Transparency is not part of their brief.

His run-down office building is located in an expansive government compound on the edge of town. The site is lined with trees and fenced by armed sentries. It's quiet. The atmosphere is inexplicably nervy, like a military base during a temporary armistice. A large herd of ambling goats is blocking the driveway. My taxi driver toots his horn. Both the goats and the dozing guard jump in fright.

Except for two or three staff rustling behind mounds of paperwork, the office is empty. I pick my way through a maze of pine cubicles to the Deputy Collector's room, which is situated at the far end behind a closed door. I knock and a voice invites me in. The room is painted lilac and empty of furniture but for a cabinet, a desk and six plastic chairs. The chairs are arranged in two rows of three, suggesting that the Deputy Collector is a man accustomed to receiving delegations of petitioners. I take a seat in the front row and place my notebook on the desk beside a freebie calendar from the Bank of India. The month of October is given over to the promotion of the Bank's mortgage products. 'A house is made of wall and beams,' the caption states. 'A home is built with love and dreams.' The words take me back to the collapsed building in Jeevan's village. The rudimentary house-building advice would provide the property's owner with cold comfort.

The Deputy Collector, Mr Rajendra Kanphade, is sat across the desk from me. He is not at all what I expect. Dressed in a light purple shirt buttoned to the neck, the senior civil servant has a mane of long white hair, which is combed back and tied into a ponytail. There's a slightly wild look in his eye. His skin is dark and leathery, and his body as thin as a flagpole. Pens protrude from his top pocket. There is little to his look that suggests a government bureaucrat approaching retirement. If I had to guess, I'd say he was a magician.

A tall clerk with a limp comes in. He's holding a selection of papers. Orange labels are stuck to the pages that require signing. The Deputy Collector removes one of his pens, scribbles his name in the requisite places and shunts the pile down the table. The clerk hobbles out.

'I was recently in Sweden,' he starts, as his departing assistant closes the door.

I'd hoped we could talk about rural development issues and, more particularly, about the Naxalite movement. But I'm on the Deputy Collector's turf, so hear him out. What follows is, like his appearance, unexpected. Mr Kanphade's trip to Europe was motivated not by work or tourism, I learn, but competitive sport. He is an amateur diver. One-metre springboard, to be precise. He picked up the sport nine years ago at the recreation club for government officials and now competes in the world masters series. His passion for diving has taken him to Italy as well. Gadchiroli's lack of a swimming pool hampers his practice, however. To hone his skills, he needs to travel three hours to Nagpur – something he tries to do on a weekly basis.

The story has a purpose beyond showing me his certificates (which he does). Several purposes, in fact. The first is to stress his alternative credentials. It quickly becomes clear that there is little orthodox about the Deputy Collector. For starters, he claims to have joined the civil service with a desire to 'mend the system'. In a similar vein, he maintains an absolute abhorrence of violence, 'legal or illegal'. Likewise, he says he's vehemently opposed to corruption. Sitting in his government office, he cites example after example of crooked behaviour by his colleagues. Such sentiments have not made him popular. Early on in his career, he tried to put a stop to an illegal timber operation. The loggers were in cahoots with local officials, paying them off to turn a blind eye to their chainsaws as they stripped bare an area of protected forest. His boss reprimanded him. If he didn't like the way things were done, he was told, then he should 'go back to teaching' (a reference to his former profession).

The Deputy Collector's long trips to Nagpur contain a wider message too. Gadchiroli lacks more than just a pool. According to the senior official, the district's one million inhabitants are served by only eighteen kilometres of railway track. They are also short on doctors. Twenty-five of the thirty-one senior medical posts in the region remain vacant. The state of the schools is woefully substandard too. Nearly four hundred school buildings are judged to be 'on the verge of collapse'. A similar number have no electricity.

In terms of industry, there's a large pulp and paper plant seventy kilometres out of town. The rest is small fry: a bakery, an ice-cream factory, a rice mill, a tile manufacturer, a couple of furniture makers. None is a big employer. Several mining companies have talked of developing the region's rich iron-ore deposits. That would be a shot in the arm for the local economy. Were they to start digging, that is. As yet, none has.

Three-fifths of the district's inhabitants qualify as 'rural'. Gadchiroli boasts almost one thousand seven hundred villages. The vast majority (ninety-eight per cent) of their inhabitants are tribals: mostly Gonds, plus a splattering of Madia, Pardham and Kolam tribespeople. In as much as they can, they live off the land.

Yields are poor, and hunger common. All bar a few subsist below the poverty level. According to the Indian government, Gadchiroli is officially classified as a 'Backward Region'.

I tell the maverick administrator about my trip to Chavela and its lack of amenities. He doesn't seem surprised. He knows far worse cases, he tells me. Three months back, for example, he visited a village called Beenagonda. Located at the very limits of the Gadchiroli district, in the dense forests of Abujmarh, the isolated settlement is home to thirty-five huts and two hundred and nineteen residents. Beenagonda has no roads and no electricity. The nearest market is fifty-seven kilometres away.

The only evidence of the State is an ashram school and a rural health centre. Of the fourteen teachers on the payroll, he found only three at their posts. The Deputy Collector's assessment report talks of blocked school toilets, roofless bathrooms and leaking classrooms. The health centre earned an equally unfavourable verdict. It lacked both a doctor and medicines. Undocumented, the village's tribal residents have never benefited from a government welfare scheme. Beenagonda has two wells: one dry, the other clogged up. Its inhabitants make do with muddy water from a stream.

The remote village has another defining characteristic. It is situated deep in the heart of 'Naxal infested' territory. According to army intelligence, the left-wing guerrilla group runs training camps and explosive-manufacturing units in the surrounding forests. The hillsides are said to be planted with landmines to keep the army at bay.

The nearest settlement is the village of Leheri, about twenty kilometres away. It has a small police barracks. A year before the Deputy Collector's visit, Naxal gunmen ambushed the remote outpost and shot seventeen policemen dead. The road runs out in the same spot. So it was there that the official alighted from his jeep and began his trek into the hilly forests to Beenagonda. He was on government business. His boss, the Collector, had ordered an appraisal of all the tribal schools in the region and had assigned the inaccessible adivasi village to his deputy.

The Deputy Collector is frank about his reasons for going. Fulfilling his assignment was, at best, only a part of his motivation to risk his life trekking through hostile terrain to reach Been-agonda. A secret, ulterior motive drove him too. He hoped to run into some Naxals. Startled, I ask why. His overriding interest, he reiterates, is the development of the district. Gadchiroli's 'back-wardness' is often blamed on the guerrilla insurgents. They scare away investors, it's said, and hold the tribals back. He wanted to hear from them if that was true.

The local police chief said he couldn't guarantee his safety. A team of government-funded welfare officers had tried carrying out a census of Abujhmad's tribal population earlier in the year. The Naxals had forcibly refused them access. The only other serious attempt to map the area had happened during Akbar's reign, five centuries ago. That, too, had been stymied by the aggression of its inhabitants. The Deputy Collector resolved to take his chances. With considerable persuasion, he managed to persuade seven others to join him.

What followed has become the subject of much talk in the district. After forty-eight hours, no word had been received from the senior government official or his team. Local villagers reported seeing the group wading through a river a short way out of Le-heri. After that, nothing. Total silence. The security forces feared the worst and hit the panic button. A call was put in to the home minister. A police search party was dispatched. Local scouts were recruited. Within hours, news of a major kidnapping on the Ma-harashtra–Chhattisgarh border was running across TV bulletin boards.

Then late on the second day, the white-haired diver walked out of the forest. Tired and wet, but otherwise unharmed, he was surprised by all the fuss. He was immediately escorted back to Gadchiroli. A press conference was hastily arranged. The Collect-or bustled him out in front of the cameras and ordered him to scotch the rumours of a kidnapping. The Deputy obliged. But he went further. Not only did he say that the Naxalites had caused him no harm, he accused the security forces of inciting violence.

The comment was occasioned by an experience on the drive back, when a uniformed policeman ordered him out of his official car at gunpoint. 'In the so-called "dreaded Naxal area", no Naxal attacked me with a gun,' he explains. 'But when I came back into my own area, my own police showed me the gun.'

The listening journalists lapped it up. A second media frenzy ensued. His superiors went ballistic. An official case was launched against him for 'demoralising' state security forces and 'glorifying' the Naxals. The investigation remains ongoing.

We both sit in silence for a few seconds. A government official apparently sympathising with the enemy. The Deputy Collector really is an intriguing mix. Has he always harboured such feelings, I wonder, or did his trip into the forest spark some kind of Damascene conversion? The thought sparks another question: did he achieve his hidden objective? Did he actually meet with the Naxals? I ask him straight.

The question is met with an ambiguous reply: 'I didn't meet anyone who declared themselves to be a Naxal.'

'So you did meet with the Naxals, then?'

He merely repeats the statement again, although this time with a knowing smile.

And so it is that we fall into a hypothetical discussion about what the Naxals might have said had he met them. The conversation becomes peppered with caveats and comic conditionals. 'There are reports that . . .' 'Some people say . . .' 'Everyone knows . . .' For all his attempts at subterfuge, his true feelings lie close to the surface. The Naxals, he'd ultimately concluded, are not against development. 'They are against exploitation.' It's true that they might oppose roads and bridges. This, he maintains, is only because better transportation is designed for the authorities to get into the forest and not for the tribespeople to get out.

Nor does he subscribe to the general view that the Naxals abuse tribal communities. They're 'friendly', he says. If they were to ask for food, 'let's suppose', then they'd pay for it. The only ones at risk are teachers. 'Teach well,' they tell them, 'or you'll be in trouble.' Perhaps that's why so many absented themselves,

I suggest. He shrugs. Naturally, he 'wouldn't know'. He's merely repeating what he's heard.

I shift tack. If he can't tell me directly what the Naxals say, what do the villagers say about them? Are they sympathetic?

He lightens up. Speaking to the villagers was, after all, part of the official reason he'd been sent to Beenagonda. Some of them do support the Naxals, he confirms. I ask why. He takes one of the pens from his pocket and begins to scribble doodles on a sheet of paper. 'The old generation of adivasi, they are content,' he eventually responds. 'But this new generation has no direction. They have no employment or means of livelihood. Yet they are exposed to the luxurious life. They are confused and . . .'

He drops into Hindi, struggling for the word in English.

'Frustrated?' I suggest.

'Yes, frustration. They have very much frustration.'

He draws two mountains on the sheet of paper in front of him. With the tip of his pen, he points to the valley between them. The tribals are on one side and the 'civilised' world on the other. One in the light, he says, the other in darkness. 'They have their own traditions, values and culture, but they have been told that they must come into the mainstream. They are being shown luxuries they don't know how to achieve.' The Naxals play on that, he says. Their tactics are sometimes crude. They pay new recruits a start-up fee, for instance. Unlike Dr Kopulwar, he's prepared to put a figure on it. Three thousand rupees. 'It's an open secret.'

In other ways, their methods show more subtlety. Many adivasi groups oppose plans to develop the region's mineral deposits on the grounds that it will mean the appropriation and denuding of tribal lands. The guerrilla group took up their cause and made it their own. Posters began appearing that pledged never to concede an inch to 'Capitalists and Imperialists'. The tribals remember the guerrilla for previous interventions too: fights for fairer pay for forest products like tendu leaves (the base ingredient for beedi cigarettes) and bamboo; protection from heavy-handed forestry officials; retaliation against murderous paramilitaries.

Faced with an indifferent, often violent State on the one hand, and an illegal but armed defence force on the other, the choice for many tribals is simple. As the Deputy Collector concludes: 'In a sense, they [the Naxals] are the messiahs of the poor.'

I turn the conversation to the district's other gun-touting group, the security services. With mention of the police, he relaxes his charade of impartiality. Perhaps because of what he sees as his own unfair treatment or perhaps because he no longer cares, he's content to speak his own mind. 'The police are more violent than the Naxals,' he insists. 'Ask anyone in Gadchiroli and they will tell you the same.'

He has his own theory as to why this is. He thinks the police are exaggerating the movements of the Naxalites to spread fear among the population. Fifty-seven deaths in three decades. The Naxalite rap sheet in Gadchiroli is bad, he admits, but it doesn't merit the huge security resources being poured into the area. There are currently around nine thousand state and paramilitary forces in the district, ranging from everyday police to specially trained anti-terrorist commandos. No one can be sure how many fully fledged Naxals there are, but official estimates put it at no more than three hundred. The Deputy Collector spies a racket. 'In defining this as a "Naxal-affected district", the security forces get more funds and facilities. That's the root cause.'

As corruption stories go, it's one of the more extreme I've heard yet: the police misrepresenting the terror threat so as to keep their budgets augmenting. I have a hunch his mind is set and, without any evidence to the contrary, I leave it there.

Instead, I focus the time we have left on the positive spin he gives the Naxals. Before arriving in the backwater town, I'd done a quick survey of newspaper reports from the district. Stories abound of tribals being dragged from their homes by guerrilla soldiers. Each account finishes in the same fashion: with the individuals being branded 'informants' and summarily executed. The Deputy Collector does not refute the practice. 'I never said the Naxals are good,' he insists. 'My version is that the police are worse.' The Naxals, he continues, carry out 'targeted killings'.

The violence unleashed by the police, in contrast, is 'unlimited' and 'random'.

Just two days ago, a fire-fight had broken out between security forces and a Naxalite unit in the tribal village of Sawargaon, not far from Gadchiroli. During the confrontation, a grenade was lobbed into the school. Four died instantly – two pupils, a female cook and a villager. Another pupil died later of his injuries. All the reports suggest it was the Naxals' doing. What's that if not random violence? The Deputy Collector sees things differently. Who's to say it was the Naxals who threw the grenade? The police. And who's to say they can be trusted? I feel myself being drawn into his web of distrust and double-guessing. As with all conspiracy theories, suddenly nothing seems clear-cut. I sense it's time to finish off.

We've been talking for over three hours as it is. Outside, the last of the light has long passed. The Deputy Collector toys with his top button, smiling as he does so. He rocks back in his chair.

There is something I should know, he says confidentially. He is currently on suspension. His salary has been frozen for the last three months. His debts are mounting (he paid for his Swedish trip by credit card). A second investigation has now been brought out against him, this time for 'unauthorised leave'. His bosses allege that his diving vacation in Europe had not been officially sanctioned – something that the indicted official fiercely disputes.

The Deputy Collector is evidently something of a loose cannon. How much truth there is to his theories of duplicity and state-sponsored violence is unclear. I have my doubts. If Gadchiroli was such a lucrative posting, for example, why are roughly half the senior posts in the collectorate vacant? Yet his description of the tribals' wretchedness rings true. And the idea that the Naxalite movement (though far from being messianic) might be somehow related to that wretchedness sounds plausible too.

What seems certain beyond doubt is that the system the Deputy Collector once hoped to change is now turning in against him. His questioning of official doctrine – namely, that Naxals are a nihilist menace and a stain on the face of New India – has lost him any support that he may once have enjoyed.

The censured official is not the only one to fall foul of the establishment. Booker Prize winner Arundhati Roy recently wrote a cover story for the popular weekly magazine *Outlook* in which she linked the Naxal phenomenon to the 'downward spiral of indigence' experienced by India's tribal population. The article elicited a furore of abuse. One leading academic compared her to Carl Schmitt, Hitler's apologist. The Chhattisgarh police even threatened to charge her under the state's draconian Public Safety Act. In the case of Dr Binayak Sen, a human rights activist and vocal Naxal sympathiser, the authorities delivered on their threat. The sixty-one-year-old was recently convicted for sedition and sentenced to life imprisonment.

Naxals are not welcome in New India. That much is understandable. Yet the Naxals' cause and the tribals' plight are not one and the same, however the guerrillas or the government try to spin it. It's possible to object to the first and still support the tribals' struggle. Yet the space to do so is shrinking. As the two issues continue to be confused, so the Red Corridor will carry on being a place for outsiders – be they armed or otherwise.

The next day, I travel out to Mendha Lekha. I had been feeling out of sorts ever since leaving the Deputy Collector's office the previous night. After so many months on the trail of New India, such an abrupt return to the Old had left me confused and despondent.

Returning to the spartan hostel, I'd spent a sleepless night. The desperation still apparent in India's forgotten hinterlands depressed me. Travelling through India provides endless scope for wonderment in face of the poverty and inequality, which remains so transparently evident.

The blueness derived from somewhere else, though. Perhaps it was the sheer extent of the mess in Gadchiroli that had dampened my spirits? The forgotten tribals, the duplicitous administrators, the aggressive police, the outcast guerrillas. The district seemed stuck in a never-ending mire of poverty and recrimination. Elsewhere there had always been hope, a chance to leap the fence. The problems here seemed not only widespread, but intractable too.

As I lay awake, I'd tried telling myself that the development quagmire of this little-visited corner of Eastern Maharashtra should come as no surprise. Sucking in resources, seeing them disappear without trace. It was frustrating to watch, but hardly a novelty. Old India had been at it for decades. Did I really expect it to loosen its grip so easily? Only fools – and some quarters of the foreign press – still bought the 'Shining India' story. Everyone accepted it was mostly myth and marketing, and only a small part truth.

India is a nation on the up. Until now, this sense of transition, of a country on the move, had given me a degree of assurance. The theory had served me well. As much a defence mechanism as an explanation, it provided a way of comprehending the contradictions hurled at me, a means of stopping India's daily discrepancies from overwhelming and consuming me.

I hold to it still. As I do to its corollary – the idea of India having yet to arrive. That much seems indisputable. The uneven pace of change announces itself at almost every turn. The nation is cluttered with pillars of progress and signs of stasis. Nor, I'd wager, will the country arrive together. India is travelling at multiple speeds and, as often as not, in multiple directions. New India is a story of fits and starts, not linear progression.

This and more I'd repeated to myself. But unlike before, the reasoning provided little succour. Sleep stubbornly refused to come.

As I waited for dawn, listening to the scratching of mice in the darkness, I'd had to concede that life in this blighted corner of Central India had caught me off-guard.

Maybe it was partly my fault, this cultural blindsiding? In coming here, I had broken with routine. Usually, I travel by land wherever practical. In India, that invariably means the train. I like its steady, predictable pace. I enjoy the reassuring sound of its wheels rattling along the tracks. Land travel helps me adjust too, allowing me to gradually sink into whatever waits ahead as the world slips by outside the window.

On this occasion, however, for reasons of time and logistics, I'd flown. Catching a morning shuttle from Delhi to Nagpur, I'd plopped in from the sky. The experience proved disorientating. Physically, I arrived with my baggage, but my thoughts and tempo remained in the country's energetic, non-stop capital.

Tuned to a faster frequency, my antenna for the New had instinctively begun twitching as soon as we touched down. It honed in on the chrome trusses of the airport arrivals hall. It drew my eye to the widely publicised slogans of a local conglomerate: 'Vision Unlimited. Growth Infinite' (beside a picture of electric pylons), 'Illuminating Lives' (alongside a power plant), 'Strengthening the Nation (beside a steel plant). Three days in Gadchiroli district and my mind had finally caught up with me. It had brought with it a restless night and a suitcase of questions.

Dislocation explained much of my mood, but not all of it. A sense of ill ease lay at its fringe, a circle of what I could only describe as foreboding. The first trickle of morning light brought with it a possible source. It came as a revelation. No, more of a warning sign. I was in danger, I realised. In danger of pushing India further than it wanted to go.

It was my old mistake. As a starry-eyed backpacker, I'd longed for this land – so exotic, so far from home – to romance and entice me. It hadn't always, of course. But like an obdurate lover, blind to his partner's spurning, I'd ignored all hints of disaffection. Now I found myself beginning to desire something from India once again. Not to embrace me, this time. I was seeking something else. I was seeking it to dazzle me. I wanted it to regale me with its new wardrobe of glittering modernity, and prove to me just how snugly the costume fitted.

On leaving that morning, a sign at the door of the government hostel had temporarily lifted my spirits. It detailed 'six impressive words' in bold print. The list was devoted to common courtesies, such as 'I made a mistake' and 'If you please'. Their 'unimpressive' antonym was tacked onto the bottom, the 'ego-cage' of which the Bhagavad Gita speaks, the one-letter word 'I'. The sign's intent seemed so far from common practice that it made me chuckle. But it was a sardonic kind of pleasure that passed as soon as it arrived.

Any residue of good humour had been wiped clean by my visit to Gadchiroli hospital. In a whitewashed ward illuminated by crude striplights and smelling of disinfectant and sadness lay four survivors from the grenade attack. Their wounds were cosseted beneath bandages. Their faces, blank and unresponsive. They had no idea who was responsible for the attack. Only that five of their classmates were now dead. I left, glummer than ever.

So, sat in Mendha Lenka's IT centre, watching twenty-seven-year-old Charandas tap away at a computer keyboard, it took me a while to plug in to what he was saying.

The son of one of the community's leaders, Charandas follows Jeevan in looking much younger than his years. Dressed in grey cotton trousers and a green T-shirt, he is wearing a scarf despite the heat. 'Love Rd', his T-shirt reads. 'One Way: Do Not Enter.'

'People outside think of us as backward,' he remarks, swivelling his chair away from the computer screen and addressing me directly.

I'm sat on the floor. There's that word again, 'backward'. Its mention pulls me back to the present. I ask if he agrees.

'They think we can't be like them,' he says. 'But we can.'

Charandas has just completed a six-month computer repair course at the Oxford Institute in Gadchiroli, thirty kilometres away. As with Chavela, Mendha Lenka is a tribal village. No one owns a car, so to get to class he'd walk to the nearby highway and catch the bus.

'The backward people are coming to the front right now. And our people don't come in front just so we can improve agriculture. Here, look at this.'

He turns back to the computer, clicks the mouse and brings up a short video. The film is bucolic, scene after scene of rural harmony and Gandhian simplicity: women drawing water from wells, a herd of healthy-looking heifers (out of respect for mother and calf, the adivasi don't milk their cattle), children in blue uniforms hopping to school, oxen pulling carts of hay, villagers threshing rice, a community meeting in the village square. All the while, a simple folk song is playing out in the background. For the final frame, the camera closes in on a message carved onto a board just outside the IT centre. 'We have our government in Mumbai and Delhi,' it proclaims. 'But in our village, we ourselves are the government.'

Mendha Lekha is no ordinary adivasi village. Under the decades-long tutelage of Baba Ante, a recently deceased community activist, it has become a model for self-empowerment. Charandas's father, the serious and bespectacled Devaji, had earlier taken me through the village's guiding philosophy.

Sitting in the community hall, a fan keeping us cool, he'd talked me through the battle to reassert their traditional rights and livelihoods. He'd spoken of how they'd blocked a large paper mill from extracting bamboo at penurious rates, how they'd rebuilt the road from the highway, how they were harvesting forest fruits and how they were generating cash from bottling purified honey and making soap. The village is currently embarking on a plan to make electricity from biomass. It's also launching a line in bamboo furniture and other forest-based handicrafts.

There were two achievements of which Devaji was particularly proud. The first occurred the previous year. After much agitation, Mendha Lekha finally won the right to manage its traditional forest lands. Other villages would follow, but for once Gadchiroli district could claim to be leading the way. The governor himself had come in person to preside over the transfer. The landmark event made the front page of the *Times of India*.

By way of background, Devaji had handed me a booklet describing the fight. It was, it would appear, a long one, dating back to the 'period of slavery' under the British and the 'encroachment [on] natural and traditional rights'. The document went on to describe how, after Independence, the country's forests had fallen entirely under government control. Adivasi like Devaji saw this as a calumny. From one moment to the next, a tribesperson became a criminal for collecting wood. 'Indians became free,' he'd continued, talking of the onset of democratic rule. 'The tribals, though, we became slaves.' A legal amendment in favour of community-managed forests is at last reversing that injustice.

Devaji had given me another booklet too. It was entitled 'Consensus Decision Making' and it constituted Mendha Lekha's second accomplishment of note. 'Everyone makes the decision for everyone. That is the option that this village had opted for,' he'd explained. Wasn't that a touch utopian, I'd asked? That has been the view of many in the past, he'd admitted. The booklet contained thirty-seven pages, each one of them a guide to how such an approach could be achieved. He and his fellow villagers were proving its effectiveness page by page. Could he give me some examples? 'Everything,' he'd said. He wasn't lying. From banning alcohol in the village right down to the brand name for the handicraft business ('Bamboo Vishwa', or 'Bamboo World'), every decision had passed through a public vote.

Back in the IT centre, I ask Charandas about city life. What does he think of it? Would he like to live there? As with Jeevan, I'm keen to know how he compares the supposedly 'developed' world to his rural reality.

He had once been to Delhi to attend a workshop. He tells me about the experience. Much of what he saw was new to him. He went by train, a means of transport he'd only previously seen on television. 'I didn't know how fast it goes. I didn't know, for example, how to buy a ticket. I didn't know how the bathrooms would be. All these things I learned.'

Delhi left him with other lessons too: the fact that Indian women could smoke (in Mendha Lekha, such a practice is frowned upon), that the only potable water comes from a plastic bottle, and that too much traffic makes the sky turn grey.

Charandas came back unimpressed. He saw nothing in the national capital that he would like for his village. Everything there is dirty and dangerous. 'If we made houses like they have in Delhi, we would have a water problem. And it wouldn't be good to dress here as the people do in Delhi.'

I'm not sure quite whether to believe him, and ask if there really is nothing that he saw that would improve life in the village. He thinks for a while. Some more computer hardware wouldn't go a miss, he admits. Especially a fax machine and Internet. 'This would facilitate communication with others.' It's the same desire to reach out that Jeevan had expressed in his longing for a road.

The two men have other views in common. Charandas also identifies lack of employment opportunities as a burden on his village. 'Our lives can change only once our economic status changes,' he says. He repeats Jeevan's scepticism about government programmes too. Right now, development schemes are dreamt up by people in Delhi and Mumbai, he complains. 'What do they know about the situation in the villages?' If Charandas could have things his way, he'd have all public funding given directly to the villages themselves. Not even the Gram Panchayat should get their hands on it. 'This would help avoid corruption,' he insists. 'People get elected, then all they care about is their own needs.'

Despite their commonalities, the two young men are actually cut from very different cloth. Brought up on a diet of political theory and self-empowerment workshops, Devaji's son is as confident as Jeevan is diffident. The computer technician doesn't reject 'developed' India because it has no space or jobs for him. He rejects it because he and his fellow villagers are creating their own version of the future. That is why he has no time for the Naxals either. Their goals ('people's progress') are the same, he states, but their methods are different. Whereas the Naxals believe in change through violence, the residents of Mendha Lekha advocate dialogue. 'Discussion takes time. But a gun takes just five minutes.'

He laughs, and I laugh with him.

Listening to Charandas is lightening my mood, I realise. It's partly what he says. His thinking is undeniably cogent and progressive. To cite just one example: the villagers drink from the village well every day, yet when the water goes bad or dries up, they never think to resolve the problem themselves. Why? Because it was the government who built it and therefore it's the government's job to fix it. 'Development can't come from the government, it has to come from us,' he tells me.

Policies for the people by the people. Taking responsibility. Governing for themselves. Creating a sense of ownership. It's all inspiring stuff. He is indeed his father's son.

Yet, it's how he speaks, that slowly rekindles my confidence in the Newness of India. Every word arrives primed with self-belief and optimism, a sucker punch of hope. He's not bowed by the breadth and depth of the problems facing him and his community. Nor does he waste his energies in blame games and criticism. Everything is poured into bringing about change to the realities around him – thinking of it, planning it, effecting it.

He clicks back to a computerised catalogue for Bamboo World and enthusiastically takes me through the pictures. Product after product flashes up: chairs, soap holders, spoons, lampshades, fruit bowls, ornaments, place mats, jewellery, beds, cupboards, garden chairs, even a bar counter. The village has just struck a deal with a local exporter, he tells me.

As Charandas finishes and closes the computer, my attention drifts off to the noises outside. With most out at work in the fields, the village is left to the animals. Nearby a goat is bleating. Two dogs bark at each other, one gruff, the other screechy. Behind us, far off, a cockerel lets out a shrill, distant crow. I realise with shame that the only alien noise is the tinny sound of the radio in my taxi driver's car.

It would be easy to idealise the rustic simplicity of Mendha Lekha. In reality, life is far from perfect. Like anywhere else, residents fight and the best-laid plans sometimes fail. Many of the adults remain illiterate and the ill can lack proper care. As for facilities, the primary school could be bigger and the health centre better equipped. For many core amenities – a hospital, a bank, a secondary school, a dentist, a market, even a shop – they have to travel miles. And the public transport is slow and unreliable.

Even so, sitting there, on the floor of the IT centre, with its one computer and single scanner-printer, I utter silent thanks to Charandas. A thanks for renewing my focus, for reminding me that progress isn't quantified only in the material, for reawakening me to the upbeat, optimistic spirit of New India. It's that which dazzles so.

I pick up Devaji's booklets and move towards the doorway. As I turn to go, a final question occurs to me. Are there more examples like Mendha Lekha? Charandas shakes his head. He wishes there were. Why not? Lack of knowledge, he replies in a shot. 'Many are still not educated.'

The comment reminds me of my conversation with Dr Kopulwar. Education, he'd said, is the gateway to development. The Deputy Collector's disgust at Beenagonda's ashram school was similarly motivated. Could education really be so fundamental to breaking the curse of India's so-called 'backwardness'?

I leave Gadchiroli the following day. Next time I'm close to a computer, I look up the key statistics for India's educational performance. The facts are startling. Literacy levels among the adivasi are among the worst in India. The problem does not end there, though. A third of the world's illiterates live in India. Around one in four (twenty-seven per cent) of young people between thirteen and thirty-five cannot read or write. Hidden within those numbers is a learning divide. Literacy rates are only rising half as fast in the overcrowded cities as they are in rural areas. Girls, meanwhile, are ten per cent less likely to enrol in secondary school as boys.

India's leaders are not blind to the gulf between the educational 'knows' and 'know-nots'. The fact that the ranks of India's poor, malnourished and generally disadvantaged are filled with illiterates is now widely recognised. In Delhi, moves are under way to try and resolve the problem. With much fanfare, Parliament recently passed a bill enshrining every Indians' fundamental right to education. From now on, the law holds that all those aged between six and fourteen years must be given a shot at formal schooling. Crores of rupees are being thrown at the target.

Any changes will take time to kick in. For the moment, India's public education system remains permeable, leaking teachers and losing some children altogether. I travel across the country to meet a voluntary group trying to plug the holes.

9

Teach for India

[education]

'My shoulders are aching from carrying books. My father says if
you get 99 per cent you get a watch, if you get less than that you
get a cane.'

Lyrics to a popular Bollywood hit

Vijayawada

Jayaraj pulls up on Sri Konada Prakash Rao Road. The narrow
street is devoid of shops and unusually empty for an Indian city
in the mid-afternoon. We alight and edge past a couple of rusty
parked cars. A destitute-looking cow is nosing through the roadside rubbish. His coat is patchy and his hind legs caked in mud.
He turns his head, appraising us with a stare that's both jealous
and threatening, as if warning us to beat it from his patch and go
find our own to pilfer.

A brick wall runs up from the junction of the road. We follow
it as far as a doorway. The gate rests ajar. Slumped with his back
against the gatepost sits Guravaiah. He is an adivasi, from the
Dommara community, one of millions of tribals to have gravit-
ated to India's cities in search of work. Verging on the obese, the
middle-aged migrant sports a bushy seafarer's beard. The top of
his head is equally overrun with hair, as if by leaving it to grow
wild his facial appearance can obtain equilibrium.

Jayaraj asks after his health. The two seem to know each other
a little. He can hardly move, he replies, making a show of trying
to rise to his feet and failing. His back has gone. Jayaraj commis-
erates. The two talk for a while about his condition and possible
remedies. For much of his adult life, Guravaiah has worked as

a rickshaw puller. In more recent years, he traded up the hand-drawn cart for a cycle version.

The gateway gives way to a courtyard. Guravaiah invites us in. A small, padlocked bungalow is situated on the left. Behind, running down the slope towards the banks of a canal, is an attractive, tree-lined garden. The immediate area is paved, with a smart black jeep parked in one corner. The car belongs to the landlord.

Guravaiah acts as gatekeeper. The task extends to his wider family. Three women – one per generation by the looks of it – lie strewn on the tiles. A jumbled assortment of infants and young children are sprinkled among them.

Guravaiah's son-in-law works as a servant in a low-grade hotel. His income is pitiful and falls far short of what's required to keep everyone fed. The younger two women – the gatekeeper's wife Jamalamma and twenty-year-old daughter – go out to earn as well. During the day, they work as rag-pickers, sifting through the city's garbage bins. At night, they prostitute themselves.

The family's adopted home of Vijayawada in Andhra Pradesh serves as the main train junction for southern India. Hundreds of passenger and freight trains pass through this hot, dog-eared city every day. It has a sprawling business park for heavy industry, an automotive district for the production of car body parts and very little else. Vijayawada's tourist office must have a hard time selling the place.

Because of the city's role as a rail hub, however, people are always passing through. Most are men, lorry drivers in the main. The sex trade is, as a consequence, one of the few boom industries in this city of transients. Rates of HIV/AIDS also run frighteningly high. For the most part, Jamalamma and her daughter don't have to tout for work. The city's canal banks (Vijayawada has three canals in total, all of them black and swollen with filth) have a reputation as red-light areas. Both women have regular clients.

It's Jayaraj, not Guravaiah, who gives me the family's back-story. Many Dommara women work in the sex trade, he tells me. For them, as for a handful of other tribal communities, prostitution has become a 'traditional occupation'. Like carpentry or shoe-mending or rag-picking even.

Jamalamma stretches and wakes from her afternoon nap. Surprised to find her husband with visitors, she quickly rises to her feet and brushes down her hair with the flat of her hand. She straightens her sari, which is wrinkled from her nap but otherwise perfectly set. She approaches with a diffident smile. Short and plump, she resembles her daughter, who also begins to stir. Then a baby wakes and soon the entire courtyard is brought to life.

I ask Guravaiah if we might see the canal. He nods to his wife, who offers to accompany us. She heads across the courtyard to a brick wall that runs the length of the garden. A section has fallen down, providing a convenient way through to the next-door lot. Through the rubble-strewn gap lies an empty plot. The earth is bare except for some piles of redundant building materials and a cluster of weeds.

The barefooted Jamalamma ushers us through the gap. A line of industrial sacks balances against the wall on the other side. Each is full of used plastic bottles and other recyclable goods, the product of her daytime labours. A short distance in front stands a makeshift tent. It's the family home. Constructed with plastic sheeting and supported by a bamboo frame, it is held down by bricks and contains everything they own. There is no bed. Nor is there any side netting. There are, however, several more bags of scrap.

Parked next to the tent is Guravaiah's cycle rickshaw. The frame is chipped and the seat much worn, but it looks still to be in working order. 'Care and Share', the name of the Catholic charity for whom Jayaraj works, can just be made out on the metal base of the rear passenger cabin. Guruvaiah bought it through a discounted loan scheme.

A high wire fence runs along the bottom of the lot, separating the land from the water's edge. The boundary is riddled with holes, each just large enough for an adult to squeeze through. On the legal side of the fence, a group of women is washing their

TEACH FOR INDIA   261

laundry. The wire doubles as a clothes line. The opposite bank
is strewn with discarded rubbish. The open garbage heap covers
every inch of space, a contagion of plastic and general detritus. A
man is squatting at the water's edge, defecating. I've seen enough
of the canal and Jamalamma shepherds us back.

Before leaving, Guravaiah calls Jayaraj aside. He has a favour
to ask. The charity worker bends down to hear him better. The
bearded adivasi presses his hands together in the sign of petition.
In a quiet, pleading voice, he mentions his two youngest sons,
Chinna and Pullaiah. He beckons them over. The pair are lurking
on the edge of the courtyard, watching inquisitively. They wander
over to their father's side and position themselves shoulder to
shoulder as if for inspection.

Aged seven and eight respectively, both boys are slightly built
and dressed in little more than rags. Their heads are shaven and
their faces blistered with heat spots. Neither goes to school. Could
Jayaraj take them, Guravaiah wants to know? Find a place for
them in one of the charity's care homes? He would dearly wish
to see them educated. The charity worker promises to do what he
can and bids farewell.

Jayaraj restarts the engine and drives off. He talks breezily of
the day's agenda. He's arranged for me to visit a selection of Care
and Share's education initiatives around the city. The first is just
across the other side of the canal. We traipse into Ginny's Home.
The kindergarten occupies a collection of bare rooms above a
noisy mechanic's workshop. Around fifty tribal children attend
regularly. All are the offspring of commercial sex workers.

'You see the showers here,' he says. 'The children have a wash
at the beginning of every day.' I peer into the miniature shower
block. 'Every week, their hair is washed with a special shampoo.'
He itches his head. 'For the lice.'

Ten minutes later, we traipse out again. Jayaraj is efficient.
Anxious for us to keep to time, he almost jogs to the car. I follow,
my heels dragging a little. I am still trying to process our brief
stop at the river bank. A jumble of thoughts is running through
my head, not least the description of prostitution as a 'traditional'

career. Wouldn't 'indentured' be a fairer description? Isn't that the truth of being born into such a life, a life in which choice is limited to hunger on the one hand or degradation on the other?

I want to ask Jayaraj, but sense he wouldn't understand. Not because he doesn't care. He does. His manner may be mild and his speech sometimes curt, but these traits conceal a generous and giving heart. It's just that for him – working in Vijayawada's slums, spending his days with those on the very lowest rung of the Indian ladder – such realities mark nothing new. For his constituents, hard choices represent the daily norm. That may be unpleasant, but it's a fact.

What would confuse him, I suspect, is that after so many months in India I should continue to be surprised.

Jayaraj is not resigned either. He would like to see things change. And it is for that reason, among others, that I have come to see him.

'We used to take poor children from wherever,' says Jayaraj, as we head up the stairs to Care and Share's main office. 'But now we focus specifically on children from slum communities.'

Vijayawada is a city of over two and a half million people. At the last count, it had more than one hundred slum communities. To make the demands on its resources more manageable, the charity prioritises orphans and the children of single parents, widowed or otherwise. Care and Share makes no distinction on the grounds of religion or caste. Pure demographics mean the majority end up being Hindu and dalit. The process leaves it with over thirteen thousand children on its books.

A sizeable proportion of that number appears to be in the main room of its headquarters. We open the door to a scrum of children. The densest section centres around a long line of desks, where registration formalities for the new school term are taking place. The charity runs a number of pre-school literacy centres, such as the one by the canal. Research shows that knowledge of basic alphabetisation in Telugu and English reduces school dropout rates later on. In addition, Care and Share has a couple of large residential schools outside town for older children picked off the street. The bulk of its work, however, concentrates on pupil sponsorships. Government schools are officially supposed to provide tuition, lunch and textbooks free of charge. The charity helps with the remainder: uniforms, notebooks, stationery, school bags and travel money where appropriate. It's cash well spent. In India, many a child's schooling is disrupted for want of a proper pair of shoes or money for the school bus.

I mingle in the queue for registration. Naga Srinivas, a bright-eyed boy scarcely big enough to see above the registrar's desk, proudly hands over his report card from the previous term. 'You have been consistent and hard-working. Promoted to Class V. Congratulations.' The plaudits earn him a smile and a tick beside his name and code number, 04-A-14. Contented, he makes his way to a round table nearby and begins writing to the Italian housewife who sponsors him. It is one of three obligatory thank-you letters he sends every year. His script is round and rudimentary, but perfectly legible. 'My Dear Mummy . . .' the note begins.

At the back of the room, another queue snakes along the wall. I follow it to the front and discover that it leads to a well-stocked storeroom. Inside, a team of exhausted-looking charity workers is frantically dispensing kits for the term ahead. For the lucky few, gifts from their sponsors are waiting too. The children take possession of the presents gingerly, as if suspecting a mistake has been made and any minute they'll have to hand them back. Most of the packages contain clothes or toys or stationery. Propped behind the door, however, stand two brand-new bicycles. They earn an envious glance from every child who enters.

Jayaraj has come to find me. We're running late. 'Shall we go?' he suggests.

As he nudges me towards the exit, a gaunt woman of around thirty approaches him. A well-built younger man stands behind her, flanked by two timid boys in their early teens. The boys' hair is combed carefully and parted. Their clothes are old but ironed. They've travelled all morning on the bus, the woman explains.

She is holding a piece of paper, which she thrusts towards Jayaraj. He takes it and reads, one ear still listening to her as she continues to speak. Her husband died ten years ago, she recounts. She does seasonal work when it's available, picking fruit for the most part. Her brother – she indicates the tall chaperone behind her – is a schoolteacher. He smiles. Her children attend the Catholic-run Don Bosco school, in Nandigama. In unison, they step forward a pace, like conscripted soldiers on military drill. She places a loving hand on their shoulders. The school is a long journey from their village, she explains. Someone told her that Care and Share might be able to help. Is this true?

Jayaraj looks up. She points to the letter. It describes her church attendance and the boys' diligence at their studies. 'It's from the headmaster,' she emphasises.

'Yes,' Jayaraj says. 'Very good.'

So can he help? He'll do what he can, he promises, explaining that she'll have to fill in some forms and indicating where to do so. Before moving on, he turns to her two sons and, looking each in the eye in turn, asks what they would like to do when they grow up. 'Priest,' answers Aravindu, the older of the two. 'Teacher,' says his younger brother Ashok. Both are well prepped.

'Good, good,' Jayaraj says again, offering each an affirming smile.

It's the second such petition that the charity worker has received in less than an hour. As we head back down the stairs, I ask him about the likelihood of the boys securing support. It all depends on finding a sponsor, he answers. 'Frankly, the eldest is probably too old already.' The younger boy might just stand a chance. It's a long shot though. 'People prefer sponsoring younger children.' Again, Jayaraj's matter-of-factness is not evidence of him being callous – just realistic.

From the headquarters, we drive out to Bombay colony. Situated on barren wasteland on the edge of town, the new development resembles a poor man's version of Mahindra World City. It is built by the government and has one road and no amenities. Hulking great apartment blocks are deposited one after another, like concrete bollards hastily constructed beside a highway. The formulaic towers are each equipped with ten flats to a floor, all uniform in shape and all identical in size. Twenty square feet per family, roughly the size of a bathroom in one of Mahindra World City's duplexes. The barren rooms have no furniture, little ventilation and, as yet, no occupants.

For the moment, the buildings' future residents are camping outside. Rounded up from the city's slums, they have been unceremoniously dumped here in the outskirts. The fact that the buildings are yet to be finished did not halt their eviction. Quietly but determinedly, the government is building ghettos of permanent exclusion for these people. It calls the policy 'slum resettlement'.

Jayaraj approaches a low-hung brick building amid a row of squalid shacks. The cramped, single-room structure houses another of Care and Share's literacy centres. Inside, a gaggle of obedient three- and four-year-olds is studiously repeating the alphabet. Our arrival sparks a frisson of excitement. Space is limited. We stand at the door. I take some photos. The children squeal. And then we take our leave.

At the next stop, we tarry longer. NSC Bose Nagar is likewise located on the city's fringes. An older, low-rise version of Bombay colony, the neighbourhood has the advantage of being bounded by open fields on one side. The school, regrettably, is on the other. Hedged by an open sewer and the main trunk road into town, its three classrooms are, to my surprise, a haven of orderliness and calm.

Again, class is under way. The alphabet and days of the week are written in red chalk on the blackboard. The children sit at individual desks, watching the teacher and then, as soon as she turns, whispering and giggling among themselves. A girl of about five, with gap teeth and blue bows in her hair, is instructed to come to the front. The teacher scribbles a short ditty on the board. She is instructed to repeat it.

'Butterfly, butterfly, where did you go?' the girl recites in a nervous but clear voice. 'House in the garden. Dancing, dancing.' The other pupils stand up and collectively shake their hips. The teacher compliments the girl, who proudly walks back to her seat.

Since it is an English lesson, Jayaraj invites me to address the class. I say a little about myself: where I'm from, my age and how many brothers and sisters I have. They look at me blankly, forty faces of total incomprehension.

Undeterred, my guide for the day asks if I have any questions for the teacher. 'Why does she feel teaching is important?' I ask. She too stares at me with the same blank expression. I ask again, slower this time. Still not understanding me, she turns to Jayaraj in search of help. The two converse in Telugu for a moment. 'With more information,' he repeats back to me, 'the children can develop themselves.' The teacher nods in affirmation.

Education and development. Back in Gadchiroli district, Charandas had made the same connection. That the two men should concur is perhaps not so surprising. The notion that learning opens horizons and provides fresh opportunities is the basic premise of most education systems. The poor understand that as quickly as anyone.

The conclusion to our visit proves as much. In a small classroom at the rear of the school, a group of young women is attending a tailoring class. Most have children in the school. Surisetti has two – a child of four, and another of five. She is twenty. She quit school on getting married, at the age of fourteen. Her husband works in an aluminium factory, earning one hundred and fifty rupees per day. Surisetti hopes tailoring will add an extra fifty to the tally. It's the limit of her aspiration. Yet for her children, her hopes know no bounds. She would like to see them both become doctors.

Big ambitions are by no means limited to parents. A few days later, at a residential school run by Care and Share in the countryside, I'd meet eighteen-year-old Sasha. He has no parents, or none he can count on. His mother died when he was he was ten. His father abandoned him shortly afterwards. They'd been travelling by train from their native Gujarat. Pulling into Hyderabad station, his father had sent him off to buy water. When Sasha returned to the platform, the train had gone. His father had gone with it. He waited for three days for him to return. He never did. Speaking only Urdu and partially sighted, Sasha found his way to

Vijayawada, where Care and Share took him in. He's now fluent in Telugu, Hindi and English. A successful cataract operation had also restored his sight to normal. He wanted to go on to study medicine. His heart's desire, he'd tell me, is to become an eye surgeon.

Care and Share does everything it can to facilitate such ambitions. It encourages all its sponsored students to go on to further education. In doing so, they are already breaking the mould. Three in four literate Indians never go beyond school matriculation. For reasons of financial pragmatism and – to an extent – academic reality, most of the charity's school leavers end up on courses that are relatively short, comparatively inexpensive and highly vocational. That's to say, easy tickets into the job market.

For male students, this translates to trades such as plumbing, car mechanics and gas-fitting. The more academically minded might be pushed towards a degree in mechanical engineering, metallurgy or technical laboratory studies. As for female students, they typically fall into one of two streams: teaching or nursing. The gifted might find their way on to an accountancy or computer science course. Such examples, however, remain the exception.

In that sense, Korlaiah represents a model case for the charity. A year or so older than Surisetti, Korlaiah is one of a small band of new graduates that Care and Share has helped finance through college. At Jayaraj's request, he and his fellow students are waiting promptly at the school gate. We all file into the principal's empty office.

Korlaiah is the first to share his story. He is medium-height and dark-skinned, with a strawberry-shaped mark to the left of his mouth and the wispiest of moustaches. I ask him about his background. The youngest of five siblings, he moved to Vijayawada with his family fifteen years ago. 'We migrated because we had no land in our village, so we faced many problems to get food.' At first, the family lived as 'roadside dwellers'. For five years, home was a shack on the banks of the Eluru irrigation canal. Then the government relocated them, here to NSC Bose Nagar. It's better, he says. They don't pay rent.

Not that their struggles are over. I ask if his parents work. His father is 'old', he explains. His mother works in the market, selling vegetables. Neither, he adds, is literate. And his siblings? His sisters are married off. Both brothers work as cleaners in a hotel. Of the five, he is the only one to be educated. Giovanni Aliani, his Italian sponsor, funded him through school and college. He's recently finished a three-year diploma in electronics and communication, he informs me proudly.

I enquire about his future. Does he have a job? Finding employment is difficult, he admits. For the moment, he works as a book-keeper at a small printing firm. He hopes to find a position with an engineering firm soon. He's submitted an application to a local electronics manufacturer that specialises in making digital meters. He found the opening advertised in the newspaper. He's also put his name into the ballot for Indian Railways. As yet, he's received no word back from either.

If possible, Korlaiah would like to stay close to his parents. He has a duty to care for them, he says. But he must face facts. 'There are very few jobs here in Vijayawada.' To join a good firm, he'll probably have to relocate to a larger city such as Hyderabad, Chennai or Visakhapatnam. All his fellow graduates face a similar predicament.

Education is clearly no panacea for the poverty trap. The deficiencies of the school system are partly to blame. India is getting better at churning out graduates, the statistics show, but levels of 'employability' remain low. Despite India's economic growth, the labour market itself remains tough. Even for those with strong vocational training like Korlaiah, openings are few and far between, especially in India's smaller towns and cities. Nor do poorer graduates typically have the necessary connections to squeeze a foot in the door. The prejudices of Old India have not entirely disappeared either. Caste, gender, the very poverty they are trying to overcome: all result in job applications sometimes going unreturned.

That said, there's no denying that the prospects are far better for those with an education than for those without. Schooling,

more than anything, represents the fundamental difference
between Jivan and Charandas. It explains the desperation of
Guravaiah to see Care and Share take on his children. As for Korlaiah, if he must go to another city to find work, it'll represent an
entirely different type of urban migration to the luckless journey
his parents faced.

Education is transformative, without doubt. But who are the
educators and what are they saying?

As I near the end of my journey, the question strikes me as a
critical one. New India remains only partially built. In many quarters, it remains just an idea, a hope of something better. It will fall
to the 'democratic dividend' – the five hundred and more million
youngsters under twenty-five – to construct the final edifice.

That a New India will emerge is beyond doubt. India will and
must change. The forces pushing it are too strong to resist. But
the style and shape of that new country still hangs in the balance.
The spirit of the New must still overcome the stubbornness of the
Old. Only with the right architects will that happen.

In search of such change-makers, I hop on a train across the
country to Pune – a city so full of schools and colleges, it's nick-
named the 'Oxford of the East'.

Pune

I arrive at Lt V. B. Gogate School during morning break. A deluge
of playing children fills the central courtyard. Their feet hammer
on the paved surface with the thud, thud, thud of heavy rain on a
windowpane.

I make my way to the first floor of the main, L-shaped teaching
block. Painted slogans accompany me up the wide spiral staircase.
Several have religious overtones. 'God hath made us all equal,'
reads one. 'Man proposes, God disposes,' says the next, a reminder that the divine might be generous but that he's no walkover.
My favourite appears towards the top of the stairs. 'Look before
you leap.' It's wise advice, I think, as I peer over the balcony to
the scurrying pupils below.

Ashish is behind his desk preparing for the class ahead. His laptop is open with his lesson plan neatly typed out in Word. He's dressed in a checked work shirt and casual jeans. His squarish jawline frames a set of facial features that are remarkable less for their form than their gentleness. An endearing boyishness has slunk with him into adulthood, a feature he has tried to shake off with a week's scruffy beard growth.

He spots me at the door. 'Come in, come in,' he insists, walking over and shaking my hand warmly. 'Welcome to my office.'

The last word brings a smile to his lips. Until recently, Ashish worked as a high-flying computer programmer. Every morning, he would trek into Infosys's plush Pune campus and spend his day quality-testing new versions of Microsoft Windows.

His current surroundings are somewhat different. For starters, his is the only laptop on the premises. There's no gym facility, no staff canteen and no air-conditioning. There's not even a watercooler. The decor perhaps has an edge on his former corporate environment. In place of spreadsheets and Post-it notes, the walls are brightened by a colourful ensemble of children's artwork and posters depicting body parts, geometrical shapes and collective nouns.

By the door, an attendance sheet contains the names of his Class Four charges. Next to it is a list of classroom etiquette, his equivalent of a corporate Code of Conduct. Rules One to Three: Be on time, Listen to the teacher, Speak in English.

Class Four is happily sat in circles of five or six, noisily devouring chapattis, rice and vegetable snacks from stainless-steel tiffin containers. 'Hello Sir,' they shout in unison, as I walk in. 'Have a nice day.'

Before the bell rings and lessons resume, Ashish provides some background to his class. Most of the pupils are aged between nine and ten. Class numbers are lower than usual. Fifty or sixty to a class is the typical figure. He has sixteen. The small size is a consequence of the school being relatively new, he explains. The younger grades fill up as children join. The kindergarten is now oversubscribed.

As far as income levels go, all the pupils come from uniformly poor homes, the sons and daughters of autorickshaw drivers, office peons, domestic helps and others in similarly low-skilled jobs. A few have parents who run small neighbourhood shops. Ten of the sixteen classify under the government's reservation quota for scheduled castes and tribes. That exempts them from the municipal school's administrative levy of one hundred and fifty rupees per month.

Several in his class face learning difficulties. Ashish indicates a girl sitting in a group by the window. She is staring at the wall. Her long limbs mark her out as older. 'She's thirteen,' the form teacher says. 'She's been thrown out of her three previous schools.' Others have to deal with troubled home lives. Ashish has three children who he knows suffer regular domestic violence. One of them, Ashvaraj, has a habit of attacking the other pupils. He's even punched Ashish in the past.

Another boy, with an alcoholic father, frequently turns up to school with bruises. Other times, he just doesn't come at all. The same is true for Vaishnavi, he says, pointing to a pretty girl across the room. 'Her father beats her regularly.' She's dressed in pink. It's her birthday.

Seeing us watching, she gets up and comes over. With the sweetest of gap-toothed smiles, she presents me with two Cadbury Eclair sweets. They're warm from being in her pocket all morning. I thank her and feel a lump rise in my throat.

A teacher pops his head in. There's a parents' meeting that afternoon. Does Ashish know when it starts? 'Five p.m., I think,' he tells him. He turns back to me. The parents are just concerned whether the children's school-books are filled in, he says resignedly. 'It's a shame, but most can't relate to what we're doing in the classroom.' That's a stumbling block for some. Like Basuraj, for example. Ashish reckons him one of the brightest students in the class. But both his parents are illiterate. 'They can't even write their names.' Like a well-kept secret, therefore, Basuraj's education goes no further than these four walls.

The bell goes and the children slowly filter back to their desk.

I find a seat in the last row, beside an open window. The sound of gears clanking and car horns honking drifts up from the road outside. There's no hint of a breeze.

Ashish claps his hands and brings the class to order. 'Who knows which heats faster, water or sand?' No one responds. He repeats the question. A couple of hands go up. The answers are divided. The ex-computer programmer takes two glasses from his desk – one full of water, the other brimming with sand – and places them on the window sill. 'Let's wait till the end of class and then we'll see.'

Returning to the front, Ashish picks up a piece of chalk. 'Fractions,' he says, writing the word in capitals along the top of the blackboard. 'Who remembers from the last class what an improper fraction is?'

The next half an hour or so is occupied with going over the rudiments of numerators and denominators. Ashish starts with numbers. $3/4 + 6/4 = 9/4 = 2\ 1/4$. The class watch him, at first with interest and then with varyingly decreasing levels of attention.

He switches to apples in the hope of re-engaging them. Soon the board is covered in drawings of apples, interspersed with '+', '=' and '/' signs. Some of the class show evidence of comprehension. Basuraj, for instance, is carefully copying down Ashish's pomaceous examples in his notebook. Others appear less enchanted by the mathematics of divisible fruit. Nilambari, the girl with learning problems, has returned to staring at the wall.

Ashvaraj, meanwhile, appears to have fainted. Vaishnavi volunteers one of her Eclairs. Under the rush of sugar, her classmate gradually revives. He'd gone through break without a snack. Ashish tells him to remind his mother to always prepare his tiffin. Then he instructs the class to open their textbooks to Chapter Six and to attempt the questions on the final page. As they set to work, he goes over to Nilambari and repeats the fundamentals of what he's just taught.

Ashish is one of a hundred or so Teach for India fellows. Based on an innovative programme first piloted in the United States, Teach for India encourages young professionals to take time out of their careers to try their hand in the classroom. The scheme is sold to their companies as an opportunity to equip their high-potential graduates in soft skills such as communication and leadership. A roster of leading firms has bought in. Some, like ICICI Bank and the Indian Premier League sponsor HDFC, even provide paid sabbaticals to their volunteers.

Teach for India's purpose is to breathe some new life and fresh thinking into the country's education system. Narrowing the educational gulf between rich and poor is the programme's most immediate goal. Integrating well-educated professionals into the school system will, the theory runs, improve instruction in the basics.

The scheme's organisers have a more strategic aspiration too. By focusing on the top crop of young managers, they're setting their sights on influencing India's long-term educational standards. Today's volunteers, it's hoped, will become tomorrow's leaders.

As far as the first part of that equation goes, Ashish is doing his best. He concentrates particularly on improving Maths and English. A poor understanding of both subjects is the main cause of students like his flunking their Board exams, which await them in a couple of years. Although ostensibly an English-medium school, none of Ashish's Marathi-speaking class could read or write a word of the language when he took over at the beginning of the year. Now their notebooks are lined with Roman-shaped consonants and joined-up diphthongs. After school, he runs extra classes for students struggling with pronunciation and spelling. Aside from that, he's conscientious in setting homework and diligent in marking it. He tries to find interesting ways to teach the syllabus than simply reading straight from the textbook.

He's making progress. On the wall is a list of promises. Each pupil has written a personal pledge. Rohan, for instance, has promised to 'do writing properly'. Manish has given his word to 'listen to my what teacher say listen to them'. Ashvari, meanwhile, has committed to 'come to school every day'. Tacked on to the end are the words '. . . and on time'.

Beyond basic arithmetic and grammar, Ashish has a second goal for the sixteen pre-adolescents under his instruction: Exposure. It's a word he uses frequently and liberally. He means it in its broadest sense: exposure to new ideas, to alternative viewpoints, to different careers, to the numerous possibilities out there. Exposure to life in general, beyond the bounds of a menial job in a hard-up corner of town.

Ashish's passion for expanding his pupils' perspectives is partly a reaction to the blinkered education that he himself received. Although not affluent, his own background is much more advantaged than those of Lt V. B. Gogate School's Class Four. His father enjoyed a comparatively comfortable career with India's National Thermal Power Corporation. The state-run firm has a tie-up with the country's best private schools, so Ashish was educated at an on-site affiliate of the prestigious Delhi Public School. He graduated with honours, but not with any real sense of the world around him.

That was partly the fault of his location. His father worked in Vindhyanagar, home to Asia's largest coal-mine and situated in the remote tribal state of Madhya Pradesh. Ashish had made a few brief trips to visit family in Lucknow and Varanasi, but otherwise knew little of the country at large. Life on the company's compound was safe and closeted. He never once competed against another school in sports and crime was more or less unheard of.

It was in the classroom where he felt the keenest sense of confinement. Engineer or doctor? The orientation of his entire learning was a choice between the two. Ashish opted for the former and, like Sunny, spent a year studying to crack the entrance exam for the Indian Institute of Technology. He got through the first round but not the second, so ended up going to a well-respected state engineering college instead. It wasn't until he was into his mid-twenties that he gave any thought to what he himself might want from life. By that stage, he was five years into a lucrative career with Infosys.

Exposure is the reason why he leaves his laptop open during recess. He actively wants his pupils to tinker with it. In class, he uses it to show them photographs and videos as well. Anything to spark their imaginations. In the same spirit, he's also invited some of his graduate friends to come in and talk about their jobs. A former classmate who works at a power plant in Indore was the first to visit. The children wanted to know how he didn't get electric shocks all the time. Ashish has a policeman, air hostess and fashion designer lined up for future talks.

Ashish leaves Nilambari and strolls around the room. He looks over the shoulders of his students and checks the equations in their exercise books. He congratulates some and corrects others. After five minutes, he tells them to close their books. 'Your homework for tomorrow is to finish the questions, okay?' The class groans in protest.

Then he walks over to the window and takes the two glasses from the sill. He puts them on Tejas's desk. 'Which is warmer?' The boy tentatively touches the contents of each glass. 'Water, sir?' he answers, with an almost visible question mark. Ashish congratulates him on a correct answer and then explains the science behind it. Tomorrow, he tells them, they will discover which of the two materials cools fastest.

He turns to me. 'Before we finish, I would like to invite our guest to come to the front. I am sure you have lots of questions for him. Who wants to start?'

I make my way to the front of the class. For the next ten minutes, I field an array of quickfire questions, from where I live and what I do through to my preferred cartoon and my favourite god. Ashish then passes the baton to me. Ask whatever you like, he says. How many of you know about computers? All the hands go up. How many of you know how to use a computer? Three hands go up. In each case, one or other of their parents received a hand-me-down machine from the offices where they work.

Thinking of Ashish's efforts to broaden their horizons, I ask about his former employer. Who's heard of Infosys? About half the class puts up their hands. Closer inquiry reveals that they are all thinking of a nearby college with the same name. Ashish explains that Infosys is of one of India's most successful firms. 'It's

a company that works with computers.' They receive the information without expression. For children whose direct experience of
the job market is almost exclusively manual, perhaps the notion
remains too abstract. Still, I like to think that his explanation has
sown the seed of an idea.

I try another line. A poster on the classroom wall describes
various jobs. I ask who would like to be an astronaut, one of the
featured options. Most of the boys put up their hands. A teacher? Another good spread. A rickshaw driver? Not a single raised
hand. The idea of following in their fathers' footsteps clearly does
not appeal. Businessman? This time, not a hand stays down, boys
and girls.

Ashish calls time. Reminding them about their homework, he
adds that there will be a science test tomorrow. 'No one to be absent, heh. Now off you go. Class dismissed.'

We'd arranged to have lunch after class in a nearby restaurant.
Before we leave, I ask if I can meet the principal. Ashish had previously mentioned the possibility of a brief interview with her. Now
he doesn't seem so keen. 'I am not sure if she'll agree,' he says.
Then he backtracks and suggests we at least pass by her office and
see if she's in.

Ashish is one of five Teach for India participants in the school.
Relations between them and the mainstream staff are, it would
appear, a touch tense. With a base stipend of fifteen thousand rupees per month, the programme affiliates earn more money. The
salary marks a large drop from their corporate wage. Even so, it's
still five times more than a newly qualified teacher might earn.
Some resentment is only natural.

More than the money, the young professionals are seen as a
threat to the status quo. The majority of teachers have only a
minimum level of education themselves. In Ashish's home state,
statistics from a few years back showed that unqualified 'contract'
staff filled more than half (fifty-three per cent) of teaching posts.
The reason the pupils' English is so bad, Ashish contends, is because the teachers' own command of the language is so poor.
He cites a note that the principal sent to parents about sending

snacks for break time. Instead of 'snacks', however, she'd written 'snakes'.

The same is often true for mathematics. Government inspectors recently undertook a spot-check of teachers across the state of Maharashtra. They were tested on their seven times table. A sizeable minority failed. The results sparked outrage among parents' groups. Less predictably, the teachers' unions were equally incensed, claiming that the tests had been unfair. Their members had not been forewarned.

As part of the Teach for India programme, volunteers are required to undertake extra-curricular initiatives. Ashish has set up a series of training workshops in curriculum development. Using project-planning skills learned at Infosys, the idea is to instruct teachers in putting together a creative twelve-month syllabus plan. The course has attracted one hundred and twenty participants from fifty-five schools. Only now it wasn't running any more. The municipal official responsible changed posts. His replacement thought the initiative 'inappropriate' because Ashish was unqualified. He pulled the plug. Another case of Old India obstructing the New.

As Ashish had warned, the principal proves frosty. She grants me the shortest of audiences, most of which is occupied with questions about my identity and reasons for being there. 'Who are you?' 'What are you doing?' It's like being back in the class again, only distinctly more hostile. Ashish is given a dressing down for not obtaining proper permission for my visit. ('If I'd asked,' he says afterwards, 'she'd just have said "no".') As for the Teach for India recruits, she eventually concedes that they are 'doing okay' although they have much to learn. She re-emphasises that the young volunteers are 'not qualified teachers' and, by inference, substandard. Her points made, I am duly excused.

Ashish and I have lunch at a mid-range hotel in the centre of town. The menu is orientated towards an international palate. Slowed-down, elevator versions of popular Hindi soundtracks drift across the almost empty restaurant. The air-conditioners are set several degrees too low. The lighting is, by a similar measure, too bright. The waiter, meanwhile, is ever-present and then nowhere to be seen. Everything feels slightly out of sync, yet oddly familiar, as if the hotel owners had visited an Indian restaurant in small-town England and tried to import the export back home.

I ask Ashish how he heard about the Teach for India position. He'd seen an advertisement in the newspaper, he says. Had he thought about being a teacher in the past? He almost chokes. 'No, never.' Teaching, he'd been brought up to believe, was a profession you did when 'you were unsuccessful in every other career'. If you failed your exams or couldn't find employment elsewhere, then you became a teacher. It was a job of last resort. 'We used to think of it as a noble profession and all,' he admits. 'But from a career point of view, it wasn't even on the list.'

Teachers have not always been so poorly viewed in India. By tradition, education is a Brahmin profession. Students of his parents' generation studied under highly educated teachers, Ashish points out. Back then, the school principal would occupy a similar rank in society to, say, the commissioner of police. 'The day that teaching as a profession gets that kind of respect, it'll be the day that India really starts changing.' The drop in standards is partly the result of expanding educational opportunities. Fifty years ago, when Ashish's parents were studying, there were far fewer schools. The teaching pool was therefore smaller and more selective. That worked well for those who got an education. Many, however, went without.

Ashish feels that the main reason for the fall in teaching standards lies elsewhere. India's guiding ethos, he believes, is no longer what it was. He sees the shift among his peers. India is a very commercialised nation right now, he tells me. 'Our daily routine just concentrates on the profits and losses that we are making.' With everyone keen to get on and make what they can, traditional concerns for the country's wider social welfare are diminishing. 'Out of a thousand,' Ashish says, referring to those with a college education, 'hardly one turns up and says they are ready to sacrifice something.'

I wonder if he's not being overly harsh. India is not without its charitable pursuits. I'd seen as much in Vijayawada. The notion of sacrifice is an interesting one, though. The idea of giving something up for a greater good is deeply rooted in the Hindu scriptures and Gandhian tradition. Is India's nascent materialism eating away at such thinking?

I ask Ashish if taking up his voluntary teaching job has been a sacrifice. I presume it has. When he left Infosys, he was earning just shy of forty thousand rupees per month. It was 'fast money', he'd told me earlier. With no responsibilities, no worries, he could buy – within reason – whatever he liked. His father had had to wait until he was forty before he could afford his first car. Ashish could persuade the bank to extend him sufficient credit with his first salary cheque.

The question appears to make the young programmer uncomfortable. He even winces ever so slightly. Sacrifice, I surmise, is a subject to be discussed in the generic sense. As with acts of charity, using the first person has the unseemly effect of turning a private virtue into a public boast.

I try another route. You must miss the extra cash? Ashish is visibly happier discussing the matter in monetary terms. 'Who wouldn't?' he responds with a long-suffering smile. He's learning to live on less again. He actually quite enjoys the forced downsizing, he says. 'It's like being a student.' If he feels any sense of sacrifice, then it's related to his career path. He enjoyed his job. Signing off software products that would then be released to consumers around the world gave him a buzz.

I thought back to the Infosys training campus that I'd visited in Mysore and the glittering careers that the company promised. Becoming a volunteer teacher – if only temporarily – cast doubt over such a future. When he told his friends that he was leaving, they thought he was mad. Why was he abandoning 'corporate' to work for an NGO, they'd ask? 'It's a highly unusual decision for someone with a background like mine,' he admits. I ask what he means. Financially speaking, he clarifies. 'I mean, my family, we're not that strong, so it's a risk.' But it was a risk with several important mitigating factors, he'd resolved. He's twenty-seven, so still young. Plus, he could always go back to Infosys or sell his IT experience elsewhere. 'So, no, it's not been a big sacrifice in that respect.'

Eventually, the waiter reappears. He is carrying our food. We're both hungry and tuck in ravenously. Several minutes pass in silence.

The break in conversation provides Ashish with a moment to reflect. He wants to clarify something. No one forced him to leave his job. It was a step he chose to take himself. In fact, he was already doing some voluntary teaching while he was at Infosys. Every Saturday and Sunday, he ran a small English and maths class in Pune's Aundh slum. It was originally his girlfriend's idea. 'You're always talking about the country's problems and society, and all,' she'd told him. 'Why don't you do something about it?' So he did.

The result was a charity called Prarambh (meaning 'beginning'). He hired an apartment and taught the lessons from there. By the end, around forty children were coming along regularly. Teach for India, he felt, represented a perfect opportunity to 'scale up' what he was already doing. 'It gave me a scope to utilise my potential completely and create something good out of it.'

Couched though it may be in corporate-speak, it is hard not to admire the sentiment. Especially given how Ashish delivers it, free from self-satisfaction or sanctimony. From what I can tell, the young programmer simply feels drawn to the classroom. Teaching gives him a personal, tangible sense of the value of education – an activity in which, in terms of its societal repercussions, he clearly believes.

I'd seen a similar blend of personal fulfilment and ideological belief in Daniel and Ritesh, two other volunteers on the Teach for India programme. We'd met a few days previously, on the outdoor terrace of Cafe Coffee Day in the city's trendy Koregoan Park district. Immediately around the corner lay the shell of the German Bakery, a popular eatery with tourists and the scene of a recent bomb blast. The attack, which left nine dead, was thought to be the work of the dissident Indian Mujahidin. Like the Naxals, the

Islamic terrorist group is unhappy with the direction that India seems to be taking. The Bakery's charred interior had reminded me of the extent to which the country's future still hangs in the balance.

As with Ashish, both the young men came across as extremely articulate and evidently well educated. Daniel, a middle-class Catholic from Bengaluru, used to work at the huge IT advisory firm Tata Consultancy Services, designing software solutions for the digital TV station Tata Sky. Ritesh, on the other hand, is on leave from his job designing power plants with a Dutch engineering company. Both studied engineering.

Each had had their own reasons for trading in their careers to teach. In Daniel's case, the decision was prompted by a desire to escape the rat race. Seeing the advertisement in the newspaper, it had got him thinking: did he really want to be designing software solutions for digital TV when he was forty? He didn't.

Ritesh's motives were more idealistic. Like Ashish, he enjoyed his job. Brought up in a tribal region of the mountainous eastern state of Jharkhand, it had cost him a lot to 'get this'. He'd pointed round at the mall where we'd been sitting as though the brand-name stores represented a physical emblem of his change in station. His parents, both primary-school teachers, had scrimped and saved for him to have private English lessons. He was one of the few from his home town to score a lucrative corporate job. It was precisely these struggles and his sense of good fortune that made him, as he'd put it, 'realise my responsibility to society'. Again, the words are spoken without self-regard.

As I listen to Ashish in the restaurant, what comes back to me from that earlier conversation with his fellow affiliates is the strategic vision with which they view education. For Daniel's part, he wanted to see a more unified 'citizen culture'. Such a prospect, the young Catholic believed, remained impossible as long as caste and religion pushed Indians into separate camps. Only education could broaden minds. Like Ashish, he was a firm believer in the 'exposure' method of teaching.

Ritesh's hopes had been even more ambitious. India, he'd felt, had the opportunity to grow into a superpower. The country must believe that, he'd said, as if losing faith would cause the dream to slip away. Yet India had a long way to go. He spoke passionately about his home town, which lacked a rail network or proper road system. 'People are under the illusion that things are good, but look at rural India. If anything, it is falling further behind.'

It was a claim I'd heard up and down the country. Ritesh's benchmark, like that of many others, was China. Huge investment in public education had much to do with the meteoric rise of India's eastern neighbour, he felt. Meanwhile, policy-makers in Delhi are busy drawing up twenty-year plans for the country's development. If education standards aren't tackled, Ritesh believed, then such plans would come to naught. India, he'd concluded like a good engineer, needs solutions. 'If we don't come up with them, who will?'

Daniel had decided to carry on in teaching. Ritesh would probably head back to his power-plant job, for now at least. I ask Ashish about his future plans.

'I'm not sure if I'll go back,' he admits secretively, as though fearful his employers might somehow get wind of his possible defection.

The revelation surprises me. Taking time out from work is one thing. Leaving for good is quite another. Daniel's family had the financial wherewithal to support him if necessary. Ashish's didn't.

His future, for the moment, is fluid. He's asked Teach for India if he can continue with his placement. He could work part-time for them to help make ends meet, he hoped. It looks unlikely that the charity will agree. His father, meanwhile, is putting pressure on him to come home. If his son is to carry on with teaching, he'd like to see him properly qualified. He'd then be in a position to take up a job in the local school. Ashish can't decide. It sounds as if his corporate days are numbered, though. If not education, then he's thinking of a switch to the voluntary sector.

The waiter returns and we ask for the bill. As we wait, the socially minded programmer tells me about another idea he's toying with.

'It's called AwakIND,' he says, his expression brightening. 'It's the world's first socio-political forum.' He lays out the concept, which revolves around the creation of an online platform for all 'stakeholders of society' – everyone from common citizens and civil-society representatives to local leaders and government agencies. The idea is to enable everyday Indians to engage with their leaders.

'Take me,' he says, pointing to himself as an illustrative example. 'I might never get the opportunity to speak to my local Member of Parliament. This platform will allow me to do that.' He hopes such interaction will enable everyday Indians to voice their concerns and obtain resolutions to them. He's already rolled out the idea on Facebook, he says. He and a programmer friend have put together a Beta site as well. They have almost six thousand preliminary users so far. He passes on the web address so I can look it up when the website goes public. 'www-dot-awakIND-dot-com,' he spells out. 'Awaken India, you see?'

I like the idea and tell him so. The end goal – the hope of raising awareness, of changing perspectives, of allowing others to envision the possibility of change – strikes me as similar to what he is trying to achieve through his school placement. He nods enthusiastically. 'Exactly, exactly.'

The thought turns my mind back to the sixteen faces watching him at the blackboard. Ashish is passionate about awakening them to the possibilities that lie ahead. As a product of the New India dream himself, he firmly believes in it. But will Class Four be part of that same story?

Ashish takes a long breath. There's an edge of sadness to his voice when he comes to speak, as if already mourning the day he has to leave them. 'Right now, they're so eager to learn. They are ready to take on each and every thing.' He cites the example of the pupils experimenting with his laptop. He worries about the standard of schooling that awaits them, though. 'The students that can study themselves might be able to sustain. But only sustain.' As for the likes of Nilambari, Ashvaraj and Vaishnavi, he fears they will fall back.

As for life beyond the school gates, he's equivocal. Opportunities in India may be growing, but competition remains cut-throat. 'There's only a little space at the top and a lot of people trying to grab it,' says the Infosys graduate, who'd fought off thousands of eager young programmers to land his former job.

Even so, he holds out hope for the three or four brightest students in his class. 'They are sure to go on to do something in their life.' Like what? It's impossible to know, he says. At a minimum, he hopes they'll continue to further studies. And then? 'Who can say?' he says. He's confident of one thing, though. 'Whatever it is, it'll be something better than what their parents or their relatives have ever even thought of.'

I leave Pune for Mumbai on the morning train. The journey gives me time to reflect on my time with Ashish and his volunteer colleagues. They are by no means the only young people in India who are pouring their energies into educating the next generation. I'd read in the paper about a seventeen-year-old in the Bengali village of Berthampore who ran his own free school. He currently had eight hundred students enrolled. A further two hundred are on the waiting list. He started when he was nine. The staff room is filled with his teenage friends.

Nor is Teach for India the only initiative applying innovative techniques in the classroom. Several months earlier, I'd spent a few days visiting schools on the outskirts of Bengaluru. The headmaster of one these – Indus International, an exclusive private school with state-of-the-art facilities, attended by the children of India's elite and those of foreign expatriates – had set up a parallel community school for children from the local village. He'd instructed that the classrooms should be built with natural materials indigenous to the area, and had equipped them with the latest in multimedia gadgetry. Revenue from Indus International's fee-paying parents ensures one hundred per cent subsidy for all the attendees. Each child is provided with his or her own laptop and studies under the rubric of the International Baccalaureate system.

On the other side of the city, at Valley School, I'd found a very different but equally innovative approach being put to the test. Nestled into the grooves and contours of a native forest, classrooms peeked out of hillsides and dormitory blocks stood hidden in the trees. The school's administrators took their steer from Krishnamurty, a Hindu philosopher and ardent proponent of holistic, secular education. His method for 'dynamic living' gives priority to two main factors: direct contact with nature, and the encouragement to question. Only then, he argued, would young people grow to live fully developed lives, free of greed and unimpeded by fear.

Valley School could not be further from the unimaginative teaching and rote learning experienced by so many of India's schoolchildren. School uniforms are banned, rewards and pun-ishments done away with, organic food insisted upon and 'land work' (cleaning, gardening, sweeping, et cetera) integrated into the timetable. Students' creative sides were nurtured in a specially con-structed 'art village' situated in a wooded dell. Drama classes take place in an open-air amphitheatre, with an emerald-green lake for a backdrop and an audience of curious woodland animals.

On the day I visited, the double period before lunch was given over to a concert by a folk band devoted to the ancient songs of the poet Kabir. As for the syllabus, Valley School has no tests and no curriculum until Class Eight (when students are around thir-teen years old). It all sounds very hippy. The headmaster insisted it was not. Come graduation exams, its pupils do as well as or better than their conventionally educated peers. As well as law-yers, doctors and engineers, the headmaster was gratified to count the school's first professional scuba-diving instructor among its graduates.

Ashish helped me clarify what these other examples had intim-ated: that the essence of change lay in exposure to new thinking and fresh perspectives. This, along with getting the educational basics in place: the ability to understand, to question, to get the full measure of things. Provided together, these two educational inputs make a powerful mix for the future. And an important one too. Because of course, it's not only in the classroom where vision-ary educators are exposing India's youth to what the future might hold. Change is there on the television, in the playground, along the High Street, at the mall.

As India opens its borders, the world is flooding in. For now, it's fighting for the country's wallet. But ultimately it could make a grab for its soul.

India's future hangs in the balance. Much will depend on which influences it embraces, which it rejects, and which it takes and makes its own. The stakes are staggeringly high, too high to be left to chance or private interest. Individual Indians must choose for themselves and do so wisely. That requires the tools to decide and the courage to act. Leading from example, India's change makers are striving to provide both.

10

Gandhi's Talisman

[change agents]

'It is probably true that we are a slow-moving elephant, but it is especially true that with each step forward we leave behind a deep imprint.'
   Prime Minister Manmohan Singh

Mumbai

Back at Pune's railway station, I'd picked up the latest edition of *India Today*. The cover story of the popular weekly had caught my eye as I passed the newspaper wallah. Splayed out along the platform, amid all the other magazines, newspapers, crossword books and medical supplements, beamed a bright-eyed huddle of young go-getters. 'HARVEST OF HOPE', ran the headline, in yellow block letters. From the four hundred and fifty-nine million Indians aged between thirteen and thirty-five, the magazine has identified three dozen individuals that it thought captured the 'innovation, gumption and determination' of New India.

Towards the end of the short train ride to Mumbai, I pick up the magazine and begin reading the editorial. The piece starts with some comparative statistics that reinforce the demographic advantages that the Mahindra Lifespaces president had first brought to my attention. In 2020, the average Indian citizen will be aged twenty-seven. That's a decade less than the predicted norm in China, and almost two decades younger than the average European.

The magazine is optimistic about what lies in store for the current generation of young Indians. The economy is growing and social attitudes are slowly shifting. Two in three literate young people, for instance, support assigned quotas for women in parliament – the subject of a legislative proposal that is presently splitting India along fault lines of Old and New. Right now, the upbeat editorial concludes, 'the world's largest democracy can afford to dream.'

The subsequent pages are given over to profiles of the magazine's high achievers. So what are they dreaming about? I flick through.

Some names I recognise. There's Sushil Kumar, for example, the Delhi-based wrestler who shot to fame after becoming world champion. And Karun Chandhok, the young racing driver who became a household name when he broke into Formula One.

The others are mostly new to me. The selection partly reflects the interests of the age. Film dominates, with a significant portion of the list devoted to rising actors and those earning reputations behind the screen as producers, film-makers, scriptwriters and music directors. The director of the dance troupe that won the reality show, *India's Got Talent*, earns a mention. Inevitably cricket makes it in too, with the inclusion of Cheteshwar Pujara, an upcoming batsman.

Writers, dancers, poets and musicians occupy a second category. Many are contemporary champions of classical art-forms. There's a sattriya dancer and a Carnatic vocalist, for instance. A professional historian, architectural conservationist and writer of historical fiction win a look-in as well. Evidently the powers that be at *India Today* – part of the powerful, pro-establishment *Times of India* group – have a message to plug: by all means, refresh, renew, even reinterpret, but, in the headlong rush to modernity, don't forget India's roots, its history and its traditions.

With thoughts of my school visit still fresh in mind, I wonder if any of today's crop of high-flyers share backgrounds like those at Lt V. B. Gogate School. Do Class Four, I'm still wondering, really stand a chance?

From the text of the magazine, it's not immediately obvious which have battled against the odds. At least one, Ajjay Agarwal, is a school drop-out. He's since gone on to set up Maxx Mobile, a fast-growing mobile-phone retailer. A number of the sportsmen and women come from humble beginnings too, further proving the role of sport as a social leveller.

One example stands out above the rest: Uttam Teron. Born in a remote hamlet in Assam to a train-driver father and an illiterate homemaker mother, he took up private teaching as a stop-gap after graduating from college. His bamboo classroom became a school. It reminded me of the teenage headmaster in West Bengal that I'd read about. Teron's Parijat Academy now has more than five hundred pupils. Precisely half are girls. I'd like to imagine he's the kind of person that could have been sitting in Ashish's class.

The list includes no other schoolteachers. 'Roboteacher', the only other hopeful, turns out to be a mechanics whizz from the Indian Institute of Technology in Mumbai. Not that the title is entirely disingenuous. Twenty-nine-year-old Gagan Goyal now runs a successful robotics company producing 'hands-on education tools'. The battery-powered devices are designed to expose children to a different approach to teaching science. Ashish would, I'm sure, be impressed.

Approaching Mumbai's city limits, I turn the page to Vivek Gilani's profile. He occupies a third category of entrant, those explicitly committed to making New India fairer and more inclusive than the Old. Most operate in the social or developmental sectors. One, Indrani Medhi, works with Microsoft to tweak new technologies for the needs of illiterate communities – essentially doing to smartphones and netbooks what Unilever is doing to shampoos and detergents. Another, Rikin Gandhi, is a US-born aerospace engineer using basic video cameras to help farmers voice their problems and share their success stories. Vivek, on the other hand, runs a website.

MumbaiVotes.com emerged from Vivek's confusion about who to vote for. Mumbai's voting patterns are, generally speaking, split along caste and religious lines – much as Daniel had complained about back in Pune. It's not uncommon to see apartment enclaves with saffron flags and bunting hung across the entrance gate, an indication of a block vote for one of the Hindu-dominated nationalist parties. For those wanting to make a more discerning choice, however, information on individual candidates is sparse. Mumbai Votes sets out to address this by keeping tabs on all the city's one thousand four hundred and forty-four politicians.

As with all the other individual profiles, Vivek's magazine profile finishes with a question about his Mission. His goal is to produce an annual 'report card' for all elected officials. This would 'allow room for positive debate between politicians and the civic community'. The comment makes me stop short. I'd heard the phrase before. It's Ashish's AwakIND idea, is it not?

I think back to our conversation in the hotel restaurant. There was something about the online idea that had confused me at the time. It wasn't the general objective. I could see how that broadly fitted with Ashish's hopes for Class Four. It was more the leap from classroom teacher to web-based activist. It struck me as an impossibly large one. Education and politics operate in different spheres. How did Ashish propose bridging the two?

Reading about Mumbai Votes, the answer – or the possibility of an answer – occurs to me: information. Ashish's hope for influencing the ambitions of his students lay in exposing them to ideas, theories, facts, opinions, perspectives, life experiences. Information, in other words. Could exposure to the same shift political thinking as well? The more I think about it, the more it seems to make sense. Was access to information not the cog that whirred Indrani's 'tweaked' technology? Was the same not true for Rikin's videos? Excited by the possibility, I resolve to track down the creator of Mumbai Votes and find out if the theory holds true.

That evening, I log on to the featured website and fill in the online contact form. An answer pings back the next day. Later in the week, I find myself traveling down a residential street in a middle-class area of Juhu.

Dressed in jeans and a T-shirt, Vivek's frame is narrower and his cheekbones sharper than suggested by the *India Today* photographer. Also escaping the camera's lens is the American inflection to some of his vowels, a hangover from years studying and then working in the United States. Where the magazine photograph of him was spot-on, however, is in his aura of quiet, calculated intelligence.

He shows me to a seat in the main room of his family's moderately sized flat. No sooner has he sat down than he's up and fretting over the knotted mess of cables outside the large sliding window looking out onto the street. He's on to the local authorities to come and remove them. He is pushing the residents in the block to join in a petition. It used to be that you could fly a kite in Mumbai, he says. Now, the clutter of electric cabling makes even a clear view of the sky difficult. 'It seems all people care about these days is having cable TV.'

He speaks quickly and precisely, his features animated and his attention wholly absorbed by the glut of cabling – what he sees as an infringement on his basic citizen's rights. There's nothing theatrical about the performance. Just pure, concentrated intensity of focus – the same intensity he's channelled into Mumbai Votes.

He returns to his seat and begins to outline how the Internet venture works. Vivek runs a detailed search of a dozen or so daily newspapers, Parliamentary sources, party manifestos, individual politicians' websites, records of budgetary spending and whatever else is available in the public domain. He then collates the findings and publishes them in a searchable online database.

It's all very user-friendly. Voters can click on and track the record of their elected representatives. They can see their attendance in Parliament or in the Municipal Legislative Assembly, their record of public speaking and their priorities in public spending. Mumbai Votes asks for an interview with each politician once a year, an online link to which is also provided. The end goal, as Vivek puts it, is to ensure their 'promises remain on file'.

It's not a one-man job. Vivek has a network of around two hundred voluntary researchers and analysts around the city. Most are students. Cleverly, he's struck a deal with a number of universities around the city. In return for helping him, they collect credits towards their degree. Coursework activism, you could call it.

As if on cue, Sonita walks in from the neighbouring room. A journalism undergraduate and a student leader, she's been heavily involved in Vivek's Web venture for several years. She is having problems getting online, she says. 'Mind if I sit by the window?' She finds a place on a mattress by the open sliding door, her laptop on her knees. Above her head, on the balcony side of the glass, hangs a bird feeder.

Vivek's eye is drawn to the hanging container. His attentions briefly shift to Mumbai's lack of bird life. He is disappointed. He'd hoped that the feeder might attract more birds to the neighbourhood. Other than the odd hungry sparrow, however, sightings have been sparse.

Mumbai Votes is a different story. I ask how he's persuaded so many volunteers to help out. They 'get' the website's objectives, he says. For the next half an hour, he lays out exactly what these are. It's an ambitious vision of citizen-led political reform. He's completely caught up in the idea, looking at me dead in the eye, speaking almost without pause. I'm reminded of Gopi back in Bengaluru and his infectious enthusiasm. Vivek has an activist's passion for bringing 'accountability' and 'transparency' to the electoral process. He talks enthusiastically about the 'polity' reaching out to their elected representatives. He wraps up with a picture of 'political self-cleansing' as the electoral process moves towards becoming more genuinely democratic.

I'm impressed by his apparent lack of political ideology. Mumbai Votes has 'absolutely no agenda', according to Vivek. He doesn't care whom people vote for, only that they vote 'intelligently'. Unlike many other politically oriented movements, his isn't driven by anger or dogma. Quantifiable data is his tool of choice, not protest banners or hunger strikes.

Ultimately, he'd like to see everyday Mumbaikers become 'citizen lobbyists', as he puts it. Not in the 'khadi kurta' sense of full-time activists. Closer to his thinking are politically engaged men and women armed with the necessary facts to hold their elected representatives to account. That's why he's against smart-matching – namely, websites that allow voters to plug in the issues that concern them and then automatically calculate the best-fitting candidate. In his mind, that's just drive-thru voting.

His guiding concern is to make India the world's most evolved democracy. Whenever he gives a presentation about Mumbai Votes, that's the message he puts on the first slide. At the moment, India is the world's largest democracy. That, he suggests, is nothing to boast about. 'Being the largest is simply down to bad family planning.'

It's a rare joke for him and it makes me laugh.

Gradually, I find myself being drawn in by Vivek's vision. 'Delhi', Chennai', 'Telangana', I jot down, as the Web activist lays out his hopes for a franchise model spreading across India. Dotting my notebook are other aspirations: 'Never have to go to the electoral booth with that sense of shame again,' 'An end to dynastic politics,' 'A silent revolution, click by click.' On the page, they read as a little clichéd, like a politician's soundbites. There's nothing of the sloganeer about Vivek, though. His vision comes across as sincere and heartfelt. It's not just me who thinks so. He's winning over others too.

Vivek talks of the website's volunteers. As he does so, I'm struck by a related thought: the allure of a great idea. His is a generation that has grown cynical about the political process, he says. All politicians are perceived as venal. Voting is seen a choice between 'the worst of two evils'.

He is more optimistic about the number of young Indians with a social conscience, however. A large number of his peers have a desire to 'give something back'. (He mimics the quote signs as he says the phrase. It's an ironic gesture that acknowledges how the sentiment itself has become saturated with cynicism.) Mumbai Votes appeals to many of these. 'Without making a huge hue and cry, they see it as a way to revolutionise how politics is done in our country.' Web-savvy voters are buying in as well. At election time, newspaper journalists cite the website's candidate profiles. Supporters spread the word through their social networks. 'People who felt there was never any hope in the way politics is done in Mumbai or in India now see in us a workable model – a way to crack the problem in some way.'

Vivek hopes to see Mumbai politics becoming cleaner. A cursory glance at the newspapers suggests the inner workings of power are as murky as ever. Political representatives still vote along party lines, not following private conscience. Party hierarchies are still lined with the brothers, sons, wives and third cousins of political potentates. Objectively, just how much difference is he making? Vivek admits that it's early days. The website only became fully functional less than two years ago. Metrics for success are difficult to gauge as well.

That two hundred students are becoming advocates for change – 'in their families, among their relatives, on their campuses' – marks one of his positive benchmarks. What gives Vivek most heart, however, is when politicians telephone to complain. 'It shows what we're doing bites.' The thought that he might be getting under their skin brings a wry smile to his face.

'What do they call to complain about?'

'Oh all sort of things. Some object on principle to what we're calling for,' he says. 'They claim that our demands are unrealistic. "Listening to voters is all very good," they say, "but we have more urgent matters. There are slums to clear, poverty to alleviate and jobs to create."'

For most, however, their chagrin is of a more personal nature. What riles politicians, he says, is the website's publication of their criminal records. More than a third of Mumbai's elected representatives are convicted felons or have criminal cases pending against them. One local legislator, a well-known gangster, even ran for national office from his prison cell. Rioting and causing injury comprise the most common allegations. But at least half a dozen current representatives are under investigation for murder. Like it or not, Vivek says, politicians can't stop these facts seeping out. 'Even in slums, people in cybercafes are Googling politicians' names and this information comes up.'

Vivek pauses. He looks to the window, to the tangle of wires, to the empty bird feeder. 'Of course, there's a long way to go.'

For the first time, he sounds downbeat. India is not about to usher in an era of enlightened legislators. That's a fact. Public good will only ever motivate the few. The rest will be lured by the prospect of power and the trappings of office, as they always have been. Then his optimism returns. There is one sign of hope, he says. Not why people run for public office. Any change there lies outside the hands of man. It requires a 'spiral revolution', he maintains. Progress, instead, is revealing itself in the how: how politicians win power, how they use it and, ultimately, how they retain it. The key, according to Vivek, is information: finding it, organising it, spreading it.

I wish Vivek well and head up to the Indian capital for the final time.

Delhi

There are two people I want to meet: Rajesh Jala, a documentary-maker, and Arjun Pandey, a conservationist and owner of a small media company.

I have met both before, on my earlier trips to the capital. This time, I return with a specific question for them. Ashish and Vivek had convinced me of the latent power of knowledge and information sharing. Ideas and facts, together they have the potential to transform minds and initiate change. My gut and my experience confirm this to be true.

The question I have for Rajesh and Arjun is one of access. Information needs to be transmitted for its power to be unlocked. Alone, it's useless. How can they ensure that information reaches all Indians?

The issue of access marks the beginning of a journey, not the end. India is bubbling with talk of change. The twenty-first century is, potentially, there for the taking. Which way will it go, though? Who in India will decide? Right now information is controlled by a minority. Supposing that all one billion-plus Indians gain equal access. What destiny would they choose? What kind of country would they build for themselves? Such a prospect, the very opportunity to decide, would constitute a revolution in itself.

As my train rattles northwards, I realise that the question is as much about the message as the medium – and no message is

ideologically neutral. Few facts arrive without their accompanying arguments. In today's India, as the billboards, cinema screens
and TV channels profess, it is commercial interests that dominate.
Are the streets of tomorrow's India to be lined with Cafe Coffee
Days and clothed in Levi's? Are the voices of the elite – the business tycoons, the God Men, the cabinet ministers, the celebrities –
to win out?

In a sense, that's not my concern. It is for Indians themselves
to decide their future course. Yet New India deserves a balance,
a full spectrum of ideas from which to pick. Alternative messages
do exist, but picking them out requires determined listening. Their
proponents are sidelined, their arguments muted. Every now and
then, a lone voice does break through the mesh of mainstream
media. Well-known social activist Anna Hazare provides a celebrated case in point. His decision to go on hunger strike in early
2011 kicked off a nationwide debate about governmental corruption. Politicians were due to vote on a new corruption bill. Hazare
feared it would be watered down. The public agreed. The protest
call of 'I Am Anna Hazare' spread throughout the land. His fears
were realised. Hazare went on hunger strike again, lasting two
hundred and eighty-eight hours and causing him to lose seven and
a half kilograms. The combination of man and message, timing
and tactics, combined to force the issue onto the front pages. But
Hazare is the exception. Search the airwaves for the voices of dis-
possessed tribals or indebted farmers and the silence is profound.
Flick through the newspapers for the views of radical environ-
mentalists or human-rights activists and the column inches are
scant. So who exactly is bringing fresh perspectives to the ear of
the masses? Too few, I fear.

In this context, schoolteachers are crucial conduits of information and ideas. Do enough have the vision to help their pupils
probe and question? From what I've seen and heard, my confidence is low. Is the Internet the answer? Websites such as Vivek's
will no doubt contribute towards shaping the future, yet for the
moment Web access remains limited. Mumbai Votes can count
one hundred and twenty thousand unique visitors. That's im-

pressive. Still, it's less than one in every hundred of the city's population. While people may well be Googling in the slums, my hunch is that most of Vivek's visitors are educated, engaged citizens like him.

The battle for hearts and minds is being fought in the mainstream. Twenty years ago, India had five television channels. Today, it has more than five hundred. India's newspaper readership is the only one in the world that is actually growing – a consequence in large part of the penetration of the local-language press. Over one hundred million newspaper copies circulate daily in India. But what messages are they bringing to the masses?

Flicking through the mainstream television channels leaves me despondent. Filling the breaks between the advertisements is a lacklustre diet of soaps, sport, film reruns and general daytime mediocrity. Not that TV listings elsewhere in the world are substantively different. All the same, it remains true that the content is primarily engineered for minds to vegetate, not to cogitate on. To their credit, the national news channels are constant and ubiquitous. Ultimately, however, they too are structured with ratings in mind. Run an in-depth story and viewers are as likely as not to switch over. Risk a hard-hitting exposé and the lawyers' phones start ringing. As for local or regional stories, only the absurd or macabre find their way on to the national channels.

The newspaper industry is largely the same. Editors are as anxious to entertain as to inform. Easy targets are attacked as virulently as India's sacred cows are protected. The lines between private and public interest are also blurring. Advertising in India's printed press brings in just shy of three billion dollars a year. The *Hindustan Times*, for instance, openly admits that its journalists help write advertorials. *The Times of India*, meanwhile, has recently had to defend its practice of private treaties (essentially, strategic investments in mid-level companies that guarantee advertising and editorial exposure in return). Television majors like NDTV and CNBC reportedly have similar deals in place. Tellingly, the story broke on Doordarshan, India's lone publicly funded channel.

Of course, there are exceptions. India has many visionary editors and courageous journalists. Abrasive political weeklies like *Tehelka* offer them a platform from which to be heard. Almost by definition, however, these are non-mainstream, minority mouthpieces geared towards challenging the voice of the established press.

Earlier in the year, I'd attended a prize-giving ceremony organised by broadcaster CNN-IBN. It provided me with an illuminating insight into how things stand.

We'd all gathered in suits and ties in the conference hall of a five-star Delhi hotel to celebrate the year's top 'Citizen Journalists'. I'd gone along full of hope. Citizenship journalism – everyday people voicing their concerns, reporting realities from street level, bringing the spotlight on injustices and wrong-doings – surely this was a route to change, a shot in the arm for the democratic process?

Admirably, CNN's powerful Indian joint venture gives air-time to such amateur reporters. The winning clips, all shot on handheld cameras, made for heart-rending, eye-opening footage: the woman who escaped after years of forced prostitution, the father who tracked down the speeding lorry driver who ran over his son, the schoolgirl who fought for under-age factory workers to return to class, the ninety-year-old Freedom Fighter who'd battled to have her pension reinstated, the man who brought officials to book for siphoning off funds from government schemes. Many had used provisions of the Right To Information Act, an innovative law that allows members of the public to request information withheld by officialdom, to build their cases. If the evening had finished there, I'd have left inspired by the possibilities ahead.

Then Amitabh Bachchan, the Bollywood superstar and the evening's guest speaker, stood up and damned the broadcaster with his praise. In sonorous tones, the actor-statesman eulogised the broadcaster for cultivating the 'nascent seed' of citizen reporting. An elaborate discourse on citizens' rights and their reciprocal obligations to the body politic then followed. 'These individuals amongst us . . .', he'd said with in-character gravitas,

'. . . possess the native intelligence to think for themselves, the will to inform themselves accordingly, a higher justice beyond immediate self-interest, the heroic valour to act, and a belief in the possibility of change.'

The corporate executives in the front row began to squirm. The addendum was not in the script. If they'd been in their control rooms, they'd have pulled him off air. But, trapped in their seat, they could do nothing but sit and listen to the King of B-Town lecture them on journalism's 'code of ethics'. Their painted smiles looked grimacing.

At the podium, India's biggest superstar still had more to say. Audiences, he railed, deserve more than info-tainment, saccharine emotionalism, hackneyed language, hysterical rumour-mongering, shallow punditry, blind partisanship and 'hyped-up, dumbed down, scooped out, frivolous conjecture'. All responsible journalists would agree, would they not? Citizen journalism was 'at best a modest redress', he rounded off, dagger now truly bloodied. Indeed, some might argue that more 'cynical' elements of the news media embrace it so as to 'dissimulate' its threat, 'lavish such praise . . . as to kill it smilingly'.

The King of Bollywood sat down to applause that, for once, was less than ecstatic. Even among griping celebrities, such a vitriolic gnashing at the arm that feeds them is rare. More so for someone like Bachchan, who has the media to thank for a good part of his hyperbolic fame.

All the same, I found it odd that his high-profile speech should have gone more or less unreported in the next day's press. In the following weeks, I'd watched CNN-IBN's mainstream bulletins in vain, waiting for a citizen journalist to crop up. Repeated requests to speak to the broadcaster about the initiative went unheeded.

Bachchan may not be the most objective of commentators, but nor, I began to sense, is he the most misinformed.

Rajesh Jala operates at the other end of the film spectrum. Whereas the Bollywood icon lives his life in the glare of the spotlight, this quiet, clear-eyed pundit from Kashmir strives and struggles in the shadows. As a documentary-maker fascinated by the human condition and the plight of India's underclasses, both his medium and his message fall outside the remit of the popular.

At our first meeting, he was in good humour. After a dozen years devoted to full-time film-making, his work had finally won some recognition. His recent film – *Children of the Pyre*, a stirring, evocative portrayal of the 'untouchable' Dom community that service the cremation ghats of Benares – had won a number of accolades including the special jury prize at the prestigious National Awards.

Six months on, he is in more sombre mood. I find him in a 'tricky spot', he says, when we meet for coffee in Delhi's South Extension. He's keen to do a film on his home state of Kashmir, he tells me, but unrest in the disputed border area keeps forcing him to stall. He's scoping out a second documentary on Benares too. This time, his focus will be on the widows who travel to the holy city to die. This project is running into difficulties as well. One of the women who he'd planned to film has just passed away.

As for *Children of the Pyre*, he'd successfully applied to Plan, an overseas grant-maker, to run an awareness campaign in Benares about caste discrimination. Twelve months on and internal problems with his local partners mean it is still waiting to get off the ground.

There is some good news, though. Four of the seven adolescent boys around whom the film revolves are now in full-time school. Two others are learning to become drivers. That gratifies him enormously.

I ask him how the film has been received in India. It hasn't been, he reluctantly admits. It's won plaudits on the international festival circuit, everywhere from Amsterdam and Rome to Montreal and Leipzig. But the film has yet to have its Indian debut. He has some screenings planned for the coming months. But venues for documentaries are limited. As for cinema halls, forget it. Television offers an outside chance. One in ten documentaries might get picked up by a national network. 'Even then, the pay is peanuts.'

He spent his life savings on producing the film, topped up with substantial loans from his friends. He is hoping to recoup the money through the sale of overseas rights and DVDs abroad. He has an international distributor, Fortissimo Films. Channels in Poland and Hong Kong already plan to screen it. Isn't there funding from the government? There is, he says, but it requires a 'lifetime's patience' to extract it. Nor is it very much, just five hundred thousand rupees. 'You can't make a film on that.' Plus only five per cent is paid up front, subject to the film-maker depositing a similar amount as a guarantee. To add insult to injury, the government takes twenty per cent off the top. 'As a culture tax.'

I don't have the heart to ask Rajesh how he thinks messages like his can best be conveyed to the public. He is fighting against a system that seems reluctant to listen. So instead I ask why he bothers. The forty-three-year-old sighs. It's a question he must have asked himself more than once.

'Films can't bring revolution,' he eventually states, 'but they can change perception.'

'Yet . . .'

I hesitate. An obvious rejoinder jumps to my lips. I'm not sure how to phrase it. I admire Rajesh enormously, both for his human sensitivity and his gifts as a cinematographer.

Last time we'd met, he'd loaned me a copy of his award-winning film. I watched it and was as impressed by its technique as I was moved by its subject-matter.

Earlier in the year, I'd stood at the same burning ghats on the River Ganges where he'd shot. I'd watched bodies placed on the high stacks of sandalwood, seen the mourners crowding round. I'd smelt the sweet incense of butter oil as the first flames flickered, felt the warm blast of air as the fire built, heard the pop as a skull exploded. I'd stood there mesmerised, for as long as I could bear the heat, right on the edge of the cremation ground.

Thinking back to the scene now, I can picture a shaven-headed man, the eldest son, clothed in a white dhoti. His chest naked, tears in his eyes, he rakes the coals for the last of his father's earthly remains. I can see him turn his back for the last time, eyes cast heavenwards. Biting his top lip, he throws a small clay water jug over his shoulder, shattering it into a hundred tiny fragments, severing in a single move the mortal ties with his father and releasing his spirit from the cycle of Samsara, from the circle of suffering and rebirth.

My recollections of those working at Benares' famous Manikarnika Ghat come back far less sharply. I have vague visions of a gaunt, bearded man carrying logs up the crematorium steps, dropping them beside a smouldering pyre and then silently returning below for more. I've an image of another man, sad and faceless, perhaps shrouded in a headscarf, keeping the burning embers alive with the prodding of a stick.

It is these men – the stagehands of the deathly saga, not its protagonists – who had stirred Rajesh's empathy. It was their untold story that he described with such vivid, compassionate eloquence.

And so it is with trepidation that I continue with my question, unwilling to sound facetious or disrespectful, but compelled to ask all the same.

'. . . Yet in order to change perceptions, people will need to actually see your films, right?'

Rajesh merely smiles and acknowledges the logic. Of course, he's thought about that, he says. He knows documentary-making in India isn't commercially viable. He's aware his audience will only ever be limited. But what is he to do?

'I've wanted to make films since I was ten years old. I used to bunk off school to go to the cinema. It's all I've ever wanted to do. And it's now all I do. I'm not an activist. I'm not a philanthropist. I'm just trying to address the issues that concern me in the best way I know how.'

Film-making is his vocation. I understand and respect that. It's the tirelessness with which he pursues his craft: it's that which I can't quite fathom. Has he not thought about going overseas? He has a commitment to India, he says. 'It's no good being somewhere else. You have to be in the current system if you want to correct it.'

Perhaps I look unconvinced or maybe he feels a burden to share. Either way, the gentle, soft-spoken film-maker sighs once more and then, in whispered tones, starts slowly describing his past.

His mother died when he was thirteen. His father . . . well, let's just say, he grew up from then on with his uncle and aunt. In December 1989, aged twenty-one, incursions by militant Kashmiri nationalists forced him to flee his homeland. In total, more than three hundred thousand Indians, mostly Pundits, packed up and left. Most went to neighbouring Jammu. Rajesh headed for Delhi, to a refugee camp.

'Close to where we are now,' he says, pointing out of the window, across the highway. 'The conditions were subhuman.' Twenty-seven families under one roof. Two toilets between one hundred people. He lived there for eight years, working part-time as a technician for All India Radio.

I look in the direction of his pointed finger but can see only shops and flats. 'No, further off,' he says. 'But it's gone now, anyway.' Eventually, he moved to Mumbai. He hoped to land a job under a well-known director, 'to gain some experience, you know'.

As with struggling acting student Naval, he soon discovered the loneliness of being a 'nobody' in India's film capital. He ended up at TV Today, a production house, trotting out meaningless half-hour shows for the Hindi news channel Aaj Tak. He returned to Delhi. A decade of corporate videos, travel shows and 'stupid films to survive' followed. It wasn't until his mid-thirties that he managed to direct what his calls his first 'meaningful' film.

'What was it called?'

The Floating Lamp of the Shadow Valley, he says with a note of wistfulness. 'It's about a nine-year-old boy on Dal Lake in Srinagar. He's a boat boy.' A boat boy? A ferryman, the film-maker clarifies. His name is Arif. He rows passengers across the lake.

Rajesh had spotted him one day on his flat-hulled canoe and followed him home, to a wooden shack on the lake-side where he lived with his mother, sister and three small brothers. 'He alone kept that family of six.' His father was absent, an ex-militant in the clandestine war for Kashmir.

It struck me that, as with his film on Benares, the story revolves around a fatherless boy. Was that an important theme in his work? Rajesh mulls over the question. How families interact fascinates him, he says quietly. He grew up not knowing what fatherhood was. He still doesn't. His voice grows almost inaudible.

'No one knows this.' He stops, collects himself. Knows what, I wonder? I try and fathom what might be coming next. 'My father . . . my father was a spy.' The words emerge slower and more deliberate than ever. 'He was caught.' The tip of his finger presses hard into the wooden table top until it grows crimson around the quick. 'For seventeen years, he was incarcerated in a Pakistani prison. The nation, this nation, forgot about him.'

As my mind processes the revelation, Rajesh wraps up his story. His father was eventually released in a prisoner exchange, he explains. He now lives in Delhi. With you? No, not with him. Somewhere else. He's a broken man. The two see each other, although they have no real relationship. His father has tried to gain some sort of legal restitution, a regular state income at least, but he lacked the money for the lawyers' fees. 'So you see, I can't give up.' Making films, 'sensitising people', as Rajesh puts it, is not only what he does. It's *who* he is.

Arjun is altogether different. He's an ideas man. He's also a relentless, first-class strategist. He knows what he wants and has a savvy sense of how to get it. Tall and broad-chested, he is a product of India's best schools and the country's highest social grooming. Arjun's wife's aunt is married to the Raja of Patna. 'She has a palace,' he'd said as an aside. As for his family, his landowning lineage is written into the fertile soil of Uttar Pradesh. In his early thirties, he has the confidence of someone born into privilege, of someone who can talk of 'our ancestral home' without a hint of irony. A friend in the British diplomatic service had put us in touch. The two had met in Germany, at a global youth leaders' summit.

I liked Arjun from the start, mostly because he was the antithesis of what he could have been. Generous-spirited, modest and

unapologetically idealistic, he disabused me of the worst stereo-
types associated with India's social elite. He'd studied welfare
economics, not finance. He worked for himself, not a large corporation. And, above all, he cared passionately about the destiny
of India, his homeland – both for its people and its natural environment.

We'd met at the five-star Imperial Hotel, a revamped British-
era relic with exquisite Victorian art on the walls and foxhounds
on the bar-mats. The corridors were full of Indian gentlemen in
brass-buttoned blazers and the kind of well-heeled tourist who
travelled the world in a Panama hat. From the soft-carpeted
splendour of the Imperial, we'd moved on to the Press Club of India. A complete contrast, the journalists' clubhouse was an earthy
joint full of sweat and boozy laughter. Located close to Parliament, the low-roofed refuge kept its affiliates happily fed, watered
and within stumbling distance of evening press conferences.

Sitting in the dusk-lit courtyard, drinking a beer and nibbling
on masala chips, Arjun had revealed the roots of his eclecticism:
how his father was Hindu and his mother Sikh (he himself read
the Gita but felt drawn to Buddhism), how his parents had been
born in East Africa but had migrated back to India, and how a
commitment to change ran in his blood.

His father (now deceased) and uncle both enjoy reputations
as pioneers in wildlife cinematography. *Shores of Silence*, a film
made by his uncle, Mike Pandey, prompted a nationwide ban on
the hunting of whale sharks. The film-making pair helped win
protective sanctions for a host of other native species, including
the Indian elephant, the Indian vulture and the humble horseshoe
crab.

Arguably their most significant legacy comes through
EarthMatters, a weekly television bulletin about environmental
issues. In India, it runs on public broadcast television in twelve
different languages. It goes out in localised formats to another
fifty-five countries around the world. Its impact – the programme
has spawned two thousand 'eco clubs' and generates over five

thousand letters per week – earned his uncle the title of 'Hero of the Environment' in *Time* magazine.

Arjun has inherited his father's passion for India's rich cultural and natural heritage. He is not the older man's clone, however. For one, their characters are dissimilar. His father had, he remembers, enormous patience. One of his best-known documentaries depicts a lone tree on a deforested hillside in Jharkhand. He filmed it every day for a year. Arjun, in contrast, is manically active on numerous fronts. A film on tiger conservation, a website on India's primary health risks, a hidden camera exposé about e-waste and a regional network of community radio stations were just some of the projects he'd mentioned to me last time.

Arjun's hyperactivity reflects the youthful spirit of his generation. It's also a symptom of the times in general. In his father's youth, people fished in the Yamuna River. Today, industrial waste and raw sewage have robbed Delhi's main watercourse of all life. The time for patience, Arjun feared, had passed. 'India may well become the next superpower,' I remember him saying. 'But what good is it if we have no drinking water?' It's not just environmental degradation that has sped up. Technology has accelerated too. Twenty years ago, a trunk call to Mumbai had to be pre-booked and routed through an operator. For today's mobile-phone millions, it's there in the press of a speed-dial button.

With last orders called, I'd asked Arjun if he had a guiding philosophy, a maxim that brought direction to his numerous ideas and copious energy. He'd answered vaguely at first; something about 'making an impact', about leaving India a better place for his daughter. Then, almost embarrassed, he'd mentioned 'Gandhiji's Talisman'.

Coined towards the end of the Mahatma's life, the short phrase used to appear at the front of every schoolbook. 'It's just a simple thing,' Arjun had said. Growing up, he and his classmates used to 'hack it'. As an adult, it came back to him differently. What does it say? Picking up the bill and pushing back his chair, he'd suggested that I look it up.

Afterwards, I had done so. The Talisman represents a plea

for all Indians to think of the wider collective before themselves. When in doubt, the Father of the Nation advises, apply the following test. Recall the face of the poorest and the weakest man whom you may have seen, and ask yourself if the step you contemplate is going to be of any use to him. Will he gain anything by it? Will it restore him with control over his own life and destiny? In other words, will it lead to swaraj [freedom] for the hungry and spiritually starving millions?' His mention of the Talisman is one of the reasons I'd like to see Arjun again.

This time round, we meet at his office. His company, 24 Frames, is housed in a windowless basement along a residential street in the capital's downmarket Chittaranjan Park area.

'Rent's cheap,' he says, as he unlocks the door and shoves it with his shoulder. His uncle's offices have a fish tank in the roof with twenty koi carp. Arjun's has an arthritic fan and a damp problem. Yet it's his own venture and its success or failure rests on him alone.

Judging from the extensive to-do list on the whiteboard beside his desk, the environmentally minded media executive has clearly lost none of his zeal for work. Short films, 'docos', press releases and various media campaigns are sketched out in hurried marker pen. 'New projects?' reads the penultimate entry, as if he didn't already have enough on his plate.

The final addition to the list anchors Arjun in the real world: 'Bills pending'. To keep afloat, he takes on a range of purely commercial projects to cross-subsidise his other interests. 24 Frames is a 'for-profit social enterprise', in Arjun's words, a very modern, very New India concept.

He opens his laptop to fill me in on his latest venture. A sticker on the reverse of the screen rears into view. '24 Frames: Empowering Visual Communication', it says. He loads up a track by Swaransh Mishra, a young music artist. 'Smoking is like hanging yourself,' the unlikely first line rings out to a boom-box beat. The lyrics continue in a similar vein. 'You grow tired, but your cough doesn't.' The song forms part of an anti-tobacco campaign that

Arjun is spearheading. Smoking kills millions of Indians every year, he insists. 'Many have absolutely no idea of the risk.'

The anti-smoking song is currently playing 'on FM'. It comes with an accompanying video, released on YouTube, depicting a happy smoker who ends up in a hospital bed. It sounds like a license for a lawsuit. But Arjun doesn't seem overly concerned. He's persuaded Agnee, an Indie pop band, to record another track for him. He's working towards an album. 'Once the tunes get on the radio, they create a life of their own,' he says, his eyes sparkling at the thought. His roll-out strategy also includes a tie-up with iTunes, a series of ring-tone downloads and a competition for school bands. Anti-smoking messaging on matchboxes form part of his plan too, although he's yet to resolve how to action the idea. 'We'll run it through social media,' he says, jumping back to the band competition. And the prize? 'A slot on the album, of course.' It will, Arjun is sure, be 'absolutely huge'.

As with Rajesh, Arjun has anticipated my question before I have the opportunity to ask it. His tactic for getting his message out is straightforward: take each and every media form, new and old, and, as far as funds permit, exploit them to the full. The mainstream press won't run stories like these, he says, referring to his various projects. It confirmed my existing impression of the media.

'The tobacco lobby has an enormous budget. We don't.' Yet Arjun remains a staunch believer that information can create the ripples of change. 'All it takes is a small nudge to give rise to an awakening.' I'm struck by his use of the term, a carbon copy of Ashish and Vivek's thinking.

I think back to our last meeting and the dire picture that Arjun had drawn of India's environmental predicament: forests being stripped, rivers being dammed, water courses being polluted, industrial waste proliferating and greenhouse gases escalating. Isn't it too late? It's never too late for anything, he insists, an optimist to the end. Indians have a deep respect for nature. 'It's there in our scriptures and folk stories.'

He recounts the case of the Bishnoi community in Rajasthan, who, he maintains, would 'sacrifice their lives' before seeing a single tree cut down. Or the tribes of Goa's sacred groves, who remove their shoes before entering the forest. 'Such is the respect they have for nature,' he says passionately. 'This is the country that has all that too.'

I'm reminded of *India Today*'s message about ensuring India's heritage informs its future. Arjun, meantime, repeats his belief about how ideas, once they're out there, burst into the public consciousness and call individuals to action.

I raise my eyebrows involuntarily. 'You don't think so?' he asks, probing my reaction. I agree with the premise, I tell him cautiously. I mention the comparatively low hit-rate for Mumbai Votes and Rajesh's uphill battle to get his films aired. Aren't the barriers just too high? The young change-maker looks unconvinced. The domino effect, unseen consequences, the power of the collective. All result in impacts of which we are often not aware, he insists.

Then he reaches for his Blackberry. 'What are you doing this weekend?' No plans, I tell him. He puts in a call. Five minutes later, he's arranged for me to fly with him to Ladakh.

We are off to plant some trees.

Leh

The streets of Leh are already busy as our small convoy snakes through the city's narrow streets shortly after breakfast. The air is cold and crisp, invigoratingly so, like plunging into an ice bath after a leisurely sauna. On the roof of the world, the stifling streets of Delhi feel a world away.

A contingent of army trucks rattles past, bound for the nearby Chinese border. Townspeople shuffle along the pavements, their high cheekbones and oval faces hidden beneath winter hats and woollen mufflers. A family of Punjabi holidaymakers stands on a corner cocooned in fleeced clothing. They look lost and are huddled around a tourist map as though wishing it were a warm camp fire.

Ladakh's mountain-cradled capital soon disappears from view as we head up the Indus River valley. Our destination is the village of Changa, a couple of hours' drive away. The road is flat and the sky as blue and clear as glacial melt. The river, still young and full of mountain vigour, cuts a straight, frothing path along the valley floor. Vivek would approve: there are no offending cables to spoil the view, just two rocky mountain ranges that encase the valley like distant fortress walls. Their granite tips are doused in snow, archers' posts painted white. I imagine border guards crouched behind them, holed up in insulated bivouacs, eyeing one another through frosted binoculars and dreaming of home.

Arjun is sitting up front in the passenger seat of the hired jeep. His cameraman, a photographer and I occupy the seats behind. The driver, a local man lost inside an oversized jacket, drives in silence. At one stage, he turns on the radio, flits between channels, locates some crackling pop music and then, with a grunt of displeasure, turns it off.

The quiet returns. We journey on, no one speaking, all of us adjusting to the altitude and the vast, impregnable stillness of the landscape.

Arjun breaks the silence to point out the Dalai Lama's summer palace, lying in the valley below, across the Indus. Nestled amid a copse of slender willows, a rarity in the desert terrain, the retreat itself is hard to make out. Prayer flags flutter among the leaves, yellow as custard, waiting tentatively for the wrenching hand of autumn. Further along, Arjun calls our eye to monasteries perched impossibly above on mountain clefts, serene Buddhas locked away in their own meditative bliss. Stupas stand as sentinels around them, warding off the world outside.

About halfway into the drive, we approach a small roadside hamlet. Arjun requests the driver to slow down. He indicates for us to look to the right. Lining the road is a row of single-storey buildings. Square and squat, they match the houses in other wayside settlements along the way. Yet these are different. They are all squashed beneath a snowdrift of black, stony earth, each building frozen in time, as if captured on black-and-white camera film and then forgotten on the cutting-room floor. Several roofs have collapsed. One house has the boot of a car projecting out of what was presumably the garage.

'Mudslide,' Arjun says. The driver recognises the hateful English word and wrinkles his forehead grimly.

Nearing an army outpost, we drop down from the road into Changa and cross the fast-flowing Indus via a solid steel bridge. Doubling back along the river, the jeep climbs up and out of the drab, colourless village and trundles towards a ridge in the road. Prayer flags stand at intervals along the route, the Buddhist equivalent of traffic cones. Other than us, the road is empty of vehicles. Across the brow of the hill ahead, a faint dust cloud rises. The driver shifts down a gear and brings the car to a halt. Arjun alights and walks towards the ridge, camera in hand. He returns a couple of minutes later, his face aglow.

As we pull out, the source of his excitement comes into view. Down below, spread out over a huge field of scrubland, is a sea of white. Thousands upon thousands are gathered, too many to count. So many people, so much life, it's as though the gods have pitched a fairground in the desert. Were it a mirage, the scene could not be more surprising.

The photographer winds down the window and immediately starts shooting off frames in rapid succession. He doesn't stop, not even when we reach the waiting crowds and friendly hands of welcome mob the jeep. We pull up in a caravan of buses and trucks. Vehicles have been arriving since first light, bringing men and women – young and old, Buddhist and Muslims, monks and nuns – from every corner of the valley. Each volunteer is dressed in a white prescription T-shirt and is awaiting the starting bell.

We make our way to the field, pressing through the crowd of onlookers at the entrance gate. Individual teams, five or six people strong, stretch down to the banks of the Indus. Each group stands in the square plot assigned to them. Everyone has an implement with which to dig: some have spades and picks, others nothing more than sticks and stones. They sing and pray and talk and laugh, a burble as sweet and pure as a mountain stream.

A local reporter is interviewing the Chief Forest Officer. The excitable official is talking ten to a dozen. Trees firm up the soil, staving off soil erosion and preventing landslides, he's explaining to the camera. He numbers off their other benefits on his finger: more tourism, less 'toxins from cars', a nice aesthetic.

The reporter thanks him and turns the microphone to Arjun, whom he recognises as part of the event's organising committee. 'So, a *Guinness Book of Records* attempt here in Ladakh today,' he says. 'Tell us, how did this come about?' Arjun repeats the account he first gave me back in Chittaranjan Park: about his initial idea to offset the carbon emissions of the Commonwealth Games, about how one million trees will need planting and how his Holiness the Gyalwang Drukpa had agreed to help. Twenty-seven thousand trees planted in one hour is the current record, he clarifies. 'Today we're aiming for fifty thousand.'

A sudden shout goes up. The crowd surges forward. Cutting Arjun short, the reporter mumbles his appreciation and rushes off. His Holiness has arrived.

We too edge forward. Shaven-headed monks with gleeful faces strain to catch sight of their spiritual leader. Villagers too stand on tiptoe, levering themselves up on the shoulders of those in front. As they stretch, the brightly coloured cummerbunds holding their robed garments in place poke out from under their T-shirts. As one, the crowd inches forward toward a scaffolding dais in the middle of the field. Their every step is accompanied by the blare of trumpets and crash of cymbals.

Ahead walks a stately entourage of a dozen men and women, ceremonially attired in traditional Ladakhi costume: flowing robes of silk and velvet, elaborate brocade, black fur headgear, all with loops and twists, bright buttons and silver piping. His Holiness climbs the dais steps. He salutes the crowd. A green flag is raised and the Indian national anthem sung. Then, with a sudden explosion of digging and dust, the record attempt is under way.

I stand there in awe, seeing the seed of Arjun's idea take root before my eyes. I turn to congratulate him, but find him gone. I look around. Bent-backed volunteers radiate out in every direction, all of them clouded in dust as they scrap frantically at the earth.

I look back and forth, until I finally spot him. He's off to my left, several plots away, crouched down beside a young woman with pigtails running down the length of her back. A child sits at her side, three years old at most. Arjun is watching the little one as she stretches forward and places the tiniest of saplings in the hole her mother has dug. New India is being born. His face is turned away, but I can tell that Arjun is smiling.

Conclusion: The Darjeeling Express

The jeep pulls up along the kerb and I clamber out onto Ghoom high street. Perched on a windswept ridge along the winding road to Siliguri, the air is thin and damp.

Darjeeling would be visible in the foothills below if the clouds were not so attached to the place. The hilly contours and chill winds draw them to Ghoom, just as harbours call in ships from the sea. Today, as usual, a soggy blanket of wet cloud drapes the mountainous settlement in grey. It sits there heavy and snug. There is no sign of it lifting.

Outsiders rarely stop here. Tourists pass through in the pre-dawn mists, racing to see sunrise at nearby Tiger Hill. The narrow-gauge steam train tarries longer, pausing for breath before its descent into Darjeeling. Its passengers huddle in the warm cocoon of their carriages beneath wool scarves and thermals. They rarely, if ever, alight.

It is fifteen years since I was last here. I remember the day I first arrived. It was early evening. A former monk had driven me pillion on his motorbike along a precipitous back road from town. The power supply had just ground to a halt throughout the valley, as it would do every day thereafter. Night came early to Ghoom back then.

I recall entering the monastery and how a flickering candle flame illuminated the abbot's office in an autumnal glow. The rest was pitch-black. I fought back the tears as I sat in the cold, bare room that was to become my home. Washing was impossible. The water bucket in the outside bathroom had frozen over. I climbed into my sleeping bag that first night and tried to sleep. In the early hours, I woke to the tinkling of a small bell. It was coming from the next-door room. My neighbour was undergoing a lengthy spiritual retreat, I'd later learn. Every few hours through the night, the self-styled hermit rose to pray and ring his bell. Tomorrow would be better, I told myself.

And it was. Gradually, I fell into the rhythm of monastic life. My teaching load was slight. I had time to read, think and sleep. Over the months, my reclusive neighbour and I grew accustomed to one another, my radio in the morning compensating for his nocturnal incantations.

It feels strange to be back. Despite myself, I'd expected everything to be familiar. It isn't. Recollections filter back to me, faint and blurred – the bend in the road, the railway track, the feel of moist air on my face. I wait for a bolt from the past. It doesn't come. I feel disappointed and a little cheated.

I stroll back up the road and pass the shop fronts of Ghoom's rudimentary high street. The place feels bigger than before, like an overweight version of itself. New buildings have cropped up. Old ones have expanded. Phone repair booths, an ATM and several cybercafes now mix among the time-worn convenience stores and roadside eateries. I look for the post office. Back then, before the world went global and shrank, the post office was my lifeline to home. I find it gone. Or not where I remember it.

As I near the end of the village, my feet urge me left up an inclining side road. I obey the impulse and turn off the high street. The lane passes a dimly lit butcher's hut, half shop, half abattoir. The low-roofed building is grimy. Its unsanitised morbidity feels almost like an intentional affront to Ghoom's vegetarian residents. Further up the hill, around a sharp bend, my feet come to a halt. A narrow slit opens between two houses, giving way to the tiniest of alleyways. I peer into the shady gap. It somehow seems familiar and I leave the road.

The track is overgrown. Its muddy path cuts behind a row of houses, over a foul-smelling stream and alongside some terraced vegetable patches. Dogs bark from behind gates and wire fences. The route climbs up gradually in gentle zigzags. The general direction feels right and yet wrong. I'm on the verge of turning back when I see a gate above. A white *stupa* rises grandly from a plinth to its right. It's shaped like a sugary pear drop. 'Sakyaguru Monastery', reads a welcome sign – the site of my erstwhile teaching post.

I touch the gate and it swings noisily open on a pair of rusty hinges. A short flight of steps rises up in front. I remember a grander entrance, with a gabled arch and prayer flags. Unsure of myself, I ascend all the same. The steps lead into the monastery's main courtyard. What used to be the main gate has been relegated to a side door, I now realise. Taking its place on the front side of the courtyard stands a new entrance. It faces directly down the valley. From the courtyard edge, a series of twisting, concrete steps leads to a sturdy road bridge, which crosses a muddy ravine and gives direct access back onto Ghoom's high street. Another fifty yards and my winding ascent could have been avoided. My feet were right, but out of step with the times.

I find the monastery enveloped in fog. It feels empty and abandoned. Its physical edges are blurred, as if the building were sketched in soft-tipped pencil and then smudged with an eraser. Gradually, a thin film of dampness descends and settles on my clothes. It's not long before the cold starts nibbling at my fingers and ears. I sit there in the clouds' silent folds, hands clamped under my armpits, rocking to and fro against the chill air, as the past begins to peak out of the haze – first as suggestions, then as images clear and sharp. I close my eyes. There's no sound except for the muffled sigh of the wind. For the briefest of moments, I'm eighteen again, my early life unveiling itself before me.

The experience is intoxicating: Morning *pooja*. The Lasar Festival. Breakfasts of unleavened bread. Chess in the sunshine. My classroom. Weekend escapes into Darjeeling. Tintin in Tibet. Steaming *momos*. Stodgy *thukpa* stew. Prayer flags. Conches. Cymbals. Walks in the hills. Home sickness. Kanchenjunga at dawn. The biting cold. Salty tea. Clouds, always clouds. Then it's gone. The memories fall out of focus.

Feeling the chill creep into my bones, I get to my feet and walk around the courtyard edge.

The gate is not the only modification. A three-storey classroom and accommodation block now stands where the secretary's office used to be. Bamboo scaffolding still clings to one end. Across the courtyard, an old storeroom has been converted for an electric generator. The former kitchen, a subterranean burrow stained black with wood smoke, mercifully looks to have fallen into disrepair.

Not everything has changed. The temple, square and resolute, is parked firmly in the centre of the courtyard where it has always been. Its paint looks more weather-beaten than before, but structurally it is identical. Its signature prayer-wheels still cling to the perimeter wall, reminding me now, as then, of giant spools of bronze thread.

Around the corner of the temple, an elderly monk appears from a bank of cloud. His tread is slow, his back stooped. He reaches up a frail hand and pushes each wheel in sequence. The motion is gentle, a soft caress just strong enough to set the metal capsules briefly spinning. For a few seconds, his muffled mantras sail off on the wind, before the wheels stop turning and draw still once more. His arthritic circuit takes him around the next corner and out of sight.

I watch him disappear, wondering how many laps a lifetime's circumambulations must come to.

My attention is diverted by the sight of a small novice monk skipping down the steps of the new accommodation block. His head is recently shaved and his maroon robe stained with dirt marks. He is wearing a pair of plastic sandals over thick socks.

I beckon him over. He trots across the courtyard and stares at me in amicable silence.

'Is Tashi Sangpo here, do you know?' I ask.

He looks me up and down, smiles ever so slightly and then scurries back inside without a word.

Tashi was my closest friend at the monastery. He'd have been twelve or thirteen years old then. Assigned as my aide, he would wash my clothes, bring me my food (I ate alone in my room) and collect my post. All the senior monks had a similar arrangement, the monastic equivalent of army officers and their batmen.

This servile relationship made me feel acutely uncomfortable. And so I'd try and find ways to offer Tashi something in return, to balance things out. I taught him to play cards, lent him my Sony Walkman and shared whatever gifts – mostly chocolate and boiled sweets – that arrived for me in the mail. Each of my interventions probably went against the monastery's rules, which were strict and unbending back then. The novices had only a few weeks' holiday per year, were permitted to watch television only one evening per week and would regularly feel the sting of the teacher's cane.

In fact, one of the most graphic and lasting images I have of my time at the monastery is Tashi's thrashing. I was sitting in my room, which was located on the second floor above a small courtyard. The elevated position gave me a good view of the classroom below. The sound of yelping reached me first. As I neared the window, I saw Tashi being dragged through the classroom door. The prayer master, an ox of a man, had him by the ear. I watched as he tied a rope around Tashi's wrists and tethered him to a wooden pole in the yard. Tashi let out a gut-wrenching scream. The burly teacher ignored him, turning around and pacing back to the classroom. He returned brandishing a thick wooden stick.

What followed next has shamed me ever since: I retreated to my bed. Pressing my hands over my ears, I fought to shut out Tashi's cries and wish myself somewhere else. Anywhere but there. It wasn't my place to intervene, I told myself. Even so, it was a long time before I could look Tashi in the eye again.

Another monk emerges down the steps. He is in his late twenties and his hair is receding sharply at the temples. Above his robe, he's wearing a Manchester United tracksuit top in regulation red. Like the younger novice, he too looks at me quizzically.

'Tashi?'

'Yes,' he replies hesitantly.

'You don't recognise me?'

He looks at me blankly.

I hand him a piece of lined paper torn from a child's exercise book. I'd found it hidden among the sheaves of a diary from my time at the monastery. The page contains a letter to Tashi's uncle.

A practice exercise in his twelve-year-old hand, marked up with my red pen:

Dear Akula, Amila is comes in Sonada to grandmother . . . I think your exam is finished. How like exam? I think your exam is good . . . Ani Ikhcho marriage has finished because I did not goes in marriage because this time I am goes to puja.

Gradually he puts the pieces together. I watch with anticipation. He looks up and grins. 'Mr Oliver?' His face lights up in surprise. In his wide smile, I catch a sudden glimpse of the young boy I'd once known. A wave of emotion washes over me. We shake hands (monks don't hug). 'But you cut your hair!' He holds his hands around his head, imitating my curly bouffant of the time. The recollection gives us both cause to laugh and, more importantly, to adjust to the passage of time.

Tashi, I learn, no longer lives in Ghoom. He hasn't done so for more than a decade. Not so long after I left, he transferred to another monastery further down the valley to complete his education. For the last three years, he's been based in Kathmandu at the International Buddhist Centre. With enthusiasm, he tells me how he's studying to become a translator. The news heartens me. He is back at Guru Sakya Monastery for a brief holiday. His return bus to Nepal is booked for Monday first thing. Today is Saturday. He invites me to hang out with him until he leaves.

Blessed with a kind heart and gentle spirit, Tashi always struck me as being well suited to a religious life. The same could not be said for all his classmates. Some were terrors. Many have moved on to other things, Tashi tells me. A few joined the Indian army. A few others, the police. A substantial number left to get married, including Thupten Chopal. I remember Thupten well as he was particularly unruly. According to Tashi, he's doing well for himself. He now runs a clothes stall on Darjeeling's Nehru Road. Among the other names I recognise are Tempa Sangpo, who drives a taxi in Sikkim, and Gunden Sangpo, who now lives in Germany with his sister. Of his fellow pupils, one – Kunga Sangpur – has died. I try hard to recall the face of the young monk and feel guilty that I cannot.

After a quick tour of the monastery, where I find my old room covered in lichen moss and devoured by woodlice and damp, Tashi suggests we head into Darjeeling. As with Ghoom, I find the former British hill station familiar yet different. The sight of Glenary's bakery and the forlorn Planters' Club fills me with a pleasant, comforting nostalgia. So too the starry-eyed honeymoon couples and the pony wallahs in Chowrasta square, the dilapidated Oxford Book Shop and the resilient Anglican church. Much of the rest, however – the Rink Mall on Ladenla Road, the hectic Doroga Bazaar, the United Colors of Benetton store, the new-build hotels that sprout across the hillside – sits at odds with my memory of the place as a docile mountain haven.

That evening, over soup and dumplings in a ramshackle eatery back in Ghoom, Tashi and I chat about old times. Towards the end, I bring the conversation around to the beating. He looks at me curiously. What beating? Then he remembers. 'Oh, that. That was nothing,' he says, brushing off the event with a laugh. The teacher is now the abbot, he tells me. Tashi talks of him with great affection. 'Things are different now,' he assures me. 'Many of the older monks have passed away. The younger monks are more relaxed. We have our responsibilities, but discipline is less.' The students are no longer beaten, for instance.

The revelation takes a moment to sink in. The memory of Tashi's beating –for reasons both of its physical barbarity and my own lack of temerity – has hung over me for years. For Tashi, on the other hand, it is buried away somewhere in the past. Just one occurrence among thousands in the helter-skelter process of growing up. Change is like that. Helicopetering back in, every new addition seems stark and sudden to me, like looking at a 'before' and 'after' photograph side by side. The intervening years, the transitional steps, are brushed aside. To Tashi, the pace is more gradual. Over time, he's absorbed the idea of himself speaking English fluently or having a Facebook account. These things are no longer a surprise to him. No more than waking in the morning to find himself an adult and not a twelve-year-old boy.

Similarly, India itself has changed much since my last visit. In some cases, the speed of transition has been phenomenal. Cities such as Mumbai and Bengaluru are almost unrecognisable from before. Elsewhere, in the villages and smaller towns, the first rain-drops of change are only just beginning to fall. Like the seasonal monsoons, however, Indians know more is on its way. There is nothing to stop it, no power in the universe to keep the hand of globalisation at bay. Some look up to the skies and see nothing but storms and squalls. Others hear the thunder and believe in the new dawn that lies beyond. All know themselves to be on the cusp of something momentous. Only the wilfully blind remain in the dark.

On Sunday afternoon, I travel with Tashi down the mountain road to the village of Masdura. The settlement is little more than a scattering of houses clinging to a slope. It boasts only one patch of marginally flat ground. This serves as the village football ground.

Tashi and his fellow monks are down to play Ghoom police in one of the early rounds of a local competition. Sakya United Foot-ball Club, plus several reserves and hangers-on, emerge from the squash of the team jeep. In Tashi's youth, the monastery rules pro-hibited football. Today, the monks have their very own club.

We all head to the changing rooms, which are housed in a metal shed beside the pitch. Tashi, a tenacious, sure-footed midfield-er, is captain. He takes the role seriously, talking his team-mates through the four–four–one formation (the pitch can only accom-modate nine players per side) prior to kick-off and generally buoying them up.

The whistle goes.

I watch the game from the sidelines. It's impossible to see bey-ond twenty feet or so because the fog is so dense. Shouts pierce through the cotton-wool sky. Every now and then a player bursts out of the mist and charges down the wing before being swal-lowed up by the smog once again. The spectators jump up at the prospect of action, then contentedly return to their seats.

The monk next to me fills the gaps listening to David Guetta on his iPod. Two others fall into a heated debate about the English Premier League results from the day before. The match ends with the police as victors – three goals to Sakya United's one, which came late in the game courtesy of Tashi's right foot. We're treated to an extensive account of his darting run and deft finish during the ride home. The visibility being what it was, there is no one to contradict him.

The team stops for steaming *momos* and milky tea at a family-run Tibetan restaurant back in Ghoom. After eating, some drift back to the monastery. Others move through to the proprietor's front room to slouch on his sofas and watch a game show on television. Tashi and I stay at the table. He leaves in the morning. We talk about his hopes for the future. I ask if he could ever see himself living in Tibet one day. His parents fled in 1964, five years after the Chinese occupation. He doesn't think so. Tibet will not become an independent nation again. Not in his lifetime, at least.

'So you're stuck in India then?'

'India', he replies without hesitation, 'is my home.'

This populous, overstretched nation has reached out to the offspring of refugees and offered him shelter and protection. Here, he is free to travel and practise his religion, he reminds me. He has a passport and, if so inclined, the right to vote. If he could, he'd like to go back to Tibet on pilgrimage. 'To see what it's like.'

My time with Tashi has been too brief. The next morning, he's gone before I rise for morning prayers. I enter through the temple's square door to the sound of rhythmic chanting. The older monks are sat in two lines facing one another. A junior monk walks the room with a large metal kettle, filling cups with tea. Two teenage monks are prostrating themselves in the open doorway, punishment for a minor act of ill-discipline. The morning sun streams in behind them, turning their dark robes scarlet. On either side of them, with their backs against the wall, the youngest monks giggle, yawn and occasionally contribute to the recitations. Their chief animation comes at the musical interludes, when they excitedly blow or beat the instruments that they've been assigned. The result is a wild, joyous cacophony.

Watching the smaller monks, I'm reminded of Tashi. As a child, he too used to lark about during morning *pooja*. Now he's an adult monk, with official responsibilities within his religious community. He's no stooge, though. He has grown into his own man. Like any individual, he has his personal passions and desires. He longs to hone his English. He wishes to travel. He's learning Spanish. In some ways, it is easy to see the son of refugees in him. He speaks Tibetan at home. He likes football, not cricket. He tunes into CNN, not Aaj Tak. In other ways, he is classically 'Indian'. He listens to Hindi music. He watches Bollywood films. Even the religion that frames his life owes its origins to the land he now calls home.

I'd returned to India with a latent fear. The country was globalising. Its consumer classes, as Captain Gopi had profitably foreseen, were on the rise. The ubiquitous brands of the Global Village – McDonald's, Vodafone, Coca-Cola, Google, CNN, et cetera – were there on the high streets, there in people's living rooms. Would India become subsumed? Would the commodified, conforming hand of global capitalism swallow it up?

My meeting with Tashi quieted that fear. India will change. That much is inevitable. A tangible example of this had come to me a month or so before, during a weekend visit to an ashram in Ahmedabad. The monks of the Swaminarayan sect are strictly ascetic, renouncing personal use of modern technologies such as computers and internet. Yet that hasn't stopped them developing a religious theme park in Delhi, a spectacular sound-and-laser water show in Gandhinagar, a multi-media publishing house and an IMAX feature film about the childhood of the sect's founder. 'Society is progressing,' one senior devotee had explained to me. 'It's not possible to stop that process. So we try to use technology in an educating and positive way wherever possible.'

India has a gift for absorption, a wondrous ability to amalgamate, to subvert and, for want of a better term, to 'Indianise'. As a nation, it is too diverse, too full of paradoxes, too confident ever to be homogenised. India's strength, it is often said, is in its plurality. It takes from others and makes of them its own. Down the centuries, it's seen a litany of foreign 'conquerors' come and go, from the Persians and Greeks to the French and British. Today's purveyors of globalisation are simply the latest in that line. All before them have left their mark, but none ever succeeded in curbing India to their will. Yes, India will change. Yet it will do so, I'd wager, on its own terms.

I think of Tashi travelling away on his bus. The thought of him gives me confidence in the continued strength of India's absorptive nature. He is Indian, as Indian as a Goan fisherman, a Mumbai businessman or a wandering sadhu on the banks of the Ganges. In many ways, he is a direct product of this extraordinary nation – of its linguistic traditions, its cultural history, its culinary tastes, its political customs, of the whole jumble of beliefs and ideas that make India what it is. In a small way, infinitesimal though it may be, Tashi is shaping India too. The country is richer for having embraced him. Culturally, it bears the imprint of his past and the footsteps of his present. New India awaits the contribution of his future. As it does the contributions of a billion and more individual Indians like him.

With a triumphant crash of cymbals and blowing of horns, morning *pooja* finishes. I cross the courtyard with my bag and head to the new concrete steps. I am leaving Ghoom once more. It's a new dawn and for once the clouds have lifted.

Postscript

Life moves on. People's circumstances change. As with India itself, the stories of those who inspired this book continue to unfold. Below is a very brief update on how their tales are progressing.

InMobi's growth figures are speeding off the charts. Since we met, Naveen's brainchild has grown to become India's largest internet company. The ex-McKinsey recruit now has more than a dozen offices around the world that oversee 55 billion ads per month. At the last count, investors have entrusted him with around $200 million to continue growing the company.

Despite his failsafe predictions, Captain Gopinath appears to be finding the logistics business harder to crack than he anticipated. Teething troubles at his new venture Deccan 360 have seen his air cargo business grounded and several hundred people laid off.

Babu has a new job. His former boss negotiated a position for him as driver to a wealthy Mumbai businessman's wife. She owns a Honda CR-V, a solid 'good status' car. Babu continues to live in Murty Nagar slum and dutifully attends to his crippled father every Sunday. His hopes for his own private fleet remain on the drawing board.

Shortly after my visit, Svasti landed an investment worth 54.5 million rupees from a group of private lenders. New regulation has since thrown India's microfinance sector into a spin. Even so, the Mumbai startup recently garnered an additional 45 million rupees from a Swiss private equity firm. Svasti now has eight branches across the city, over 12,000 clients and a loan portfolio of 195 million rupees.

Hindusthan Unilever's Shakti programme carries on expanding, with men being enrolled alongside women. Known as Shatimaans, the likes of Srilatha's husband, Srinwas, are given bicycles and sent out to sell Unilever's products in remote villages. As for Srilatha, she and her fellow Shakti Ammas have added basic bank accounts to their list of wares. The move follows a tie-in between Unilever and the State Bank of India.

I continue to receive occasional emails from Naval. He has extricated himself from his squat in Goregaon and is living in a Hindu temple in Kalyan East, Greater Mumbai. His work experience with Home TV led to a more permanent assistant job with Doordarshan's flagship channel DD1. As for Arya Banerjee, her ascendency towards Bollywood stardom remains on course. In a case of art mirroring life, she recently won plaudits for her role as a rising actress in Milan Luthria's acclaimed film, *The Dirty Picture*.

On the cricket pitch, Yusuf Pathan's rapid-fire century helped him land a $2.1 million deal with Kolkata Knight Riders. India also went on to triumphantly win the World Cup, with the inimitable Sachin Tendulkar emerging as the team's top runs-scorer. Off the pitch, the IPL's money-making ways led to a major corruption scandal, which saw the Rajasthan Royals and the Kings XI Punjab temporarily suspended. The lucrative league bounced back for IPL4, boasting two new teams and a brand value of over $3.6 billion.

In Bengaluru, Prasanta is still diligently swimming lengths at the K. C. Reddy Swim Centre. He followed his success at the Commonwealth Games with a Bronze Medal at the Asian Para Games in Guangzhou, China. Officialdom has finally started to take notice of him. The President of India recently awarded him the prestigious Arjuna Award for his sporting achievements.

Fashion Week grows bigger by the season. Ashdeen is still writing the odd piece for *Elle* and is tickled pink because Beyoncé recently used one of his embroidered gowns for a recent music video.

Rahul (user ID 'Jet Blazer') and I remain in touch over Skype. He finally secured a multiple-entry visa to the US, although his employers at Global Infonet are dragging their feet on his relocation deal. For the moment, he's moonlighting as a freelance IT consultant and harbouring plans to crack the US all on his own.

Sunny is now the proud holder of a degree in journalism and

mass communication from Manipal University. He and his girl-friend are still dating. They recently plucked up the courage to confess all to their respective parents. The news went down better than expected and Sunny hopes to marry within a year or so.

As for Mr Kanphade, the pony-tailed Deputy Collector hit the national headlines once again – this time for denouncing a visit to Gadchiroli by the Home Minister as a 'waste of time'. It was, I fear, the last straw. My attempts to reconnect have led only as far as a LinkedIn connection with a Nagpur-based fitness instructor of the same name. I rather like the idea of Mr Kanphade persuading his clients up onto the five-metre diving board.

Ashish left Teach for India when his contract ran out and is now working as an information system specialist for an educational charity. The website for his citizens' forum, AwakIND, is now live and counts over 9,000 members.

Vivek at MumbaiVotes has teamed up with the Association for Democratic Reform, a pioneering transparency non-profit, and continues his battle to hold Maharashtra's politicians to account. Rajesh managed to complete his film about the widows of Banares and is currently touring it around the festival circuit. He plans a sequel to *Children of the Pyre*, but has as yet failed to raise the necessary funds.

I keep track of Arjun's dizzying array of projects via Twitter. The tree-planting record will feature in an upcoming documentary about the environmental work of his Holiness Gyalwang Drukpa. India's health reforms and the prohibitive cost of prescriptions is currently occupying his documentary-making energies. On the side, he's developing a SmartPhone app that converts content from environmental textbooks into video format.

Tashi is still studying in Kathmandu. After years of not hearing from him, I see him pop up on Facebook most days. He recently changed his profile photo to the Liverpool Football Club insignia, which makes me chuckle every time I see it.

Acknowledgements

India is a large country of many languages, geographies and people groups. Even its most well-travelled citizens require the occasional helping hand to see their journeys through. How much more the foreign visitor? So my first thanks goes to the innumerable impromptu guides who sprung up on trains and in cafes, on rickshaw rides and in taxis, to point me in the right direction. Dozens went far beyond the call of duty, many of whom are already mentioned in the pages of this book. Those that don't feature include: Poulomi Shah, Sudha Menon, Meera Menon, Danish Siddiqui, Gee Vishnu, Usha Imison, Daniel Imison, Tusha Mittal, Richa Nara, Rebecca Noecker, Ramesh Menon, Jim James, Alexander Treves, and many more besides.

My particular thanks to Greg Hughes and Kanika Bhattacharya in Mumbai for taking me in as a temporary lodger and treating me as a lifelong friend. Thanks too to Shruti Ponnappa in Bengaluru, and Stephen Moss and Francesca Pessina in Delhi, for their generous hospitality. A special thanks to Kumar and Pauline, who hosted our small family during many long, humid months in delightful Kochi.

This book was written in three continents over a period of eighteen months. For providing me with a desk on which to work and for silence in which to think, my enormous gratitude goes out to: Alan and June Willis in the UK, Lia and Frans Hendriks in Holland, Zsolt Buday and Jennifer Webster in Spain, Mike Legge, and Pamela Murphy in Argentina, and the kindly folk at Kashi Café, Ethnic Passage and the Abad Hotel in Fort Kochi, India. Belated thanks too to Jon and Bronwyn Ward for helping me out of a pickle.

At Faber, special thanks to my editor, Walter Donohue, who originally suggested this book and kept believing in it (and me) throughout the process. My thanks also to his colleagues Archana Rao, Kate Ward and Rebecca Pearson. I am indebted as always to my agent, Georgina Capel, for her unerring enthusiasm and implacable commitment to superlatives. This book has benefitted immensely from the close attention of my cricket-loving copyeditor, Michael Downes, and my genius friend Matt Chesterton. Early drafts were also vastly improved thanks to the insights of Salil Tripathi, Simon Gammell and Henry Shawdon.

This book could not have been written without the unstinting support of my flacita, Emma, who, among countless mini miracles, successful weaned our youngest on dhal and kept our eldest safe from the garden cobra. Seth and Bo, my two little imps, a lifetime's thanks for joining us on our journey. May your early days in India leave you with a lasting taste for adventure. And finally, Mum and Dad, Boney and Bo, thanks for your love and loyalty over so many years.

Index